COOKBOOK FOR TWO

Audrey P. Stehle

Oxmoor House, Inc.
Birmingham

Southern Living® Cookbook for Two

Copyright 1981 by Oxmoor House, Inc.
Book Division of Southern Progress Corporation
P. O. Box 2463, Birmingham, Alabama 35201

Southern Living® is a federally registered trademark belonging to
Southern Living, Inc.

7-Bone Pot Roast instructions, page 204, courtesy of the National Live
Stock and Meat Board.
Wine selections courtesy of Rick Theis, California Wine Institute.

Library of Congress Catalog Number: 81-80604
ISBN:0-8487-0532-7

Manufactured in the United States of America
Third Printing 1984

Southern Living®

Foods Editor: Jean Wickstrom Liles
Assistant Foods Editor: Susan Payne

Senior Foods Photographer: Charles E. Walton
Photo Stylist: Beverly Morrow

Test Kitchens Director: Lynn Lloyd
Test Kitchens Staff: Martha Hinrichs, Diane Hogan, Laura Nestelroad,
  Karen Parker, Peggy Smith

Oxmoor House, Inc.

Editor: Ann H. Harvey
Assistant Editor: Annette Thompson
Production: Jerry Higdon, Joan Denman

Designer: Faith Nance
Illustrator: Susan Waldrop

Cover: For an Elegant Dinner for Two, serve Gazpacho as an
appetizer followed by Fruit-Glazed Pork Chops with Rice,
Fresh Spinach Salad, and white Zinfandel wine. Complete the
meal with Lemon Poached Pears topped with almonds and
grated chocolate. Menu begins on page 83.

Page i: For a change of pace, try microwaved Sweet Potato-
Stuffed Squash (page 57) or Vegetable Stir-Fry (page 253).

Page ii: An intimate Fireside Supper features Oyster Gumbo for
Two over rice, tossed greens, and Buttermilk Carrot Cornbread. Menu begins on page 39.

CONTENTS

Author's Note

As the growing number of people confronted with cooking for one or two can attest, cooking small quantities can be either a challenge or an overwhelming ordeal, depending on how it is approached. *Southern Living's Cookbook for Two* is designed to help you meet the challenge whether you are a new cook or an experienced cook who may be cooking for one or two people after years of cooking for three, four, five, or more.

For those who may be in the process of acquiring the proper supplies or for those who may need to replace kitchen equipment, our "Guide To Cooking for Two" suggests the equipment and staples necessary for setting up a kitchen. Also included is information about food storage and meal planning, items particularly important to those who want to create interesting, yet economical, meals.

And to prove how creative meals for two can be, we have included fifty-five menus with accompanying recipes in our section "Menus for Two." These menus are geared toward everyday cooking as well as cooking for special occasions for two or more. Often they will call for fewer items than usually found in standard menus because many people find it more convenient to prepare and serve more of two or three foods than to prepare several different foods for just two people. Included are a week's worth of menus, ethnic favorites, a collection of microwave menus, several entertaining menus,

and other menu categories just for two, many of which feature wine suggestions if you wish to add an extra dimension to serving meals for two.

The recipes in this section and in "Recipes for Two" are generally for two servings so that you will not be constantly confronted with leftovers. And some of these give double batch information which is a most helpful time and energy saving technique. Double-batch recipes feature storage and freezing instructions for extra servings so that even after a hectic day, you can serve a delicious meal quickly and easily.

Cooking for two can be exciting and fun, particularly when you consider its distinct advantages: you can purchase and serve fewer items in larger quantities; you are able to plan interesting meals when satisfying only one or two tastes or palates; you are allowed greater flexibility in the type and amount of food being served; and you use less time and energy when cooking for two.

Cookbook for Two emphasizes all these advantages, and we hope that you will enjoy preparing the recipes as much as we did testing them. Many of these came from the *Southern Living* kitchens but were reduced and then tested to yield two servings. We believe the results will be rewarding for any cook who wants to provide interesting and nutritious meals for two people.

Audrey P. Stehle

GUIDE TO COOKING FOR TWO

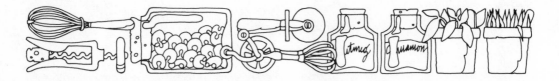

SETTING UP A KITCHEN

If you are a beginning cook, you may be overwhelmed to think about setting up a kitchen. But this activity can be fun if you plan carefully; study all the assorted equipment, gadgets, and staples available; and, most important, select only those items which fit your particular needs and space.

Your final choices should always be affected by personal habits, kind and amount of cooking to be done, personal taste, amount of money available to set up a kitchen, and the available storage space.

However, a basic rule of thumb is to buy fewer items, if necessary, but always good quality items. These will work better and function longer, thus making cooking much more pleasant and enjoyable.

Our kitchen staples list is divided into categories to help cooks decide what they want based on their particular needs. Although for some cooks, what we consider useful may be considered basic, each cook can make this evaluation based on individual needs and interests.

Oven Cooking	
Basic	Useful

Baking dishes
    13 × 9 × 2 inch
    12 × 8 × 2 inch
    10 × 7 × 2 inch
Baking pan, 8 or 9 inch square
Cakepans (two), 8 or 9 inch
Casseroles or soufflé dishes
    1 quart
    1½ quart (two)
    10 to 12 ounce
Cookie sheet, 12½ × 15 inch
Custard cups (four), 6 ounce
Loafpan, 9 × 5 × 3 inch
Muffin pan, 6 cup
Pieplate, 8 or 9 inch
Roasting pan
	Clay cooker
	Deep-dish pieplate, 10 inch
	Quiche pan with removable bottom
	Springform pan
	Tube pan with removable bottom,
	    10 × 4½ inch
	
	Note: For smaller quantity cooking, you may want to use disposable aluminum baking pans available in 8-inch round, 5-inch round, and 6- × 3½- × 2-inch loaf shapes.

Surface Unit Cooking

Basic	Useful
Dutch oven, 5 quart	Double boiler
Omelet pan	Egg poacher
Saucepans	Fish poacher
1 quart	Griddle or grill
2 or 3 quart	Metal steamer insert
Skillet, 8 or 10 inch	Pressure cooker
Tea kettle	Stock pot
	Wok

Food Preparation

Basic	Useful
Can opener	Apple corer
Chopping board	Baster
Colander/strainer	Cake rack
Corkscrew	Cheese slicer
Dry measuring cups (one or two sets)	Cookie cutters
Funnel	Food mill
Juicer	Grapefruit knife
Kitchen shears	Kitchen scale
Knife sharpener	Kitchen timer
Knives: 1 paring, 1 boning, 1 chef's, 8- or 10-inch bread knife	Meat mallet
Ladle	Mixing bowl, 4 or 6 quart
Liquid measures, 1 cup and 4 cup	Narrow metal spatula
Meat thermometer (instant registering, if possible)	Pastry bag
	Pastry brush
	Pastry cloth
Metal measuring spoons (one or two sets)	Pastry sleeve for rolling pin
Mixing bowls: 1, 2, and 3 quart	Potato masher
Pancake turner	Serrated knife
Rolling pin (ball bearing)	Skewers
Rubber spatulas	Tongs
Sifter	Trussing needle
Slotted spoon	Vegetable brush
Vegetable peeler	Wooden spoons
Wire whisk	

Microwave

Basic	Useful
Baking dishes, shallow	Bacon rack
Casseroles (microwave-safe)	Browning dish
1 quart	Instant registering thermometer
1½ quart	Muffin ring
2-cup measure	Ring mold, either microwave plastic
4-cup measure	or glass
	Roast rack

Kitchen Electrics

Basic	Useful
Coffee maker	Crêpe maker
Heavy duty electric mixer	Deep fat fryer
Skillet (with high lid or deep sides)	Electric slicer
Toaster or toaster oven	Food processor
	Hand mixer
	Ice cream machine

Basic Kitchen Supplies

Baking powder
Baking soda
Biscuit mix
Bouillon cubes or granules
Cereal
Coffee
Cornmeal
Cornstarch
Flour (all-purpose), 5 pounds
Flavorings, spices, seasonings
  celery salt
  chili powder
  cinnamon
  garlic
  ginger
  nutmeg
  paprika
  pepper

  salt
  vanilla extract
Gelatin, flavored and unflavored
Grits
Jams, jellies, or preserves
Oil
  olive
  vegetable
Packaging products
  foil
  freezer bags
  freezer wrap
  paper towels
  plastic containers with tight-fitting lids
    (a variety of sizes and shapes)
  waxed paper
  wooden picks

Pastas
  macaroni
  noodles
  spaghetti
Relishes/Condiments
  catsup
  hot sauce
  mayonnaise
  mustard
  pickle relish
  pickles
  soy sauce

vinegar, wine and white
Worcestershire sauce
Rice
  brown
  quick-cooking
  regular
Shortening, 1 pound
Sugar
  brown, 1 pound
  granulated, 5 pounds
  powdered, 1 pound
Tea
Yeast

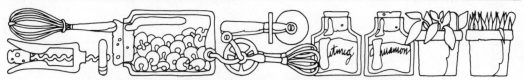

STORING FOODS AND WINES

The proper storage of foods has always been important, but with the increased cost of food and with the increased number of one- or two-person households, proper storage techniques have taken on new significance in terms of real savings.

The most important rule is to remember to buy only as much as can be consumed or adequately stored. Good shopping and food storage habits combined are the most effective way to stretch the food dollar.

The three areas commonly used for home food storage are the cabinet or pantry shelf area, the refrigerator, and the freezer. The temperature and other storage conditions are different in each of these food storage areas and each is best suited for storing specific foods.

Shelf Storage

Although often overlooked, shelf space offers valuable storage space for items that need to be stored at room temperature.

This storage area should be a cool, dry spot away from heat, light, and moisture. (Avoid storing food under the sink.) Foods stored at room temperature should be left in original containers until opened, then covered tightly for storage after opening.

Small items or smaller quantities of dried, freeze-dried, or dehydrated foods should be placed in a plastic container with a tight closure for storage. Opened containers of cereals, flour, sugar, or cornmeal should be kept tightly closed or placed in large plastic bags or canisters.

5

Food Storage Chart

Food Item	Shelf or Pantry (Room Temperature)
Fresh meat, fish, or poultry	Not appropriate
Fresh produce	A cool, dark storage area is best for onions, potatoes, winter squash, apples, citrus fruits, melon, and pineapple. Remove all wrapping to allow for air circulation; avoid direct sunlight.
Butter or margarine	Not appropriate because heat and light cause rancidity.
Cheese	Shelf storage is recommended for unopened cheese spreads and cheese foods. Refrigerate after opening. Cheeses taste better if removed from refrigerator one hour before serving.
Milk or cream	Not appropriate for fresh dairy products. Dry milk solids need a dry container or bag with a tight closure. Refrigerate reconstituted dry milk.
Baked goods	Cover with plastic wrap to prevent drying out.
Frozen foods	Not appropriate unless thawing is desired.
Other foods including oils, jams, canned foods, grains, nuts	Place in a cool, dry area and leave in original container until opened. Then place dry products in plastic bags or containers for shelf storage.

Refrigerator *(38°F to 42°F)*	Freezer *(0°F)*
Store cured meats in original wrappings, fresh meats loosely wrapped. Store in coldest part of refrigerator. Use fish, poultry, ground beef in 3 days, other meats within 3 to 5 days.	Wrap meats in moisture vapor-proof paper or plastic wrap, or place in plastic containers with tight-fitting lids. Label, date, and freeze quickly.
Wash and dry all leafy vegetables. Place in plastic bags or wrap. Place fruits whole or uncovered in refrigerator. Store berries, unwashed, in plastic bags.	Follow reliable methods of freezing all fresh produce. Package in plastic bags or material such as plastic wrap. Label and date.
Store tightly covered. Keep only as much in refrigerator as can be used in 7 to 10 days.	Wrap in moisture vapor-proof paper or plastic wrap, or place in plastic containers with tight-fitting lids. Use within 3 months.
Wrap hard and semi-hard cheese in plastic wrap to prevent drying. Store aromatic cheeses in bags with tight closures. Hard and semi-hard cheeses keep for many weeks, but cream, cottage, and other soft cheeses should be used with a few days.	Freezing causes texture changes in cheeses, but flavor will be maintained and mold prevented. Wrap in moisture vapor-proof paper or plastic wrap, or place in plastic containers with tight-fitting lids. Do not freeze creamed cottage cheese or cream cheese.
Keep in cold, dark environment to prevent bacterial growth and contamination. Cover to prevent development of off flavors. Use within 3 to 5 days.	Homogenized milk and heavy cream can be frozen satisfactorily in original paper containers.
Refrigerate all baked goods containing custard or cream fillings. Refrigerate breads to prevent mold.	Wrap cookies, cakes, and pies in moisture vapor-proof paper or plastic wrap, or place in plastic containers with tight-fitting lids. Freeze and use within 3 months. Results vary depending on product.
Freezer section inside refrigerator can be used to hold these foods for 10 to 14 days. 0°F storage is necessary for longer storage.	Store immediately and keep at 0°F until ready to use.
Cover opened cans, bottles, and jars and store in refrigerator until used. Storage time varies with the product. Refrigeration will slow development of rancidity in nuts.	Nuts can be frozen by placing in heavy plastic bags or containers. Freezing is not recommended for oils or jams.

Refrigerator Storage

Most of today's kitchens will have a refrigerator with a temperature of about 38°F to 42°F and a volume of 16 to 18 cubic feet of space. Part of this space, usually about 6 cubic feet, will be for frozen food storage.

Temperature is the most important factor to consider in refrigerator fresh food storage. Many refrigerators are frostless, and in these, the temperature throughout the refrigerator section will be about the same because of air circulation. Foods can be stored effectively in any part of this type refrigerator.

Usually, there will be an area specifically recommended for meat, fish, and poultry. These food items should be loosely wrapped and then stored for only a few days, 5 to 7 days maximum. In frostless refrigerators, all other foods should be stored tightly covered. To store cooked foods, cool them at room temperature before placing in the refrigerator. A tight cover on cooked foods helps retain moisture, quality, flavor, and nutritive value.

In refrigerators which require defrosting, temperatures vary but are coldest near the top, on either a door or an interior shelf. This is the best area for milk, eggs, beverages, and cheese. The drawers near the bottom may have a slightly higher temperature and are best suited for fresh fruits and vegetables.

Freezer Storage

This space may be a separate appliance, but in smaller kitchens it is more likely to be part of a refrigerator. Freezers and the top or side freezer sections of refrigerators with separate outside doors provide true 0°F storage, which is essential for proper long term frozen food storage.

In addition to a 0°F temperature, quality packaging material is the other item necessary for proper frozen food storage. To protect food from the freezer's cold air, use coated freezer paper, plastic wrap, or heavy plastic containers with tight-fitting lids for freezer packaging. Use only moisture vapor-proof materials. Do not use grocery plastic bags, plain paper, waxed paper, or throw away plastic containers. These provide frozen foods no protection from cold air, which will cause freezer burn.

Wine Storage

Wines are considered by many to be very fragile, but in fact they are quite sturdy. There are, however, three basic pitfalls to avoid when storing wines.

Bright light is very bad for wines, for it bleaches the wine of its color and changes the flavor. Choose a dark spot, either in a closet, under stairs, or in a wine cellar where the light remains very dim.

Sudden temperature changes also affect the quality of the wines. Experts consider 59°F the perfect storage temperature, but this temperature is expensive and difficult to achieve for home wine storage. The main factor is to avoid sudden, sharp temperature changes.

In addition to avoiding bright light and sudden temperature changes when storing wines, try to choose storage areas free of motion or vibration. Do not store wines near refrigerators, washers, or in other spots where regular motion occurs.

Along with these general conditions, there is the type closure to consider. Corked bottles should always be stored flat on their sides with their necks tilted up slightly to keep the cork wet. Wine bottles with screw caps or plastic corks can be stored safely standing upright or pointed in any direction.

In general, wines that are meant to be served chilled are best stored closest to the floor where the temperature may be a few degrees lower. Red or dessert wines can go on the higher storage shelves where temperatures may be slightly higher.

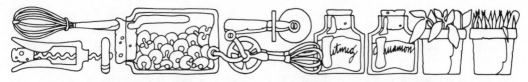

MEAL PLANNING

Cooking for two may not always be an elegant, candlelight affair, but it certainly should not be an ordinary, humdrum meal consisting of leftovers. There are an unlimited number of ways to make small quantity cooking interesting and exciting.

Planning and preparing nutritious meals is important for every family but may be considered more difficult for the two-person family. Often the person cooking for just one or two develops the attitude that "cooking just isn't worth it." This is a fallacy which need not be believed.

A quick trip through the supermarket in any town reveals a wide diversity of nutritious foods perfect for two: fresh, frozen, and canned vegetables; numerous meat, fish, and poultry choices; bread and grains of all types; and milk and milk products. These are the four important food groups around which all meals should be planned, and all can be easily purchased in the amounts needed for two.

Shopping for Two

How much to buy is often a question asked by even the more experienced cook. Get in the habit of weighing fruits, vegetables, meats, shellfish, poultry, and other foods which do not have the weight indicated on the label.

Generally about ½ to ¾ pound of such fresh vegetables as mushrooms, green beans, eggplant, and potatoes will be an ample amount for two. For greens such as spinach, lettuce, and cabbage, you will need ½ to 1 pound or enough for 4 to 6 cups to serve two. A 10-ounce package of frozen vegetables is just about the right amount for two, depending on how it is cooked and served.

Apples, bananas, oranges, and other fresh fruits served whole usually yield 1 to 1½ servings. You can get 2 to 3 servings per pound or package of grapes, strawberries, and similar fruits that are sold by the package or pound.

For meats without bone (ground meat, steaks) allow ¼ to ⅓ pound per person; for meats with bone-in (ribs, pot roast, chicken, turkey) allow ½ to 1 pound. Seafood (crab, lobster, scallops, and oysters) will yield 2 to 4 servings per pound, depending on preparation and other foods served.

Using these amounts as a guide, plan your menus for a full week so that you buy wisely and are able to take advantage of the good food buys usually associated with standard or giant-size food packages. Many cans and packages are available in small sizes, but they often cost more per unit than their counterpart in a larger, more economical size. When buying nonperishable foods, such as rice, sugar, flour, cereals, and similar items, buy the larger size when possible to take advantage of the lower cost.

Apples, citrus, and other fresh fruits can be stored in the refrigerator for several weeks, so buying them in larger quantities rather than individually is much more economical in the long run. You are also more likely to serve these items if you have them on hand.

When shopping for perishable food items, buy only the amounts you can use before they spoil. A super buy on a giant package is wasteful if the product or food spoils before you can use it.

A week's worth of menus means that you will be able to incorporate good weekly buys and specials, making substitutes at the market if necessary. Your plan either enables you to effectively use food left over from one meal in a completely different way in another meal, or allows you to buy only the quantities needed for the week.

Creative Cooking for Two

The four basic food groups are the key to successful meal planning for two. Choose a variety of these foods daily and serve them simply or elaborately, depending on your schedule, personal preference, and the time and money available. But to make cooking fun, look for creative ways to avoid monotony in meal preparation and serving.

Add appeal and interest to meals through the effective use of color, texture, shape, and different combinations of food. Remember you dine with your eyes as well as your palate. A simple carrot strip or cherry tomato may be just the touch needed to make a meal look as good as it tastes.

For easy appetizer, snack, and sandwich preparation, keep a wide variety of foods on hand. Refrigerated appetizers might include fresh vegetables served raw with a simple dip; cheese served with vegetables or crackers; herring or other fish served plain or with crackers; and various pickled vegetables, olives, and onions. Remember that canned foods also offer excellent snack, sandwich, and appetizer fixings.

Another versatile food category is salads. Almost any food can be served in a salad; the final choice of ingredients is limited only by your interest and willingness to try different foods in creative combinations. Salads can be served as appetizers, entrées, accompaniments, or even for desserts. They can be hot or cold, tossed or arranged.

Now when choosing the finale to the meal, everyone has his personal favorite. Dessert can be as simple as a plum, nectarine, or apple served fresh and unadorned; or, a more elegant cheesecake or meringue-topped pie may be chosen, depending on personal preference.

For simple dessert ideas, check our Creative Desserts chart on page 170. Here is a listing of simple dessert ingredients such as cake, ice cream, fruit, topping, and liqueurs which are likely to be on hand in many kitchens. With this guide, an almost unlimited number of desserts can be prepared using each person's favorite items.

For the main meal, try serving such vegetables as squash, cauliflower, broccoli, and spinach raw rather than cooked. Also vary your choice of cooking processes. If you usually steam vegetables, try stir-fry as a cooking technique. This cooking method, adapted from the Orient, is energy efficient, quick, and adaptable to almost any vegetable or meat.

When stir-frying vegetables, use either a wok or skillet. Season with fresh herbs, soy sauce, butter, lemon juice, or wine and top with seeds, croutons, or sliced or chopped raw vegetables for additional crunchiness.

Turn leftover cooked vegetables into a new dish by topping with an easy sauce or combining with other ingredients in stir-fry dishes; or use a mixture of cooked vegetables as a filling for egg dishes such as omelets, crêpes, or quiches. With a little imagination small quantities of uncooked vegetables can become the basis for a completely new recipe invention.

Combine leftover cooked meat, rice, and vegetables in casseroles. Use cooked meat in open-faced sandwiches or freeze small quantities of leftovers and make your own personalized "ready to serve" freezer dinners. You will enjoy the real advantage of creating two meals from one and will stretch the time and energy budget as well.

The best cooking method for meat is determined by the tenderness, size, and thickness. A description of the six meat cooking methods and cuts for which each is appropriate follows. The proper cooking method will insure proper doneness and best quality.

Meat Cooking Chart

Cooking Method	Use For	Technique
Roast	Rib and loin cuts of beef, lamb, pork, or veal; leg of lamb; smoked cuts of pork	Season meat. Place meat rack in roasting pan. Insert meat thermometer with bulb tip in lean portion of meat. Roast, uncovered, at 325° to desired degree of doneness.
Broil	Rib or loin steaks and chops; patties from beef, pork, lamb, or veal	Select broil on oven control or prepare fire on outdoor grill. Wait until coals are covered with ash. Place steak, chops, or patties 2 to 3 inches from heat. Cook until top of meat is brown. Season; turn and broil or grill second side until desired degree of doneness.
Panbroil	Rib or loin steaks and chops; patties from beef, pork, lamb, or veal	Place meat in heavy skillet. Do not add water; do not cover. Cook slowly to desired degree of doneness, browning meat on both sides. Drain drippings from pan as they accumulate. Season.
Panfry	Steaks or chops; patties from beef, pork, or lamb	Brown meat on both sides in small amount of oil. Season. Do not cover; cook at medium temperature until done.
Braise	Less tender cuts such as shank, flank, breast, tip or round steak, pork blade chops, or breast of veal	Brown meat on all sides in heavy utensil using a small amount of oil if necessary. Add seasoning, if desired, and a small amount of liquid. Cover tightly; cook over low heat until done.
Cook in liquid	Short ribs, brisket, picnic or shoulder, stew	Coat meat with seasoned flour if desired, then brown on all sides in small amount of oil. Add liquid to cover meat; cover utensil. Cook just below boiling until done. Add vegetables just long enough to cook them.

Double-Batch Cooking

Double-batch cooking describes one of the most efficient ways to save time and energy when cooking for two. Some foods almost require you to cook in standard four to eight serving sizes. Cookies, cakes, quick and yeast breads, and pies are almost always just as simple to bake in these larger portion batches. To make the portions more usable for two, use disposable aluminum baking pans which are available in a variety of sizes and shapes. Divide regular size recipes for baked goods into two and three of the smaller size mini-loaf pans. Use one of the loaves, but wrap and freeze the remaining one or two. These pans can also be used for yeast breads, muffins, cookies, and cakes which are particularly handy to have on hand, especially if you have unexpected guests. Get in the habit of having cake layers in the freezer, and you will enjoy the advantage of easy delicious desserts.

In addition to loafpans, throwaway tart pans are available and can be useful for baking meat, vegetable, or fruit pies. Divide the pastry for a 9-inch pie between two or three of the tart pans. Bake both and freeze the one you do not plan to serve right away.

Spaghetti sauces, soups, stews, and similar dishes, which require a large number of ingredients and long, slow cooking, are life savers for the busy cook to have on hand in the freezer. They are ready to be thawed, heated, and served anytime. Cool these foods completely after cooking them; package in the freezer containers with tight-fitting lids; and freeze up to three months.

It is almost always cheaper to buy whole chickens and cut them into serving portions yourself. Separate the parts and freeze what is not used immediately, remembering to label correctly. A variety of chicken pieces will then be available to be used in numerous ways.

A 7-pound beef chuck roast can be boring for two to eat if cooked as a pot roast, but follow our drawing on page 205 to cut this roast into meat for three completely different meals, all from one roast. Each recipe is certainly more interesting to serve than pot roast three or four days in a row.

When the supermarket runs a special, buy ground meat, chops, and small steaks in packages containing several portions. Separate into serving-size portions; then wrap and freeze the portions you do not plan to use right away.

In the recipes that follow, we have incorporated some of the techniques for double-batch cooking. After trying these suggestions, you can see how easily the technique can be applied to any standard recipe.

Page 13: *For a special Summer Picnic just right for two, select a bottle of Fumé Blanc to serve with Chilled Strawberry Soup, Avocado Stuffed with Shrimp, Deviled Eggs, Cocktail Cheese Biscuits, and Picnic Lemon Bars. Menu begins on page 33.*

Page 14: *Brunch, New Orleans Style begins with Milk Punch served with Eggs Benedict and fresh fruit. Menu begins on page 24.*

MENUS FOR TWO

BREAKFASTS AND BRUNCHES

Despite the fact that a good breakfast provides important nutrients and energy to start the day, many people find it the most difficult meal to prepare and serve.

However, morning meals for two can be fun to plan as well as good to eat. Use your imagination to create interesting and different breakfast menus, keeping in mind that almost any food can be served. Choices are limited only by your personal tastes and likes and dislikes.

Since time is one of the primary factors affecting these early meals, keep a supply of nutritious foods on hand. Fresh or frozen fruits and juices, ready-to-serve cereal, cheese, and yogurt are some of the foods we used in our menus. For an added touch, bake your own breads or muffins; then wrap in individual packages and store in the freezer until ready to reheat and serve. These combine quickly with eggs, cheese, and fruit for a filling breakfast that provides needed energy.

Select a brunch or one of our more elaborate breakfast menus for weekends, holidays, or vacations when your schedule is less hectic and you have more time for cooking and serving.

Pancake Breakfast

Frothy Orange Drink
Bran-Cheddar Pancakes
Cold Applesauce
Canadian Bacon
Cinnamon Hot Chocolate

This day starts with a hearty orange drink and the unusual Bran-Cheddar Pancakes. They are different and you are sure to enjoy serving them. We suggest that you serve cold applesauce as a pancake topping in place of the usual syrup, or choose any other cold fruit from your personal favorites.

Frothy Orange Drink

1 cup orange juice
¼ to ½ cup instant nonfat dry milk
1½ tablespoons sugar

2 to 3 drops vanilla extract
½ cup crushed ice

Combine ingredients in container of electric blender; blend until frothy. Serve immediately. Yield: about 2 cups.

Bran-Cheddar Pancakes

1 egg, beaten
2 teaspoons vegetable oil
¾ cup buttermilk
½ cup pancake mix

¼ teaspoon baking powder
1½ tablespoons bran
¼ cup shredded sharp Cheddar
   cheese

Combine egg, oil, and buttermilk, mixing well. Stir in pancake mix and baking powder. Add bran and cheese, stirring just enough to distribute throughout batter.
   For each pancake, pour about ¼ cup batter onto a hot, lightly greased griddle. Turn pancakes when tops are covered with bubbles and edges are slightly browned. Yield: about 2 servings.

Canadian Bacon

To cook Canadian bacon, place desired number of slices in a heavy skillet or electric skillet at 325° (do not cover). Cook bacon slowly over medium heat, turning occasionally. Brown on both sides. Cook until done.

Cinnamon Hot Chocolate

2 cups milk	¼ to ½ teaspoon ground cinnamon
3 tablespoons sugar	⅛ teaspoon salt
1 (1-ounce) square unsweetened chocolate, cut into small pieces	1 egg, beaten
	1 teaspoon vanilla extract

Combine first 5 ingredients in a saucepan, mixing well; cook over medium heat, stirring constantly, until chocolate melts. Gradually stir a small amount of hot mixture into egg. Add egg to remaining hot mixture; cook over low heat 2 to 3 minutes, stirring constantly. Remove from heat; add vanilla, and beat on medium speed of an electric mixer until frothy. Yield: about 2½ cups.

Make-Ahead Breakfast

Peach Breakfast Drink
Overnight French Toast
Sausage Links or Patties
Coffee

Invigorating and filling describes this breakfast best. Prepare Overnight French Toast the night before and refrigerate. Serve the Peach Breakfast Drink while the toast is cooking. Sausage and coffee complete the meal.

Peach Breakfast Drink

1 cup sliced fresh or frozen peaches, thawed	1 cup skim milk
1 (8-ounce) carton plain yogurt	1 tablespoon honey

Combine all ingredients in container of electric blender; process until smooth. Yield: 3¼ cups.

Overnight French Toast

4 (¾-inch-thick) slices French bread
2 eggs
½ cup milk
2 teaspoons sugar
Dash of salt

1 tablespoon orange juice
¼ teaspoon vanilla extract
2 tablespoons butter or margarine
Powdered sugar

Place bread in a 12- × 8- × 2-inch baking dish. Combine eggs, milk, sugar, salt, orange juice, and vanilla; beat well. Pour mixture over bread slices; turn slices over to coat evenly. Cover and refrigerate 8 hours or overnight.

Melt butter in a large skillet; remove bread slices from dish, and sauté in butter 4 minutes on each side or until browned. Sprinkle toast with powdered sugar; serve immediately. Yield: 2 servings.

Sausage Links or Patties

To cook sausage, place desired number of links or patties in a cold heavy skillet. Add 2 to 4 tablespoons water. Cover tightly. Cook slowly over medium heat, 5 to 8 minutes, depending on size or thickness of sausage. Pour off drippings and cook uncovered until browned.

Extra Special Breakfast

Orange Ambrosia
Sour Cream-Ham Omelet
Blueberry Muffins
Coffee

A little advance planning and preparation can make this breakfast special. Here is our simple time plan recommendation. Prepare Orange Ambrosia the night before. If possible, bake the muffins in advance and freeze or store until ready to reheat. If muffins are prepared just prior to serving, prepare the omelet mixture while they are baking. After removing muffins from the oven, bake the Sour Cream-Ham Omelet.

Orange Ambrosia

2 large oranges, peeled and cut into ¼-inch slices
¼ cup flaked coconut
¼ cup commercial sour cream
1½ teaspoons brown sugar
¼ teaspoon grated orange rind
Pinch of salt
2 tablespoons coarsely chopped pecans

Place one-third of the orange slices in a medium-size serving bowl. Top with about one-third of the coconut; repeat layers twice. Cover and refrigerate at least 1 hour or overnight.

Combine sour cream and sugar; mix well. Stir in rind and salt; cover and refrigerate dressing at least 1 hour or overnight. Top fruit with dressing and pecans before serving. Yield: 2 servings.

Sour Cream-Ham Omelet

3 eggs, separated
¾ cup chopped cooked ham
½ cup commercial sour cream, divided
⅛ teaspoon salt
1 tablespoon butter or margarine

Beat egg whites (at room temperature) until stiff but not dry; set aside. Beat egg yolks until thick and lemon colored; stir in ham, ¼ cup sour cream, and salt. Fold egg whites into egg yolk mixture.

Heat butter in an ovenproof 9-inch omelet pan or heavy skillet over medium low heat until hot enough to sizzle a drop of water. Pour in egg mixture, and gently smooth surface. Reduce heat and cook omelet about 5 minutes or until puffy and light brown on bottom, gently lifting omelet at edge to judge color.

Bake at 325° for 12 to 15 minutes or until a knife inserted in center comes out clean. Tip skillet and loosen omelet with a spatula; slide omelet onto serving plate. To serve, slice in wedges and garnish with remaining sour cream. Yield: 2 servings.

Blueberry Muffins

1¼ cups all-purpose flour, divided
¼ teaspoon salt
½ cup firmly packed brown sugar
¼ cup shortening
1 egg
¼ cup buttermilk
½ teaspoon soda
1 cup frozen blueberries, thawed and drained

Combine 1 cup flour and salt; set aside. Cream sugar and shortening; add egg. Beat well. Combine buttermilk and soda, stirring well; add to sugar mixture alternately with flour mixture, stirring just to combine. Combine berries and ¼ cup flour; gently fold into batter.

Spoon batter into greased muffin pans, filling two-thirds full. Bake at 350° for 20 to 25 minutes or until golden brown. Yield: about 1 dozen muffins.

Note: 1 cup fresh blueberries may be substituted for frozen.

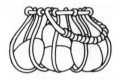

Hot, Hearty Breakfast

Apple Juice
Deluxe Scrambled Eggs
Bacon
Quick Cheese Grits
Southern Biscuits
Coffee

For this breakfast we suggest a simple time schedule. Prepare and bake the biscuits. While they bake, prepare Deluxe Scrambled Eggs and cook Quick Cheese Grits. Cook the eggs just before the biscuits are finished; then serve and enjoy.

Deluxe Scrambled Eggs

4 eggs
¼ cup buttermilk
¼ teaspoon paprika
¼ teaspoon salt
Dash of pepper

1 tablespoon butter or margarine
⅓ cup shredded process American cheese
1 green onion, chopped

Combine eggs, buttermilk, paprika, salt, and pepper; beat well with a fork.

Melt butter in a 9-inch skillet. When hot, add egg mixture. Cook over low heat until eggs are partially set, lifting edges gently to allow uncooked portion to flow underneath. Add cheese and onion. Cover; cook 1 minute or until cheese melts and eggs are set. Yield: 2 servings.

Quick Cheese Grits

1⅓ cups water
1 tablespoon butter or margarine
⅓ cup quick-cooking grits
½ teaspoon garlic salt

½ cup (2 ounces) shredded sharp
    Cheddar cheese
Salt
Pepper

Combine water and butter in a small saucepan; bring to a boil. Slowly stir in grits and garlic salt. Return to a boil; cover and cook 3 to 5 minutes. Stir in cheese and the desired amount of salt and pepper. Yield: 2 servings.

Southern Biscuits

1 cup all-purpose flour
¼ teaspoon salt
1½ teaspoons baking powder

2½ tablespoons shortening
⅓ cup milk

Combine flour, salt, and baking powder; cut in shortening until mixture resembles coarse meal. Add milk, stirring until blended well. Turn dough out onto floured surface; knead lightly 3 or 4 times.

Roll dough to a ½-inch thickness; cut into rounds with a 2½-inch cutter. Bake at 450° for 10 to 12 minutes or until golden. Yield: 6 biscuits.

Breakfast for a Chilly Morning

Sautéed Apple Rings
Fancy Baked Eggs
Fried Country Ham Slices
Coffee

This Southern-style breakfast can also be served as a Sunday night supper. Preparation and cooking time will be less than 30 minutes.

Sauteed Apple Rings

¼ cup butter or margarine
2 cooking apples, unpeeled and cut
   into ¾-inch slices

Sugar
3 tablespoons water

Melt butter in a skillet; add apple slices, and sprinkle each slice with ½ teaspoon sugar. Cook over medium heat 2 minutes. Turn apple slices, and sprinkle each with ½ teaspoon sugar; cook 2 minutes. Turn slices again, and cook 1 minute. Carefully remove apples to a serving plate. Set aside.

Add water to skillet; cook over medium heat, stirring constantly, until water evaporates and mixture thickens slightly. Spoon mixture over apple slices. Yield: 2 servings.

Fancy Baked Eggs

4 eggs
1 teaspoon seasoned salt
¼ teaspoon cream of tartar

4 slices hot buttered toast
¼ to ½ cup shredded Cheddar
   cheese

Separate eggs, placing each egg yolk on a saucer or in a custard cup. (Cover with plastic wrap to keep egg yolks from drying out.)

Combine egg whites (at room temperature), seasoned salt, and cream of tartar; beat until stiff but not dry.

Place toast on a baking sheet. Spoon equal amounts of beaten egg whites on each slice of toast, making an indentation in center of each. Carefully slip egg yolk into each indentation; top with cheese. Bake at 350° for 15 minutes or until meringue is lightly browned and yolks are set. Yield: 2 servings.

Fried Country Ham Slices

Arrange desired number of smoked ham slices in skillet. Add a small amount of vegetable oil, if desired. Cook, uncovered, over moderate heat. Turn ham slices several times until both sides have browned. Season with salt and pepper, if desired.

To use a griddle or frypan, preheat on medium or medium-high heat before adding the food. It is properly preheated when a few drops of water spatter when they hit the surface. Add food and reduce heat so that it cooks without spattering and smoking.

Brunch, New Orleans Style

Milk Punch
Eggs Benedict
Fresh Fruit
Bananas Foster
Café au Lait

If this is your choice for a breakfast menu, all you will need to capture the spirit of a New Orleans dining experience is a quiet garden setting and time to serve and enjoy leisurely.

Milk Punch

1½ cups half-and-half
¼ cup light rum

¼ cup bourbon
1 tablespoon plus 1 teaspoon sugar

Combine all ingredients in a cocktail shaker or jar; tighten lid securely, and shake well. Serve over crushed ice. Yield: 2 cups.

Eggs Benedict

2 English muffins, halved and buttered
4 slices Canadian bacon or boiled ham

4 poached eggs
Hollandaise Sauce
Paprika

Broil muffin halves until lightly browned. Top each with a Canadian bacon slice and a poached egg; top with Hollandaise Sauce. Sprinkle with paprika. Yield: 2 servings.

Hollandaise Sauce:

3 egg yolks
2 tablespoons lemon juice
½ cup butter or margarine

¼ teaspoon salt
Dash of red pepper

Beat egg yolks in top of double boiler; gradually add lemon juice, stirring constantly.

Add about one-third of butter to egg mixture; cook over hot (not boiling) water, stirring constantly, until butter melts.

Add another third of butter, stirring constantly; as sauce thickens, stir in remaining butter. Stir in salt and pepper; cook until thickened. Yield: about ¾ cup.

Bananas Foster

2 tablespoons butter or margarine
3 tablespoons brown sugar
⅛ teaspoon ground cinnamon
1 banana, peeled, halved, and
  sliced lengthwise

1 tablespoon lemon juice
¼ cup rum
2 tablespoons banana-flavored
  liqueur
Vanilla ice cream

Melt butter in a chafing dish or small skillet. Add sugar and cinnamon; cook syrup over medium heat until bubbly. Add banana slices and lemon juice; heat 3 to 4 minutes, basting constantly with syrup.

Combine rum and liqueur in a small long-handled pan; heat just until warm. Ignite, and pour over banana slices. Baste banana slices with sauce until flames die down. Serve immediately over ice cream. Yield: 2 servings.

Cafe au Lait

Hot, very strong coffee   Warm milk

Combine equal parts of coffee and milk in a serving mug. Serve immediately.

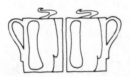

Sunday Morning Brunch

Orange Juice Special
Apple-Almond German Pancake
Hot Link Sausage
Coffee Diable

You may want to experiment with other fruits or toppings for this giant pancake. Try fresh blueberries, strawberries, or raspberries when they are available. Top with sour cream or drizzle with warm syrup, preserves, or jam.

Orange Juice Special

⅓ cup frozen orange juice
   concentrate, thawed and
   undiluted
½ cup milk

½ cup water
¼ cup sugar
½ teaspoon vanilla extract
5 to 6 ice cubes

Combine all ingredients in container of electric blender, and process mixture until frothy. Serve immediately. Yield: 2 servings.

Apple-Almond German Pancake

3 tablespoons butter or margarine,
   divided
2 eggs
⅓ cup milk
⅓ cup all-purpose flour
¼ teaspoon salt
2 apples, peeled and cut into
   wedges

2 tablespoons sliced almonds
1 tablespoon sugar
¼ teaspoon ground cinnamon
Lemon wedges
Powdered sugar
Commercial sour cream (optional)

Preheat oven to 425°. Place 2 tablespoons butter in a 9-inch ovenproof skillet or piepan; melt in preheated oven. Place eggs in blender container; blend at high 1 minute. Blending constantly, gradually add milk; slowly add flour and salt, and blend 30 seconds. Remove pan from oven and pour batter into hot melted butter. Return to oven; bake 20 to 25 minutes or until puffy.

Melt remaining 1 tablespoon butter in a medium skillet; add apples and almonds. Sprinkle with sugar and cinnamon. Cook over low heat until apples are glazed and tender; stir occasionally. Cut pancake into wedges and spoon warm apple-almond filling over each serving; serve immediately. Pass lemon wedges, shaker of powdered sugar, and sour cream, if desired. Yield: 2 servings.

Coffee Diable

1 orange
Whole cloves
1 tablespoon sugar
1 (2-inch) stick cinnamon

¼ cup plus 2 tablespoons dark rum
¼ cup brandy
2 cups strong hot coffee
Whipped cream

Peel orange carefully so that rind remains in a single long curl. Reserve orange pulp for other uses. Press cloves into orange curl, placing one every 2 inches.

Combine sugar and cinnamon in a chafing dish; place over heat, stirring until sugar is slightly melted. Stir in rum; heat, but do not boil. Drop orange curl in mixture, coating well. Raise curl out of mixture and pour brandy down it.

Light orange curl with a match and drop into chafing dish. Stir in coffee. Remove cinnamon stick and orange curl and discard. Pour coffee mixture into serving cups; top with whipped cream. Yield: about 2¼ cups.

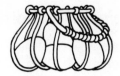

Wintertime Brunch

Sherried Broiled Grapefruit
Cheese-and-Bacon Omelet
Celery Amandine
Prune-Orange Rolls
Coffee

When this meal is planned, prepare and bake the Prune-Orange Rolls in advance. This bread is special enough to serve anytime but is perfect for a brunch. Serve with extra butter and plenty of hot coffee.

Sherried Broiled Grapefruit

1 large grapefruit, halved
2 tablespoons brown sugar

About 2 tablespoons cocktail sherry

Remove seeds, and loosen sections of grapefruit halves; sprinkle 1 tablespoon sugar over top of each. Broil grapefruit 4 inches from heat for 2 minutes; sprinkle about 1 tablespoon sherry over top of each half. Broil 1 to 2 minutes longer or until bubbly and lightly browned. Yield: 2 servings.

Cheese-and-Bacon Omelet

3 to 4 slices bacon
4 eggs
¼ cup water

½ teaspoon salt
Dash of pepper
¼ cup shredded Cheddar cheese

Cook bacon until crisp, and drain on paper towels; reserve 1 tablespoon drippings. Crumble bacon, and set aside.

Combine eggs, water, salt, and pepper; mix well. Heat reserved bacon drippings in a 10-inch omelet pan or skillet until just hot enough to sizzle a drop of water. Pour in egg mixture.

As mixture starts to cook, gently lift edges of omelet and tilt pan to allow the uncooked portion to flow underneath. When mixture is set and no longer flows freely, sprinkle bacon on half of omelet. Fold omelet in half, and place on a warm platter; sprinkle with cheese. Yield: 2 servings.

Celery Amandine

2 tablespoons slivered almonds
1 tablespoon butter or margarine
1 tablespoon dry white wine
1½ teaspoons instant minced onion
¼ teaspoon chicken-flavored
  bouillon granules

¼ teaspoon sugar
Dash of garlic powder
Dash of ground ginger
3 cups diagonally sliced celery

Sauté almonds in butter until lightly browned; stir in remaining ingredients. Cover and cook 5 to 8 minutes or until celery is crisp-tender, stirring often (do not overcook). Serve immediately. Yield: 2 servings.

Prune-Orange Rolls

1 package dry yeast
3 tablespoons warm water (105°
  to 115°)
½ teaspoon grated orange rind
3 tablespoons orange juice
3 tablespoons sugar

1 egg, beaten
1¾ cups all-purpose flour, divided
3 tablespoons butter, melted
½ teaspoon salt
Prune-Orange Filling
Orange Glaze

Dissolve yeast in warm water in a medium mixing bowl. Let stand 5 minutes to soften. Add orange rind, juice, sugar, and egg. Stir in 1 cup of flour, and mix until smooth. Add butter and salt; gradually beat in remaining ¾ cup flour to make a soft dough. Cover and let rise in a warm place (85°), free from drafts, 2 hours or until doubled in bulk.

When dough has risen, turn out onto a floured board and roll to a 12- × 8-inch rectangle. Spread with Prune-Orange Filling, leaving a ½-inch border of dough uncovered along the long sides. Starting from long side, roll up, pinching together ends of roll.

Cut into twelve 1-inch slices and place cut side down in a greased 9-inch round pan. Let rise about 45 minutes or until doubled in bulk. Bake at 375° for 25 to 30 minutes or until golden brown. Top warm rolls with Orange Glaze. Yield: 12 rolls.

Prune-Orange Filling:

¾ cup pitted prunes
⅓ cup orange juice

¼ cup sugar
1 teaspoon grated orange rind

Snip prunes into small pieces. Combine with orange juice in a small saucepan. Simmer 4 to 5 minutes or until prunes are soft and liquid is absorbed. Remove from heat and stir in sugar and grated orange rind. Cool before using. Yield: 1 cup.

Orange Glaze:

⅔ cup sifted powdered sugar

3½ teaspoons orange juice

Combine powdered sugar with orange juice in a small bowl. Stir until smooth; spread over warm rolls. Yield: about ½ cup.

MEALS TO GO

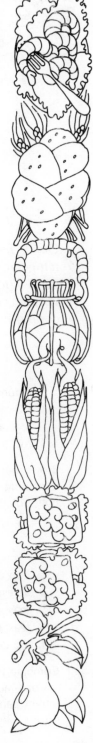

A meal packed at home but not eaten there can be fun to prepare and to eat. All you need for a successful meal served away from home are good food storage rules and a few basic containers.

When packing meals to go, you will need vacuum containers or insulated chests for soups, stews, beverages, and other foods which need to be served either hot or cold.

Salads, some sandwiches, and foods with liquid should be packaged in containers with snap or screw lids which provide a tight cover. These may be plastic storage containers, plastic bags with tight closures, or wide mouth jars with screw caps.

For transporting and packing, use baskets, sturdy canvas bags, heavy paper or plastic bags, or select from a wide variety of other tote bags which are suitable to the meal and to the person for whom the meal is being packed. If food needs to be kept cold, select an insulated chest with ample room for food containers and ice.

Hot Lunch To Go

Quick Beefy Vegetable Soup
Buttermilk Corn Muffins
Apple or Watermelon Slice
Milk

Quick Beefy Vegetable Soup can be prepared and stored either in the refrigerator for a few days or frozen for several weeks. When you are ready to pack it for lunch, heat to serving temperature and pour into a warmed vacuum container. Bake and freeze the muffins in serving-size portions; pack desired number while still frozen. They will be ready to eat by lunch time.

Quick Beefy Vegetable Soup

½ pound ground beef
1 (10-ounce) package frozen mixed
   vegetables
1 cup tomato juice

1 cup beef broth
1 cup cubed potatoes, uncooked
¼ teaspoon salt
⅛ teaspoon pepper

Brown beef in a medium saucepan, stirring to crumble; drain off drippings. Add remaining ingredients; bring to a boil. Reduce heat, and simmer 20 to 25 minutes or until potatoes are tender. Yield: 2 servings.

Buttermilk Corn Muffins

¼ cup all-purpose flour
3 tablespoons sugar
½ teaspoon salt
¾ teaspoon soda
1 cup cornmeal

¼ cup sesame seeds
½ cup wheat germ
1 egg, slightly beaten
1 cup buttermilk
⅓ cup vegetable oil

Combine first 7 ingredients in a mixing bowl; set aside.
   Combine egg, buttermilk, and oil; stir into flour mixture. Spoon batter into greased muffin pans, filling two-thirds full. Bake at 350° for 20 minutes. Yield: about 1 dozen.

Salad Sandwich Combo

Picnic Salad Rolls
Ham and Cheese Roll-Ups
Apple
Chocolate Chip-Peanut Squares
Iced Tea

Ham and cheese combine with salad-filled rolls to make a highly nutritious lunch. If you do not plan to serve both filled rolls on the same day, reserve the second filling portion and complete the sandwich on the day it will be served. The ever popular Chocolate Chip-Peanut Squares will make this lunch a favorite with everyone.

Picnic Salad Rolls

2 tablespoons chopped green
  pepper
2 tablespoons chopped cucumber
2 tablespoons chopped tomato
2 tablespoons chopped celery
2 teaspoons chopped onion
2 teaspoons chopped parsley
2 teaspoons chopped dill pickle

3 tablespoons garlic- or onion-
  flavored sour cream dip
2 tablespoons mayonnaise or salad
  dressing
Pinch of salt
2 hard rolls
Lettuce leaves (optional)

Combine first 7 ingredients, tossing well. Combine dip, mayonnaise, and salt; mix well, and fold into vegetable mixture. Set aside.

Remove a thin slice from top of each roll; scoop out center, leaving a ½-inch shell. Line shell with lettuce leaf, if desired. Spoon vegetable mixture into rolls; wrap each tightly, and chill until serving time. Yield: 2 servings.

Ham and Cheese Roll-Ups

4 (6- × 4-inch) thin slices ham
2 (7- × 3½-inch) slices Swiss cheese

2 dill pickle strips

Arrange ham slices over cheese; place pickle strip on ham. Pierce with wooden pick to hold, if necessary. Roll up in plastic wrap. Yield: 2 servings.

Chocolate Chip-Peanut Squares

½ cup butter or margarine, softened
¼ cup sugar
½ cup firmly packed brown sugar, divided
1 egg, separated
1½ teaspoons water
½ teaspoon vanilla extract

1 cup all-purpose flour
½ teaspoon soda
⅛ teaspoon salt
1 (6-ounce) package semisweet chocolate morsels
½ cup skinless salted peanuts, chopped

Cream butter, sugar, and ¼ cup brown sugar until light and fluffy; add beaten egg yolk, mixing well. Stir in water and vanilla.

Combine flour, soda, and salt; add to creamed mixture, blending well. Spread mixture in a lightly greased 8-inch square baking pan; sprinkle chocolate morsels evenly over top.

Beat egg white (at room temperature) until foamy; gradually add remaining ¼ cup brown sugar, beating until stiff. Spread meringue over chocolate morsels; sprinkle with nuts. Bake at 350° for 35 minutes. Cool and cut into 2-inch squares. Yield: about 16 squares.

Brown Bag Lunch

Sandwich Special
Chocolate Chip-Oatmeal Cookies
Cola Drink or Beer

This hearty sandwich is a combination of several standard filling ingredients, with a cabbage coleslaw topping that makes the sandwich different. Easy-to-make Chocolate Chip-Oatmeal Cookies provide the special finish.

Sandwich Special

2 tablespoons mayonnaise
1 tablespoon chili sauce
½ teaspoon instant minced onion
½ teaspoon lemon juice
½ cup finely shredded cabbage

2 slices corned beef
2 slices ham
2 slices turkey
2 slices Swiss cheese
4 slices rye bread

Combine first 5 ingredients; cover coleslaw, and refrigerate 4 hours.

Divide corned beef, ham, turkey, and cheese and place on 2 slices of rye bread; top each with equal amounts of coleslaw. Cover with remaining 2 slices of rye bread. Yield: 2 servings.

Chocolate Chip-Oatmeal Cookies

½ cup all-purpose flour
¼ teaspoon soda
¼ teaspoon salt
½ teaspoon ground cinnamon
½ teaspoon ground nutmeg
⅓ cup shortening

⅔ cup firmly packed brown sugar
1 egg
½ teaspoon vanilla extract
½ cup semisweet chocolate morsels
1 cup regular oats, uncooked

Combine flour, soda, salt, cinnamon, and nutmeg; set aside.

Cream shortening and sugar until light and fluffy; add egg and beat well. Add vanilla. Stir in flour mixture until well blended; add chocolate morsels and oats, mixing well.

Drop mixture by teaspoonfuls onto greased cookie sheets. Bake at 350° for 12 to 15 minutes. Yield: about 2 dozen.

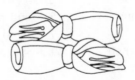

Summer Picnic

Chilled Strawberry Soup
Avocado Stuffed with Shrimp
Deviled Eggs
Cocktail Cheese Biscuits
Picnic Lemon Bars
Fumé Blanc

This meal can be really special if packed carefully to ensure safe and easy transporting. For the eggs, use a plastic container with a tight-fitting lid. There are several available with egg shaped holders that are perfect for this use. Wrap the cheese biscuits as well as the avocados in heavy-duty plastic or foil wrap. Wrap the stuffed avocados tightly enough to hold in the filling. Use a container with a tight-fitting lid for the soup, and package the Picnic Lemon Bars in a sturdy container or box to keep them from crumbling.

Pack all the individually packaged or wrapped food in a pretty basket if food will be served without much delay. If the meal won't be served for some time, pack eggs, soup, and avocado, with the wine, in an ice chest.

Chilled Strawberry Soup

1 cup strawberries, hulled and crushed
1 tablespoon lemon juice
1½ cups water

½ cup sugar
1 tablespoon quick-cooking tapioca
½ cup sweet white wine

Combine strawberries, lemon juice, water, sugar, and tapioca in a medium sauce-pan; mix well. Bring to a boil over medium heat, stirring often; cook for 15 minutes. Stir in wine; chill. Yield: about 2½ cups.

Avocado Stuffed with Shrimp

½ pound medium-size fresh shrimp, cooked, peeled, and deveined
½ cup thinly sliced celery
1 tablespoon commercial French dressing

2 tablespoons mayonnaise
Salt and pepper to taste
1 avocado
1 teaspoon lemon juice

Combine shrimp, celery, French dressing, and mayonnaise, mixing well. Season with salt and pepper; chill. Cut avocado in half lengthwise; peel and brush cut surfaces with lemon juice. Fill with shrimp mixture. Yield: 2 servings.

Note: If there will be a delay in serving, cut and peel avocado at the picnic site and fill with shrimp mixture.

Deviled Eggs

3 hard-cooked eggs
2 tablespoons mayonnaise
1 tablespoon chopped onion
2 teaspoons chopped green olives
½ teaspoon vinegar

½ teaspoon prepared mustard
Dash of salt
Dash of pepper
2 green olives, sliced

Slice eggs in half lengthwise, and carefully remove yolks. Mash yolks with mayon-naise. Add remaining ingredients except sliced green olives; stir well. Stuff egg whites with yolk mixture. Garnish eggs with sliced green olives. Yield: 2 servings.

Cocktail Cheese Biscuits

1½ cups all-purpose flour
1 cup (4 ounces) shredded sharp
  Cheddar cheese
½ teaspoon red pepper

3 tablespoons sesame seeds
½ cup butter or margarine, softened
1 egg, beaten
¼ teaspoon water

Combine first 4 ingredients, mixing well; cut in butter until mixture resembles coarse crumbs. Add egg and water; mix well with hands, and shape into 1-inch balls. Place on greased baking sheet; bake at 400° for 15 to 20 minutes. Yield: about 2½ dozen.
  Note: Store remaining biscuits in airtight container or freeze for later use.

Picnic Lemon Bars

¼ cup sifted powdered sugar
½ cup butter or margarine, softened
1 cup all-purpose flour
Pinch of salt
2 eggs, beaten
1 cup sugar

½ teaspoon baking powder
Grated rind of 1 lemon
2 tablespoons lemon juice
2 tablespoons all-purpose flour
Powdered sugar

Cream ¼ cup powdered sugar and butter until light and fluffy; add 1 cup flour and salt, mixing well. Press mixture into a lightly greased 9-inch square pan. Bake at 350° for 18 to 20 minutes.
  Combine next 6 ingredients, beating well. Pour over baked crust. Bake at 350° for 25 minutes. Sprinkle with powdered sugar. Cool; cut into bars. Yield: about 16 bars.

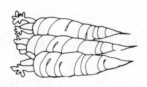

Light Lunch

Peanut-Apple Salad
Crunchy Carrot Sticks
Mint Tea

Anyone who packs lunch regularly will appreciate this change from the ordinary. The sugar can be omitted from the Peanut-Apple Salad for a reduced calorie lunch. Carrot sticks provide a nice color and texture contrast to the salad, but any other fresh vegetable can be substituted.

Peanut-Apple Salad

1½ cups diced unpeeled apple
½ cup chopped celery
½ teaspoon lemon juice
2 teaspoons sugar

1 tablespoon mayonnaise
¼ cup plain yogurt
¼ cup coarsely chopped peanuts
Lettuce (optional)

Combine apple and celery; sprinkle with lemon juice, and toss well. Combine sugar, mayonnaise, and yogurt; mix well, and fold into apple mixture. Chill well. Add peanuts, tossing lightly. Serve on lettuce, if desired. Yield: 2 servings.

Mint Tea

1 quart boiling water
5 individual-size tea bags
¾ to 1¼ cups sugar

Fresh mint sprigs
Rind and juice of 1½ lemons

Combine water, tea bags, sugar, 5 mint sprigs, and rind and juice of lemons; cover and steep 30 minutes to 1 hour. Strain and cool. Serve over ice. Garnish each glass with a sprig of mint, if desired. Yield: 1 quart.

Salads for Lunch

Chicken Salad in Tomatoes
Celery Salad
Assorted Crackers
Summer Fruit Mélange
Iced Tea

The tomato-chicken salad combination can be a welcome treat in the summer when tomatoes are at their best. To complete this salad luncheon, summer fruits are combined and seasoned with sherry and mint. These dishes may be prepared the night before to allow for thorough chilling. For transporting, place salads in containers with tight-fitting lids; keep well chilled.

Chicken Salad in Tomatoes

2 large tomatoes
3 tablespoons mayonnaise
¼ teaspoon curry powder
⅛ teaspoon salt
Dash of pepper
¼ teaspoon lemon juice

⅓ cup cooked rice
⅓ cup diced cooked chicken
¼ cup diced celery
1 tablespoon chopped green onion
⅓ cup cooked green peas
1 teaspoon chopped pimiento

Slice tops off tomatoes and scoop out pulp (reserve pulp for use in other recipes). Invert tomatoes on a plate to drain; chill.

Combine mayonnaise, curry powder, salt, pepper, and lemon juice. Add remaining ingredients, and mix well. Fill tomatoes with chicken mixture, and chill. Yield: 2 servings.

Celery Salad

3 tablespoons commercial sour
 cream
1 tablespoon vegetable oil
2 teaspoons wine vinegar
2 teaspoons sugar

¼ teaspoon salt
⅛ teaspoon paprika
Dash of pepper
1½ cups thinly sliced celery
¼ cup shredded carrots

Combine first 7 ingredients, mixing well. Add celery and carrots; toss until well mixed. Store in refrigerator. Yield: 2 servings.

Summer Fruit Melange

1 cup halved fresh strawberries
1 cup cantaloupe balls
½ cup sliced fresh peaches
½ cup seedless white grapes

¼ cup dry sherry
1 to 2 tablespoons sugar
½ teaspoon grated orange rind
2 to 4 fresh mint leaves, crushed

Combine fruit in a medium mixing bowl. Combine remaining ingredients; pour over fruit mixture, tossing lightly. Cover; chill 2 to 3 hours. Yield: 2 servings.

For an interesting change, use fresh pineapple, cantaloupe, or other shells as containers for dips and spreads. Pineapple halves scooped out are beautiful for serving cheese dips or salads. Other fruits like melon shells are nice for salads or appetizers.

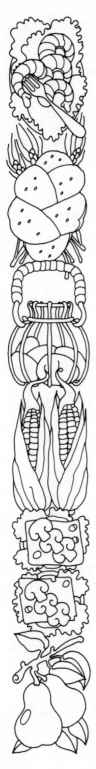

SUPPERS FOR TWO

Until recently, Southerners served supper in the evenings usually after having had their heavier main meal in the middle of the day. Today, any meal served in the evening can be called supper, but the lighter fare associated with it is most appropriate for those with hectic schedules (and whose isn't these days?) or for those who have eaten heavy noon meals—or for the traditionalist among us who just wants to hold onto the suppertime tradition.

These supper menus are planned to be somewhat lighter than our dinner menus, and several are one-dish meals, perfect for suppertime. Our main dishes are generally easy and quick to prepare. Some of the suggested desserts are fresh fruits served either plain or with toppings that require little time to prepare. Others are cooked desserts, such as the pie or fruit crunch, which complement the lighter meals for which they are suggested.

If you have not thought about supper for some time, try our menu suggestions. You may learn to appreciate this favorite meal.

Fireside Supper

Oyster Gumbo for Two
Buttermilk Carrot Cornbread
Tossed Greens with Italian Dressing
Flaming Irish Coffee
Sauvignon Blanc

Oyster Gumbo for Two makes a perfect supper, especially for Friday night, or any night when you want a hot and nourishing meal, yet one not difficult to prepare. Accompany it with Buttermilk Carrot Cornbread and a tossed salad with Italian Dressing for a simple, yet different supper. Flame the Irish Coffee for a spectacular finish.

Oyster Gumbo for Two

2 tablespoons all-purpose flour
2 tablespoons melted bacon
  drippings, butter, or margarine
½ cup chopped green pepper
½ cup chopped onion
1 small clove garlic, crushed
1 to 1½ cups water
1 tablespoon chopped parsley
¾ teaspoon salt

⅛ teaspoon black pepper
⅛ teaspoon red pepper
Dash of ground thyme
1 bay leaf
¼ pound peeled, deveined shrimp
1 (12-ounce) container oysters,
  undrained
Hot cooked rice
Gumbo filé (optional)

Combine flour and bacon drippings in a heavy saucepan or Dutch oven; cook over medium heat, stirring constantly, about 10 to 15 minutes or until roux is the color of a copper penny. (Do not let roux burn as it will ruin the gumbo; reduce heat, if necessary.)

Add green pepper, onion, and garlic to the roux; cook, stirring constantly, until vegetables are tender. Add water, parsley, and seasonings; simmer 30 minutes. Add shrimp and oysters; bring to a boil, and cook 5 minutes. Remove bay leaf. Serve over rice; add filé to each serving to thicken, if desired. Yield: 2 servings.

Note: Chicken may be substituted for shrimp, if desired. Cut chicken into bite-size pieces; brown in hot oil, and add to the roux.

Buttermilk Carrot Cornbread

½ cup all-purpose flour
½ cup cornmeal
2 tablespoons sugar (optional)
1½ teaspoons baking powder
½ teaspoon salt
2 tablespoons butter or margarine,
    softened

1 egg, beaten
1 medium carrot, peeled and
    shredded
½ cup buttermilk

Sift first 5 ingredients; cut in butter until mixture is blended. Set aside.

Combine egg, carrot, and buttermilk; add to cornmeal mixture, stirring well. Spoon batter into a lightly greased 6-inch skillet or round baking pan. Bake at 425° for 20 minutes or until lightly browned. Cool slightly; cut into wedges for serving. Yield: 4 wedges.

Italian Dressing

¾ cup olive oil
¼ cup wine vinegar
2 teaspoons minced fresh chives
1 teaspoon salt
1 teaspoon minced parsley

⅛ teaspoon black pepper
⅛ teaspoon red pepper
⅛ teaspoon dillseeds
1 clove garlic

Combine all ingredients in a jar. Cover tightly, and shake vigorously. Chill several hours. Remove garlic clove before serving. Serve dressing over tossed greens. Yield: about 1 cup.

Flaming Irish Coffee

4 tablespoons Irish Mist Liqueur
2 cups hot coffee
2 teaspoons sugar

½ cup whipping cream, whipped
Ground nutmeg

Rinse glass with hot water; dry. Pour 2 tablespoons Irish Mist into glass. Rotate over flame of Irish coffee burner or alcohol burner until liqueur ignites. Fill with 1 cup coffee; stir in 1 teaspoon sugar. Top with half of whipped cream; dust with nutmeg. Repeat for other serving. Yield: 2 servings.

The next time a recipe calls for 1 cup of buttermilk, and you have none, try this handy substitute: put 1 tablespoon vinegar or lemon juice in a measuring cup; add enough whole milk to make 1 cup; let stand 5 minutes to thicken slightly.

Eggs for Supper

Eggs Florentine
Vegetable-Thyme Salad
Baked Bananas in Orange Sauce
Gray Riesling

Eggs are among the most popular foods to serve anytime, but are especially appropriate at suppertime because they can be prepared quickly and in so many different ways. Eggs Florentine combines eggs and spinach in an open-faced sandwich and is accompanied by a nutritious vegetable salad and fruit dessert.

Eggs Florentine

2 onion-flavored buns
Softened butter or margarine
1 (10-ounce) package frozen leaf
  spinach, thawed and well drained
2 tablespoons butter or margarine,
  melted

4 slices boiled ham
4 slices tomato
4 poached eggs
Blender Hollandaise Sauce

Cut onion buns in half, and spread cut side with butter; place under broiler until lightly browned.

Sauté spinach for 2 minutes in butter. Place 1 slice of ham and 1 slice of tomato on each bun half; top with a small amount of spinach and 1 poached egg. Spoon about 3 tablespoons Blender Hollandaise Sauce over each. Yield: 2 servings.

Blender Hollandaise Sauce:

3 egg yolks
1 tablespoon lemon juice
¼ teaspoon tarragon leaves

¼ teaspoon salt
½ cup butter or margarine, melted

Combine all ingredients except butter in container of electric blender; blend until thick and lemon colored. Add warm melted butter in a slow, steady stream, and continue to process until thick. Yield: about ½ cup.

Note: This recipe may be doubled if more sauce is desired.

Vegetable-Thyme Salad

1 medium tomato, cut into bite-size
pieces
1 small cucumber, sliced
3 green onions, chopped
1 tablespoon mayonnaise

2 teaspoons fresh whole thyme,
crushed, or ½ teaspoon dried
thyme leaves
Salt and pepper to taste

Combine all ingredients, and refrigerate at least 1 hour before serving. Yield: about 2 servings.

Baked Bananas in Orange Sauce

2 firm bananas
2 teaspoons butter or margarine,
melted

2 teaspoons grated orange rind
¼ cup orange juice
2 tablespoons brown sugar

Cut bananas in half lengthwise; place cut side down in a 9-inch square baking dish. Brush bananas with butter. Bake at 350° for 10 minutes.

Combine remaining ingredients; pour over bananas. Bake an additional 15 minutes. Yield: 2 servings.

One-Dish Supper

Guacamole
Taco Salad
Garlic Breadsticks
Chilled Fresh Pineapple
Mexican Beer or Iced Tea

This Taco Salad is a complete meal and can be quickly and easily prepared. For this dish and others, get in the habit of packaging and freezing ground beef in serving-size portions of about one-quarter pound each; then it will be easy to use in recipes which call for ground beef. The Guacamole can either be served with the main dish salad or as an appetizer. Any fruit makes a good dessert for this simple meal, but we suggest fresh pineapple, well chilled.

Guacamole

1 ripe avocado, peeled and mashed
½ medium tomato, peeled and
   finely chopped
1 tablespoon finely chopped onion

1½ teaspoons lemon juice or
   vinegar
Hot sauce to taste
Garlic salt to taste

Combine first 5 ingredients; blend well. Season to taste with garlic salt. Chill before serving as a dip with corn chips or over shredded lettuce as a salad. Yield: 1 cup.
   Note: Reserve seed from avocado. Place in guacamole to prevent mixture from darkening. Remove seed before serving.

Taco Salad

½ pound ground beef
½ teaspoon seasoned salt
½ teaspoon ground cumin
Dash of garlic powder
½ cup chopped onion
½ medium head of lettuce,
   shredded
2 to 3 tomatoes, chopped

1 medium avocado, chopped
   (optional)
½ (8-ounce) package tortilla chips,
   broken into small pieces
1 cup (4 ounces) shredded Cheddar
   cheese
Commercial sour cream (optional)
Taco sauce

Brown meat with salt, cumin, garlic, and onion; drain well. Layer meat mixture and remaining ingredients on serving plates. Serve immediately with taco sauce. Yield: 2 servings.

Garlic Breadsticks

½ (9-inch) loaf bread, unsliced
¼ cup butter or margarine, softened
1 clove garlic, minced

2 to 3 tablespoons sesame seeds,
   toasted

Trim crust from bread. (Make crust into breadcrumbs for use in other recipes.) Cut bread in half lengthwise, then in 8 equal crosswise slices.
   Combine butter and garlic, mixing well; spread on all sides of bread slices. Arrange on a baking sheet, and sprinkle with sesame seeds. Bake at 400° for 10 minutes or until lightly browned. Yield: 16 breadsticks.
   Note: To double recipe, use entire loaf of bread and double other ingredients.

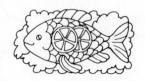

Seafood Supper

Creamy Crab Soup
Broiled Herb Fish Fillets
Golden Parmesan Potatoes
Quick Broiled Tomatoes
Chocolate Oatmeal Pie
Chardonnay

Seafood lovers will really enjoy this supper. The rich soup is perfect to begin the meal which is topped off with delicious Chocolate Oatmeal Pie. It is good enough to have several times, so we think you will enjoy the extra servings.

Creamy Crab Soup

1 cup milk
⅛ teaspoon ground mace
¼ teaspoon dry mustard
Dash of ground nutmeg
1 teaspoon grated lemon rind
½ pound crabmeat

1 cup half-and-half
1½ tablespoons butter or margarine
¼ teaspoon salt
¼ cup dry white wine
3 tablespoons cracker crumbs

Combine milk, seasonings, and lemon rind in top of a double boiler; stir well. Cook mixture over simmering water 10 minutes.

Stir crabmeat, half-and-half, butter, and salt into hot mixture; cook over boiling water 20 minutes, stirring often. Stir in wine and cracker crumbs. Serve immediately. Yield: 2 servings.

Broiled Herb Fish Fillets

2 fish fillets
2 to 3 teaspoons minced fresh dillweed
½ to 1 teaspoon minced fresh thyme
½ teaspoon salt

½ teaspoon grated gingerroot (optional)
¼ cup dry white wine (optional)
2 tablespoons butter or margarine
1 teaspoon lemon juice

Place fillets skin side down in a lightly oiled shallow baking dish. Sprinkle with dill, thyme, salt, and gingerroot, if desired. Pour wine over and around fish, if desired; set aside.

Combine butter and lemon juice in a saucepan; cook over low heat until butter melts. Pour over fillets. Broil 6 inches from heat for 7 to 10 minutes or until fish flakes easily when tested with a fork. Yield: 2 servings.

Golden Parmesan Potatoes

2 tablespoons all-purpose flour
2 tablespoons grated Parmesan
  cheese
¼ teaspoon salt
Dash of pepper
3 large potatoes, peeled and cut
  into eighths

2 to 3 tablespoons butter or
  margarine, melted
1 tablespoon chopped parsley
  (optional)

Combine flour, cheese, salt, and pepper in a bag. Moisten potatoes with water, shaking off excess. Shake a few at a time in the bag, coating well.

Pour butter into a 12- × 8- × 2-inch baking dish. Place potatoes in the dish in a single layer. Bake at 375° for 1 hour, turning once. Sprinkle with parsley, if desired. Yield: 2 servings.

Quick Broiled Tomatoes

3 tablespoons dry breadcrumbs
1 tablespoon commercial
  low-calorie Italian dressing

1 teaspoon chopped parsley
2 small tomatoes

Combine breadcrumbs, dressing, and parsley in a small bowl; mix well.

Cut thin slice off stem end of tomatoes. Spoon breadcrumb mixture over cut surface of tomatoes. Broil about 4 inches from heat for 7 minutes or until topping is lightly browned. Yield: 2 servings.

Chocolate Oatmeal Pie

2 eggs, beaten
½ cup butter or margarine, melted
1 cup sugar
⅔ cup uncooked regular oats

¼ teaspoon salt
1 teaspoon vanilla extract
2 tablespoons cocoa
1 unbaked 8-inch pastry shell

Combine first 7 ingredients; blend well. Pour into pastry shell. Bake at 300° for 45 minutes. Cool before serving. Yield: one 8-inch pie.

Oven Meal Dinner

Crunchy Baked Liver
Seasoned Fresh Green Beans
Quick Coleslaw
Cornmeal Buttermilk Rolls
Cranberry-Apple Crunch
Zinfandel

This unusual way of cooking liver is sure to make this a favorite dish. If only one oven is available, bake the Cranberry-Apple Crunch; then increase the temperature and bake the rolls and liver in the heated oven.

Crunchy Baked Liver

4 thin slices (⅔- to ¾-pound) calves
  liver
Seasoned salt
Seasoned pepper
½ cup all-purpose flour

1 egg, beaten
2 tablespoons lemon juice
½ cup herb-seasoned stuffing mix
1 tablespoon butter or margarine,
  melted

Sprinkle liver with seasoned salt and pepper. Dredge lightly with flour.

Combine egg and lemon juice in a piepan. Dip liver slices in egg mixture. Turn to coat both sides. Arrange liver slices in a greased 12- × 8- × 2-inch baking dish.

Combine stuffing mix, any remaining egg, and butter in a small bowl. Press crumb mixture onto liver slices.

Bake at 450° for 10 minutes or until cooked to desired degree of doneness. Yield: 2 servings.

Seasoned Fresh Green Beans

1 medium onion, chopped
2 tablespoons olive oil or vegetable
  oil
¼ green pepper, chopped
1 stalk celery, chopped

¾ pound fresh green beans, cut into
  2-inch pieces
¼ cup water
½ teaspoon salt
Dash of pepper

Sauté onion in oil over medium heat until tender. Add green pepper and celery; cover and cook over low heat 5 minutes, stirring occasionally. Add green beans, water, salt, and pepper; cover and cook 20 minutes, stirring occasionally. Yield: 2 servings.

Quick Coleslaw

2 cups shredded cabbage
¼ cup diced green pepper
¼ cup mayonnaise
2 tablespoons commercial sour
  cream

1 teaspoon lemon juice
¼ teaspoon salt
⅛ teaspoon dry mustard

Combine cabbage and green pepper in a medium bowl; set aside. Combine mayonnaise, sour cream, lemon juice, salt, and mustard; mix well. Spoon over cabbage and green pepper; toss well. Yield: 2 servings.

Cornmeal Buttermilk Rolls

¾ cup all-purpose flour
⅓ cup cornmeal
2 teaspoons baking powder
⅛ teaspoon soda
½ teaspoon salt

2 tablespoons shortening
1 egg, slightly beaten
⅓ cup buttermilk
Melted butter or margarine

Combine first 5 ingredients; cut in shortening until mixture resembles coarse meal. Stir egg into buttermilk; add to dry ingredients, mixing well.

Turn dough out on a lightly floured board, and knead 1 to 2 minutes. Roll dough to ½-inch thickness, and cut into rounds with a 2½-inch biscuit cutter.

With dull edge of knife, make a crease just off-center on each round; brush with melted butter. Fold each round over so that top overlaps slightly; press edges together. Place rolls on a greased baking sheet; bake at 450° for 12 to 15 minutes. Yield: 8 to 10 rolls.

Cranberry-Apple Crunch

1 cup cranberries
1½ cups chopped unpeeled tart
  apple
½ cup sugar
¼ cup firmly packed brown sugar

2 tablespoons all-purpose flour
¼ cup butter or margarine, softened
½ cup uncooked regular oats
½ cup pecans, chopped

Combine cranberries, apple, and sugar in a lightly greased shallow 1-quart casserole or 9-inch piepan.

Combine brown sugar and flour; cut in butter with a pastry blender until mixture resembles coarse meal. Stir in oats and pecans. Sprinkle mixture over cranberries. Bake at 400° for 30 to 35 minutes or until golden brown. Yield: 2 servings.

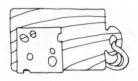

Saturday Special

Tomato-Avocado Aspic
Roast Chicken with Spinach-Cheese Stuffing
Watercress Salad
Summer Fruits and Cream
Zinfandel

Tomato-Avocado Aspic is a new version of an old favorite. It is a perfect appetizer for Roast Chicken with Spinach-Cheese Stuffing, a unique and delicious way to serve chicken. Whipped cream and currant jelly make Summer Fruits and Cream a special treat.

Tomato-Avocado Aspic

1 envelope unflavored gelatin
¼ cup cold water
1 cup tomato juice
1 small onion, sliced
1 teaspoon chopped parsley
1 tablespoon cider vinegar

1½ teaspoons lemon juice
2 whole cloves
1 teaspoon sugar
¼ teaspoon salt
½ cup diced avocado
¼ cup diced celery

Soften gelatin in cold water. Combine remaining ingredients except avocado and celery in a medium saucepan. Simmer over low heat 15 minutes; strain, discarding onion, parsley, and cloves.

Add gelatin to hot juice, mixing well. Chill until partially set. Stir in avocado and celery. Pour into a 3-cup mold; chill until firm. Yield: 2 generous servings.

Roast Chicken with Spinach-Cheese Stuffing

2 chicken leg quarters
1 (10-ounce) package frozen
   chopped spinach
¼ cup commercial sour cream
¼ cup grated Parmesan cheese
¼ cup shredded Swiss cheese
2 tablespoons fine dry breadcrumbs

1 egg
¼ teaspoon salt
Freshly ground pepper to taste
2 tablespoons butter or margarine,
   melted
Hot cooked rice

Wash and pat chicken dry. Carefully push the hand between the chicken meat and skin to loosen and lift to form a pocket for stuffing. Leave skin attached at end of leg and along side of thigh. Pat dry and set aside.

Cook spinach according to package directions. Run cold water over spinach to cool; drain and press out all excess moisture. Combine spinach, sour cream, Parmesan cheese, Swiss cheese, breadcrumbs, egg, salt, and pepper in a medium bowl. Stir to mix well. Working carefully to keep skin from tearing, press spinach mixture between skin and meat of each chicken piece.

Brush a 9-inch square baking dish lightly with part of melted butter. Arrange stuffed chicken pieces in pan; brush each piece with remaining butter. Roast chicken at 350°, basting frequently, for 1 hour or until chicken is golden brown and the leg joints move easily. Serve over hot cooked rice. Yield: 2 servings.

Watercress Salad

1 large bunch fresh watercress, torn
½ cup sliced fresh mushrooms
½ cup sliced hearts of palm
¼ cup toasted almonds

Salt and pepper to taste
¼ cup commercial creamy garlic
  salad dressing

Combine first 5 ingredients in a salad bowl. Add enough water to salad dressing to make ⅓ cup, mixing well. Pour over salad, and toss gently. Yield: 2 servings.

Summer Fruits and Cream

¼ cup whipping cream
1 teaspoon sugar
2 sponge cake dessert cups, cut into
  1- × ½-inch slices
¼ cup currant jelly, whipped thin
  for spreading

½ cup fresh peeled peaches, thinly
  sliced
½ cup fresh strawberries, thinly
  sliced
Additional whipped cream for
  garnish

Combine whipping cream and sugar in a medium mixing bowl; beat until stiff peaks form.

Arrange sponge cake slices in bottom of glass bowl. Spread with half of whipped currant jelly. Arrange a layer of peaches on top of jelly, followed by a layer of strawberries and a layer of whipped cream. Continue layering until all ingredients have been included, ending with fruit.

Using a pastry bag, decorate top of dessert with additional whipped cream. Yield: 2 servings.

Leftover vegetables go nicely in salad. Or make a chef's salad with leftover meats, cheese, and cold cuts cut in strips and tossed with leftover vegetables, greens, and salad dressing.

MICROWAVE COLLECTION

If you own and use a microwave oven, you probably already realize how valuable it is. It makes meal preparation easier, simplifies clean up, and provides flexibility in meal planning.

In our collection of microwave recipes designed for two, you will find a variety of recipes ranging from beverages and appetizers to desserts.

Remember these simple rules and follow them whether you are a novice or advanced microwave cook.

Read the manufacturer's instruction book.

Organize the menu items to allow for standing time, particularly with vegetables and meats.

Check for doneness at the shortest cooking time; then add a minute or two more, as needed.

Use your eyes and good judgment to determine doneness for foods, or test meats and meat casseroles for doneness with a microwave thermometer.

Select the appropriate container for best results. Both size and material are important. Microwave cooking containers may be oven glass, glass ceramic, or microwave plastics. A variety of sizes and shapes are available in all these materials.

Microwave Breakfast

Hot Spicy Cider
Cheese Strata
Microwaved Bacon
Hot Coffee

This time plan is designed so that all foods can be served properly. Prepare Cheese Strata. Let it stand for 5 minutes while preparing and microwaving the cider. Prepare the bacon to cook, and cook the strata. Serve the cider while the bacon is cooking.

Hot Spicy Cider

1½ cups apple cider
1½ tablespoons brown sugar
Dash of ground nutmeg
⅛ teaspoon whole allspice

¼ teaspoon whole cloves
1 (2-inch) stick cinnamon
1 thin orange slice, cut in half

Combine cider, sugar, and nutmeg in a 4-cup glass measure. Add seasonings. Microwave at HIGH for 3 to 5 minutes. Let stand 3 to 4 minutes. To serve, strain into serving mugs. Garnish with orange slices. Yield: 2 servings.

Cheese Strata

3 slices white bread, crust removed
¾ cup (3 ounces) shredded Cheddar
  cheese
2 eggs
½ teaspoon salt

1 tablespoon grated Parmesan
  cheese
1 cup milk
¾ teaspoon Dijon mustard

Place trimmed bread in a single layer in a 9-inch microwave dish. Sprinkle Cheddar cheese over bread. Combine remaining ingredients, mixing well. Slowly pour egg mixture over cheese and bread. Let stand 5 minutes.

Cover with waxed paper; microwave at HIGH for 2 minutes. Rotate dish one half-turn. Microwave at MEDIUM for 6 to 8 minutes, rotating dish halfway through microwaving. Soufflé will be puffy and set around the edge. If it still has soft spots, microwave at MEDIUM for 1 to 2 minutes. Cover wet spots with waxed paper placed directly on the surface. Serve immediately. Yield: 2 servings.

Microwaved Bacon

Arrange desired number of bacon slices on a microwave roasting rack set in a shallow baking dish. Cover with a paper towel. Microwave at HIGH according to the following times.

Number of Slices	Minutes
1	¾ to 1
2	1½ to 2
3	2 to 3
4	3 to 4

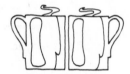

Microwave Brunch

Dixie Darling
Warmed Grapefruit
Mushrooms and Bacon in Wine Sauce
Spiced Fruit
Coffee with Lemon
Champagne

A special meal, this brunch can be served in minutes although some advance preparation is necessary. Prepare Spiced Fruit to allow for chilling. Prepare grapefruit and set aside. Assemble and cook Mushrooms and Bacon in Wine Sauce. Serve drinks, if desired, while warming the grapefruit to serve as a first course. Reheat the main dish, if necessary, before serving over toast.

Dixie Darling

½ cup bourbon
1 cup orange juice

¼ cup orange liqueur
Dash of orange bitters

Combine all ingredients, mixing well. Serve over ice cubes or allow to mellow in refrigerator and serve over ice cubes as punch. Yield: 2 servings.

Warmed Grapefruit

1 grapefruit, halved
2 tablespoons brown sugar

Flaked coconut
Maraschino cherries

Remove seeds, and loosen sections of each grapefruit half. Sprinkle 1 tablespoon sugar on each half. Top with coconut and a cherry. Place halves in small microwave bowls. Microwave at HIGH for 1 to 2 minutes or until grapefruit is warm. Yield: 2 servings.

Mushrooms and Bacon in Wine Sauce

4 slices bacon
2 tablespoons butter or margarine
½ pound fresh mushrooms, sliced
2 tablespoons all-purpose flour
⅓ cup dry white wine

Pinch of salt
Dash of pepper
2 slices toast
Chopped fresh parsley

Arrange bacon on a microwave roasting rack set in a shallow baking dish. Cover with a paper towel, and microwave at HIGH for 3 to 4 minutes or until crisp. Remove from rack. Drain on paper towel; crumble when cool.

Empty bacon drippings into a 1-quart microwave casserole. Add butter; microwave at HIGH for 30 seconds. Stir in sliced mushrooms, and microwave at HIGH for 2 to 3 minutes or until cooked and tender.

Remove mushrooms from drippings. Gradually stir flour into drippings; microwave at HIGH for 30 seconds. Add wine and seasonings, and microwave at HIGH for 1 to 2 minutes or until smooth and thickened.

Stir in mushrooms and bacon. Serve mixture over toast, and sprinkle with parsley. Yield: 2 servings.

Spiced Fruit

1 orange
1 (16-ounce) can pear halves, drained
1 (16-ounce) can peach halves, drained
1 (8-ounce) can pineapple chunks, drained

¾ cup orange juice
2 tablespoons sugar
1 (2-inch) stick cinnamon
6 whole cloves
¼ teaspoon salt

Grate and peel orange, reserving grated rind. Cut orange into 4 or 5 slices, and combine with rind, pears, peaches, and pineapple in a large bowl. Combine remaining ingredients in a 1-quart microwave casserole; microwave at HIGH for 3 to 5 minutes. Pour over fruit; cover and chill several hours or overnight. Remove cinnamon and cloves before serving. Yield: 2 servings.

Microwave Lunch

Golden Apple-Turkey Divan
or
Deviled Broccoli
Summer Vegetable Toss
Chocolate Pudding
Iced Tea or French Colombard

This menu utilizes some of the best features of the microwave with recipes calling for cooked fruit and sauces. These make Golden Apple-Turkey Divan, using either leftover or purchased cooked turkey, into a special dish. If your choice is Deviled Broccoli, you will enjoy the new way of using deviled ham and broccoli. For either meal, prepare the Chocolate Pudding in advance, leaving your microwave oven free to cook the main dish.

Golden Apple-Turkey Divan

1 apple, peeled, cored, and sliced
¼ pound cooked turkey, cut into strips
1 tablespoon butter or margarine
1 tablespoon all-purpose flour
¼ teaspoon salt

Dash of pepper
½ cup whipping cream
1 tablespoon sherry
2 tablespoons grated Parmesan cheese
Chopped parsley

Divide apple slices between 2 small individual microwave casseroles; cover with heavy-duty plastic wrap. Microwave at HIGH for 1 to 2 minutes or until apples start to turn translucent. Drain off any liquid. Arrange turkey strips over apple slices; cover with heavy-duty plastic wrap and let stand while preparing sauce.

Place butter in a 2-cup microwave measure or small bowl. Microwave at HIGH for 15 to 30 seconds or until melted. Stir in flour, salt, and pepper; gradually blend in cream. Microwave at HIGH for 1½ minutes or until sauce thickens; stir halfway through cooking time. Stir in sherry and cheese; spoon over apple and turkey. Cover with heavy-duty plastic wrap and microwave at MEDIUM for 2 to 2½ minutes or until apple and turkey are thoroughly heated. Sprinkle with parsley; recover with plastic wrap and let stand 5 minutes. Yield: 2 servings.

Deviled Broccoli

¼ cup commercial sour cream
1 tablespoon all-purpose flour
¼ teaspoon salt
1 (2¼-ounce) can deviled ham

1 (10-ounce) package frozen
  chopped broccoli
⅓ cup crushed corn chips

Combine first 4 ingredients in a 2-cup glass measure. Microwave at HIGH for 2 to 3 minutes until slightly thickened; stir well twice (do not boil).

Place broccoli in a 1-quart casserole. Cover and microwave at HIGH for 5 to 6 minutes. Cool slightly and drain well.

Combine broccoli and sour cream mixture, and place in a buttered 1-quart casserole. Microwave at MEDIUM-HIGH for 6 or 7 minutes or until mixture bubbles around edge. Top with crushed chips; microwave at HIGH for 1 minute. Yield: 2 servings.

Summer Vegetable Toss

½ pound yellow squash, thinly
  sliced
½ pound zucchini, thinly sliced
¼ teaspoon salt
2 tablespoons butter or margarine,
  sliced

2 slices bacon, cooked and
  crumbled
2 tablespoons grated Parmesan
  cheese

Place squash in a 1½-quart microwave casserole; cover with lid or heavy-duty plastic wrap. Microwave at HIGH for 4 to 6 minutes or until squash is crisp-tender. Stir once about halfway through microwaving.

Drain off excess liquid. Add salt, butter, bacon, and cheese. Toss to blend. Cover and let stand 2 to 3 minutes before serving. Yield: 2 servings.

Chocolate Pudding

2 cups skim milk
¼ cup sugar

3 tablespoons cocoa
2 tablespoons cornstarch

Pour milk into a 4-cup glass measure; microwave at HIGH for 2 minutes. Mix dry ingredients in a small bowl. Stir some of the hot milk mixture into dry ingredients. Return chocolate mixture to hot milk. Microwave at HIGH for 3 to 4 minutes, stirring at 1-minute intervals. Pour into serving dishes. Cool before serving. Yield: 2 servings.

Press plastic wrap directly on surface of custards, puddings, or white sauce immediately after cooking to prevent a skin from forming.

Microwave Dinner

Avocado Dip
Stuffed Butterfly Pork Chops
Sweet Potato-Stuffed Squash
Granola Carrot Cake
Gewürztraminer

Bake the Granola Carrot Cake and allow to cool before frosting. At dinner-time, cook the sweet potatoes and acorn squash; set aside to cool. Prepare and cook the pork chops and let stand. Prepare sweet potato filling for acorn squash and complete cooking. Heat pork chops, if necessary, before serving.

Avocado Dip

1 ripe avocado, peeled and mashed
2 (3-ounce) packages cream cheese, softened
2 tablespoons milk

1 tablespoon lemon juice
1 tablespoon grated onion
¼ teaspoon salt

Combine avocado, cream cheese, and milk. Beat until smooth. Add remaining ingredients; blend well. Serve with fresh vegetables or crackers. Yield: 1⅓ cups.

Stuffed Butterfly Pork Chops

2 (1-inch-thick) pork chops
1 tablespoon butter or margarine
½ cup chopped onion
¾ cup chopped celery
1½ cups herb-seasoned stuffing mix

¾ cup water
1 (8¾-ounce) can whole kernel corn, drained
Microwave browning and seasoning sauce

Cut pocket in pork chops.

Place butter in a 4-cup measure or microwave bowl. Microwave at HIGH for 15 seconds. Add onion and celery; microwave at HIGH for 2 to 3 minutes or until vegetables are tender. Add stuffing mix, water, and corn; blend well.

Fill pocket of each pork chop with stuffing; brush or coat with microwave browning and seasoning sauce. Spoon remaining stuffing into a greased shallow microwave baking dish. Arrange stuffed pork chops over stuffing in baking dish. Cover with waxed paper. Microwave at MEDIUM for 15 to 20 minutes or until chops are tender. Let stand 8 to 10 minutes before serving. Yield: 2 servings.

Sweet Potato-Stuffed Squash

2 medium (4-ounce) sweet potatoes
1 (1- to 1½-pound) acorn squash
1½ tablespoons butter or margarine, divided
2 teaspoons honey
2 tablespoons orange juice

½ teaspoon almond-flavored liqueur
1 to 2 tablespoons sliced almonds, toasted
Orange slices (optional)

Pierce potatoes with a fork 2 or 3 times. Microwave potatoes at HIGH for 5 to 6 minutes. Set aside to cool slightly.

Pierce squash with a fork 2 or 3 times. Microwave at HIGH for 6 to 8 minutes. Remove from oven and let stand 2 minutes. Cut in half; remove seeds and membrane, and spread each with 1 teaspoon butter.

Combine sweet potato, remaining 2½ teaspoons butter, honey, orange juice, and liqueur; mix well. Spoon into squash cavities. Sprinkle with almonds. Microwave at HIGH for 2 to 3 minutes to heat thoroughly. Garnish with orange slices, if desired. Yield: 2 servings.

Granola Carrot Cake

½ cup butter or margarine
¾ cup firmly packed brown sugar
2 eggs
2 cups grated carrots
¾ cup all-purpose flour
½ teaspoon soda

½ teaspoon baking powder
½ teaspoon salt
½ teaspoon ground cinnamon
½ teaspoon ground nutmeg
1 cup granola cereal
Cream Cheese Frosting

Place butter in a 2½-quart casserole and microwave at HIGH for 30 seconds. Blend in sugar; beat in eggs.

Combine carrots, flour, soda, baking powder, seasonings, and granola cereal in a medium bowl. Add to egg mixture.

Grease the bottom only of an 8-inch round glass or microwave plastic baking dish. Pour in batter. Microwave at HIGH for 7 to 8 minutes. Rotate dish one half-turn at 3-minute intervals. Cool; frost with Cream Cheese Frosting. Yield: one 8-inch layer.

Cream Cheese Frosting:

2 tablespoons butter or margarine
1 (3-ounce) package cream cheese

2 cups sifted powdered sugar
½ teaspoon vanilla extract

Place butter and cream cheese in a 2-quart glass mixing bowl and microwave at HIGH for ½ to 1 minute. Beat in sugar and vanilla. Mixture should be of spreading consistency. Yield: enough for one 8-inch layer.

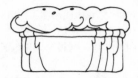

Microwave Supper

Spinach Soufflé with Cheese Sauce
Fresh Tomato Wedges
Whole Wheat Crackers
Baked Apples or Apple Betty Pie
Sauvignon Blanc

You will find this soufflé easy to prepare, and the sauce makes a deliciously rich topping. While the soufflé is cooking, prepare the ingredients for the Cheese Sauce. After removing the soufflé, cook the Cheese Sauce. Microwave the Baked Apples while dinner is served, or prepare the Apple Betty Pie in advance.

Spinach Souffle with Cheese Sauce

1 (10-ounce) package frozen chopped spinach	Dash of red pepper
2 tablespoons butter or margarine	⅓ cup milk
2 tablespoons all-purpose flour	2 eggs, separated
¼ teaspoon salt	Tomato wedges
	Cheese Sauce

Place unopened package of spinach in microwave oven. Microwave at MEDIUM for 5 minutes until spinach is thawed. Remove spinach to colander, squeezing out as much liquid as possible.

Place butter, flour, salt, and pepper in a 1-quart measure or casserole. Microwave at HIGH for 1 minute or until butter is melted and mixture can be stirred smooth. Add milk to butter-flour mixture; stir until smooth. Microwave at HIGH for 1½ to 3 minutes or until thick, stirring at 1-minute intervals. Stir spinach into sauce.

Beat egg whites (at room temperature) with electric mixer at high speed until stiff but not dry. Using the same beaters, beat egg yolks until thick and lemon colored. Add yolks to spinach sauce, and beat mixture thoroughly until smooth. Gently fold in egg whites.

Pour into an ungreased 8-inch glass or plastic pieplate. Smooth top of spinach mixture with a spatula. Microwave at MEDIUM for 5 to 7 minutes, giving dish one quarter-turn after 4 minutes. Cut the soufflé into wedges and serve with tomato wedges and Cheese Sauce. Yield: 2 servings.

Basic White Sauce:

2 tablespoons butter or margarine	¼ teaspoon salt
2 tablespoons all-purpose flour	1 cup milk

Place butter in a 4-cup glass measure. Microwave at HIGH for 30 seconds or until butter melts. Blend in flour and salt; stir well. Gradually add milk, stirring well. Microwave at HIGH for 2 minutes; stir well. Microwave at HIGH for 1 to 2½ minutes, stirring at 1-minute intervals until thickened and bubbly. Yield: 1 cup.

Cheese Sauce Variation: To 1 cup hot white sauce, add ¾ cup shredded sharp Cheddar cheese and ⅛ teaspoon dry mustard; stir until cheese melts. Serve over vegetables or hamburgers. Yield: about 1¼ cups.

Creamy Dill Sauce Variation: To 1 cup hot white sauce, add ¼ cup commercial sour cream and 1 teaspoon dried dillweed; stir well. Serve over vegetables, fish, or schnitzel. Yield: about 1¼ cups.

Curry Sauce Variation: To 1 cup hot white sauce, add 2 teaspoons curry powder; stir well. Serve over meats. Yield: about 1 cup.

Baked Apples

2 large baking apples	2 teaspoons butter or margarine
1 tablespoon brown sugar	

Core apples to within ½ inch from bottom; peel ½ inch of skin from around top. Spoon 1½ teaspoons sugar into each apple. Place the apples in custard cups or a round microwave dish. Top each with 1 teaspoon butter. Cover with waxed paper; microwave at HIGH for 2 to 4 minutes (1 to 2 minutes per apple). Yield: 2 servings.

Apple Betty Pie

½ cup butter or margarine	½ cup sugar
¼ cup sugar	1 teaspoon ground cinnamon
2 cups graham cracker crumbs	
5 cups thinly sliced apples (4 to 6 medium)	

Place butter in a large glass mixing bowl. Microwave at HIGH for about 1 minute. Add sugar and crumbs; mix well. Press half of mixture firmly and evenly to line a 9-inch pieplate.

Arrange apple slices in crumb-lined pieplate; combine sugar and cinnamon; sprinkle over apples. Arrange remaining crumbs in a high rim around edge, leaving the center open. Mold crumbs firmly into attractive peaked ridge at edges so slices of the finished pie hold their shape. Cover with waxed paper. Microwave at HIGH for 10 to 12 minutes. Cover with waxed paper, and let stand 10 minutes. Remove waxed paper; continue cooling. Serve either warm or cold. Yield: one 9-inch pie.

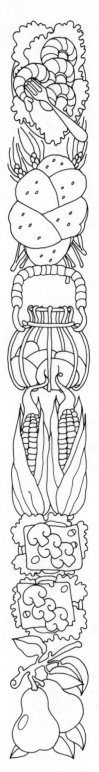

MAIN MEALS
FOR A WEEK

We have built our menus for a week around the concept of fully utilizing the food purchased for these meals. For example, a pork roast can be enjoyed for Sunday Dinner and the remainder of the meat refrigerated until Tuesday when it appears in a completely different dish.

In creating these menus, we followed the Basic Four Food Groups plan. We suggest either rice, potato, or another grain and give no bread recommendation in some menus. In other meals that call for a rich dessert, we again have omitted the bread. This balance may be important to the calorie- or nutrition-conscious cook, but others may wish to serve a bread in addition to our suggested items.

Our wine suggestions are California wines because they are readily available in most areas, but other American or European wines may be served equally as well.

Sunday Lunch

Ham and Eggs Special
Hot Mushroom Salad
Sour Cream Biscuits
Pineapple Sherbet Float
Iced Tea

This meal is easily and quickly prepared and can be served either as a brunch or for lunch. The ham and eggs are topped with a rich cream sauce, then baked in individual serving dishes. The Sour Cream Biscuits bake at the same time so that the entire meal can be served in less than thirty minutes. The salad of mushrooms, onion, and pepper is made special by the dressing and bacon.

Ham and Eggs Special

2 thin slices boiled or baked ham	Dash of salt
2 eggs	Dash of white pepper
2 tablespoons butter or margarine	¼ teaspoon tarragon
2 tablespoons all-purpose flour	¼ cup dry vermouth
⅓ cup milk	¼ cup grated Romano cheese
¼ cup chicken broth	Paprika

Line 2 greased ramekins with ham slices, trimming to fit if necessary. Break an egg into each; set aside.

Melt butter in heavy saucepan over low heat; add flour, stirring until smooth. Cook 1 minute, stirring constantly. Gradually add milk and broth; cook over medium heat, stirring constantly, until thickened and bubbly. Stir in salt, pepper, tarragon, and vermouth.

Spoon half of sauce over each egg, and sprinkle each with 2 tablespoons cheese. Garnish with paprika. Place on a baking sheet and bake at 425° about 10 minutes or until eggs are set. Yield: 2 servings.

Hot Mushroom Salad

2 teaspoons butter or margarine,
  melted
2½ teaspoons soy sauce
2½ teaspoons teriyaki sauce
½ green pepper, cut in thin strips

½ small onion, thinly sliced
½ pound fresh mushrooms, sliced
Lettuce leaves
2 slices bacon, cooked and
  crumbled

Combine all ingredients except lettuce and bacon in a skillet or wok. Cook, stirring frequently, until green pepper and onion are crisp-tender. Spoon onto lettuce, and garnish with bacon. Serve at once. Yield: 2 servings.

Sour Cream Biscuits

½ cup self-rising flour
⅛ teaspoon soda

⅓ cup plus 1 tablespoon
  commercial sour cream

Combine all ingredients in a bowl; stir until smooth. Turn dough out onto a lightly floured surface. Pat dough out to ½-inch thickness; cut with 2-inch biscuit cutter. Place biscuits on a lightly greased baking sheet. Bake at 425° for 10 to 15 minutes or until golden brown. Yield: 6 biscuits.

Pineapple Sherbet Float

1¼ cups pineapple sherbet
½ cup dry white wine

½ cup ginger ale

Combine all ingredients; stir gently until sherbet is partially melted. Serve in tall glasses. Yield: 2 servings.

Page 63: *The One-Dish Supper of Taco Salad served with Guacamole and Garlic Breadsticks calls for ice cold beer. Menu begins on page 42.*

Page 64: *Serve this simple Potato-Sprout Omelet with Spinach Salad, Bacon-Cornmeal Muffins, and Champagne for a festive Saturday Brunch. Menu begins on page 75.*

Sunday Dinner

Spiced Pineapple Pork Roast
Mixed Vegetable Dish
Tossed Fresh Greens with
Creamy Salad Dressing
Baked Sweet Potatoes
Crustless Coconut Pie
Coffee

This menu is simple to prepare, yet special enough for Sunday. The potatoes can bake during the last hour of the pork roast cooking time. Bake the pie in advance, or bake while serving dinner.

A special advantage of this meal is that any leftover roast can be used for the Tuesday Dinner menu. Freeze any pork remaining after these meals have been prepared.

Spiced Pineapple Pork Roast

1 (4-pound) pork loin roast
1 (12-ounce) jar pineapple preserves
2 tablespoons honey
2 tablespoons red wine vinegar
1 teaspoon prepared mustard

¼ teaspoon salt
¼ teaspoon ground cinnamon
¼ teaspoon ground cloves
1 (8-ounce) can pineapple slices, drained

Place roast on rack in shallow roasting pan. Insert meat thermometer into thickest part of roast, making sure it does not touch fat or bone. Bake, uncovered, at 325° for 2½ to 3 hours or until meat thermometer registers 170°.

Combine pineapple preserves, honey, vinegar, mustard, salt, cinnamon, and cloves in a small saucepan. Cook, stirring constantly, over low heat until preserves melt. During last 20 minutes of roasting time, garnish roast with pineapple slices and brush with pineapple glaze several times. Serve remaining glaze warm with roast. Yield: 6 servings.

Mixed Vegetable Dish

1 tablespoon vegetable oil
1 medium clove garlic, cut in half
1 carrot, diagonally sliced ¼ inch thick
1 stalk celery, diagonally sliced ¼ inch thick
2 to 3 green onions, cut into 1-inch pieces
1 medium-size yellow squash, diagonally sliced ¼ inch thick
½ green or red pepper, cut into ½-inch strips
2 teaspoons soy sauce
Salt and pepper to taste
2 teaspoons sliced almonds (optional)

Heat oil in a wok or heavy skillet. Add garlic, and sauté over medium heat until garlic is golden brown. Discard garlic.

Add carrot and celery; stir-fry 3 to 4 minutes or until partially cooked. Add onion, squash, and green pepper; stir-fry 2 to 4 minutes or until vegetables are crisp-tender. Add soy sauce, salt, and pepper; mix lightly. Sprinkle with almonds, if desired. Yield: 2 servings.

Creamy Salad Dressing

1 tablespoon olive oil
1 tablespoon wine vinegar
½ cup mayonnaise
2 tablespoons catsup
¼ teaspoon ground oregano leaves
¼ teaspoon garlic powder
1½ tablespoons milk

Combine all ingredients, mixing well. Serve over tossed salad. Yield: 1 cup.

Baked Sweet Potatoes

2 medium sweet potatoes
Butter or margarine
Salt and pepper

Wash potatoes well; rub with butter. Cut a slit lengthwise down center of each; wrap each in aluminum foil. Bake at 325° for 1½ hours or until tender. Serve with butter, salt, and pepper. Yield: 2 servings.

Crustless Coconut Pie

½ cup biscuit mix
½ cup sugar
4 eggs
2 cups milk
1 cup flaked coconut
1 teaspoon vanilla extract
3 tablespoons butter or margarine, melted

Combine all ingredients in container of electric blender; blend on low speed for 1 minute. Pour mixture into a buttered 9-inch pieplate. Bake at 400° for 20 to 25 minutes or until pie is set. Yield: one 9-inch pie.

Monday Dinner

Beef and Snow Peas Stir-Fry
Herbed Tomatoes
Half-a-Pound Cake with Fresh Fruit
Chenin Blanc

You will want to cook the noodles before cooking the meat mixture. Use either a wok or skillet to stir-fry beef and snow peas while the tomatoes are baking.

Beef and Snow Peas Stir-Fry

1 (½-pound) boneless round steak
2½ tablespoons soy sauce, divided
2 teaspoons sherry
2 teaspoons cornstarch
¼ cup plus 2 tablespoons vegetable oil, divided

1 (6-ounce) package frozen snow peas
1 small clove garlic, crushed
¼ teaspoon sugar
Hot cooked noodles

Partially freeze meat; cut into slices ¼ inch thick and 2 inches long.

Combine 1 tablespoon soy sauce, sherry, and cornstarch; stir vigorously until cornstarch is dissolved. Coat beef with soy sauce mixture.

Heat ¼ cup oil over high heat in a wok or skillet. Add meat, and stir-fry until meat is browned. Remove meat, and set aside.

Add remaining 2 tablespoons oil to wok; add snow peas, and stir-fry over high heat 2 minutes. Add meat, garlic, remaining soy sauce, and sugar; cook until thickened and bubbly. Serve over hot cooked noodles. Yield: 2 servings.

Herbed Tomatoes

3 tablespoons dry breadcrumbs
2 teaspoons butter or margarine, melted
¼ teaspoon seasoned salt

2 teaspoons garlic powder
½ teaspoon ground coriander
½ teaspoon ground cumin
1 large tomato, halved

Combine breadcrumbs, butter, and seasonings, stirring well.

Place tomato halves cut side up in a small baking dish; top with breadcrumb mixture. Bake at 350° for 10 minutes or until thoroughly heated. Yield: 2 servings.

Half-a-Pound Cake

1½ cups sugar
½ cup butter or margarine, softened
¼ cup shortening
3 eggs

½ teaspoon vanilla extract
1½ cups sifted cake flour
¼ teaspoon baking powder
½ cup milk

Cream sugar, butter, and shortening until light and fluffy; add eggs, one at a time, beating well after each addition. Beat in vanilla.

Combine cake flour and baking powder; add to creamed mixture, mixing well. Add milk, and beat 5 minutes.

Pour batter into a greased and floured 9- × 5-× 3-inch loafpan. Bake at 325° for 1 hour or until done. Serve with fresh fruit or other topping. Yield: 1 loaf.

Tuesday Dinner

**Pork-Wild Rice Skillet
Spinach Soufflé Deluxe
Oriental Tomato Salad
Skillet Cornbread
Apple Streusel
Rosé of Cabernet**

Serve cooked pork from Sunday's dinner to make this meal a snap and Spinach Soufflé Deluxe to make it special. Prepare Apple Streusel and the soufflé; then bake them in the same oven. The remaining menu items are appropriately simple for this meal.

Pork-Wild Rice Skillet

¼ cup chopped green onion
¼ cup chopped green pepper
2 tablespoons vegetable oil
1½ cups cooked pork, cut into
    ¾-inch cubes
1 (11-ounce) package frozen long
    grain and wild rice
1 (2½-ounce) jar sliced mushrooms,
    drained

½ cup water
2 tablespoons dry white wine
½ teaspoon chicken-flavored
    bouillon granules
¼ teaspoon dried whole basil leaves
1 tomato, cubed

Cook onion and green pepper in hot oil in a medium skillet over moderate heat until tender, stirring occasionally.

Stir in pork, rice, mushrooms, water, wine, bouillon granules, and basil. Bring to a boil; reduce heat. Cover and cook until most of liquid is absorbed, about 15 minutes, stirring occasionally. Stir in tomato. Cook over medium heat until thoroughly heated. Yield: 2 servings.

Spinach Souffle Deluxe

1 tablespoon butter or margarine
2 teaspoons all-purpose flour
½ cup milk
¼ teaspoon salt
Dash of pepper

2 eggs, separated
½ cup cooked chopped spinach, pressed dry
3 tablespoons grated Parmesan cheese

Melt butter in a heavy saucepan over low heat; add flour, stirring until smooth. Cook 1 minute, stirring constantly. Gradually add milk; cook over low heat, stirring constantly, about 6 to 8 minutes or until thickened. Stir in salt and pepper.

Beat egg yolks. Gradually stir about one-fourth of hot mixture into yolks, stirring well; stir yolk mixture into white sauce. Add spinach and cheese; stir well.

Beat egg whites (at room temperature) until stiff; fold into spinach mixture. Spoon into a lightly greased 1-quart soufflé dish. Bake at 325° for 40 to 50 minutes or until firm. Serve immediately. Yield: 2 generous servings.

Oriental Tomato Salad

2 tomatoes, thinly sliced
1 medium onion, thinly sliced
1 tablespoon soy sauce

¾ teaspoon vinegar
½ teaspoon sesame or vegetable oil
½ teaspoon sugar

Combine tomatoes and onion in a medium bowl. Combine remaining ingredients, and pour over vegetables; toss well. Chill at least 20 minutes. Yield: 2 servings.

Skillet Cornbread

Vegetable oil
¼ cup all-purpose flour
¼ cup cornmeal
1 teaspoon baking powder

¼ teaspoon salt
1 egg, beaten
¼ cup milk
1 tablespoon vegetable oil

Pour a small amount of oil in an 8-inch iron skillet; cover and heat over low heat until very hot. Combine flour, cornmeal, baking powder, and salt; stir in egg, milk, and 1 tablespoon vegetable oil. Pour batter into hot skillet; cover and place over very low heat. Cook 5 minutes; turn and cook, covered, an additional 5 minutes or until golden brown. Yield: 2 servings.

Apple Streusel

2 cups peeled and sliced apples
⅓ to ½ cup firmly packed brown
  sugar
¼ cup all-purpose flour
¼ cup regular or quick-cooking
  oats, uncooked

½ teaspoon ground cinnamon
½ teaspoon ground nutmeg
3 tablespoons butter or margarine,
  softened
Whipped cream or ice cream
  (optional)

Place apples in a greased 9- × 5- × 3-inch loafpan. Combine remaining ingredients except whipped cream; mix until crumbly, and sprinkle over apples. Bake at 325° for 35 to 45 minutes or until apples are tender and topping is golden brown. Serve warm with whipped cream or ice cream, if desired. Yield: 2 servings.

Wednesday Dinner

Stuffed Peppers
Shredded Beets
Cucumbers in Sour Cream
Bread Pudding with Lemon Sauce
Zinfandel

Plan to serve Stuffed Peppers often when peppers are plentiful. The colorful beets and chilled cucumbers complement the main dish.

Stuffed Peppers

2 large green peppers
Salt
½ pound mild bulk sausage
1 small onion, chopped
1 (8-ounce) can tomatoes,
  undrained and chopped

1½ cups cooked regular rice
½ cup (2 ounces) shredded sharp
  Cheddar cheese
2 teaspoons Worcestershire sauce
Pepper
Parsley

Slice tops off green peppers, and remove seeds. Parboil peppers in boiling salted water 5 minutes; drain. Season cavity of each pepper with salt; set aside.
  Brown sausage in a skillet; add onion, and cook until tender. Pour off drippings. Add tomatoes, rice, cheese, and Worcestershire sauce; season to taste with salt and pepper. Simmer 5 minutes.

Stuff peppers with sausage mixture, and place in a 1-quart casserole. Pack any extra stuffing around peppers. Bake at 350° for 30 minutes. Garnish with parsley before serving. Yield: 2 servings.

Shredded Beets

1 (1-pound) bunch of beets, tops
  removed
¼ cup butter or margarine, melted
½ teaspoon salt

Dash of pepper
2 tablespoons minced parsley
1 tablespoon lemon juice

Wash, peel, and finely shred beets. Combine beets, butter, salt, and pepper in a skillet. Cover and cook over medium heat about 15 minutes or until beets are tender, stirring frequently. Sprinkle with parsley and lemon juice just before serving. Yield: 2 servings.

Cucumbers in Sour Cream

½ cup commercial sour cream
1½ tablespoons minced fresh chives
1 tablespoon lemon juice
¾ teaspoon salt

Dash of pepper
1 large or 2 small cucumbers,
  peeled and sliced

Combine first 5 ingredients, stirring well; stir in cucumbers. Chill. Yield: 2 servings.

Bread Pudding with Lemon Sauce

2 eggs, well beaten
2 to 3 tablespoons sugar
⅛ teaspoon salt
½ teaspoon ground cinnamon
½ teaspoon ground nutmeg

½ teaspoon vanilla extract
2 to 3 tablespoons raisins
2 cups breadcrumbs
1 cup hot milk
Lemon Sauce

Combine eggs and sugar; blend in seasonings, vanilla, raisins, breadcrumbs, and milk. Pour into a buttered 9- × 5- × 3-inch loafpan. Bake at 350° for 45 to 50 minutes or until done. Serve with Lemon Sauce. Yield: 2 servings.

Lemon Sauce:

1 egg, beaten
1 cup sugar
Grated rind of 1 lemon

Juice of 2 lemons
1 tablespoon butter or margarine

Combine egg, sugar, lemon rind, and lemon juice in a saucepan over low heat; cook until thickened, stirring constantly. Add butter, and stir until melted. Yield: about 1½ cups.

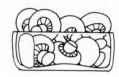

Thursday Dinner

Chicken Pillows
Mushroom-Stuffed Squash
Carrot and Cucumber Salad
Pound Cake with Ice Cream and Hot Fudge Sauce
French Colombard

Dinner in less than an hour is the advantage of this menu. Prepare and begin cooking the squash. Prepare the Chicken Pillows and cook in the same oven with the squash. Cook filling for squash, then fill, and complete cooking. Slice pound cake remaining from Monday's dinner and create a special dessert by topping it with ice cream and Hot Fudge Sauce.

Chicken Pillows

1 whole chicken breast, halved, skinned, and boned
1 clove garlic, halved
2 slices (1 ounce) prosciutto or boiled ham
2 slices (1 ounce) mozzarella cheese, thinly sliced
2 tablespoons seasoned breadcrumbs
2 tablespoons medium dry sherry
2 tablespoons clarified butter
Salt and freshly ground pepper to taste
1 tablespoon chopped parsley

Pound chicken breast pieces to a thickness of ¼ inch. Rub each chicken breast piece with cut garlic clove. Place prosciutto and cheese over chicken. Sprinkle with breadcrumbs. Roll up, starting at broader end, and secure with wooden picks. Place in a lightly greased shallow baking dish.

Combine sherry and clarified butter; heat briefly. Pour over chicken, and season with salt and pepper. Bake at 350° for 20 to 25 minutes or until chicken is done. Sprinkle with parsley. Yield: 2 servings.

Note: To clarify butter, melt butter over low heat in a heavy saucepan, without stirring. When completely melted, the butter will separate, with a milky layer atop a clear layer. Remove from heat; slowly pour the clear layer into a dish, reserving the milky layer in pan. Discard pan liquid.

Mushroom-Stuffed Squash

1 small acorn squash
Salt and pepper to taste
1 small onion, coarsely chopped
1 (4-ounce) can mushroom stems
  and pieces, drained

Pinch of dried parsley flakes
1 tablespoon butter or margarine
¼ cup shredded Cheddar cheese

Wash squash, and cut in half lengthwise; remove seeds and membrane. Place cut side down in a shallow baking pan; add boiling water to a depth of ¼ inch. Cover with aluminum foil, and bake at 350° for 40 to 50 minutes or until squash is tender. Remove from oven; turn cut side up, and sprinkle with salt and pepper.

Sauté onion, mushrooms, and parsley in butter until onion is tender. Fill squash halves with onion mixture, and top with cheese. Return to oven until cheese melts. Yield: 2 servings.

Carrot and Cucumber Salad

1½ teaspoons salt
1 medium carrot, diagonally sliced
1 medium cucumber, diagonally
  sliced

½ cup fresh or drained canned
  pineapple chunks
Lettuce leaves
Sesame Seed Dressing

Sprinkle salt over carrot and cucumber; let stand 5 minutes. Rinse vegetables thoroughly with ice water; drain. Stir in pineapple. Serve on lettuce and top with Sesame Seed Dressing. Yield: 2 servings.

Sesame Seed Dressing:

¼ cup vegetable oil
¼ cup white wine vinegar
2 tablespoons sugar
2 tablespoons toasted sesame seeds

½ teaspoon salt
½ teaspoon ground ginger
¼ cup minced green onion

Combine all ingredients, and store in refrigerator. Shake dressing well before using. Yield: ¾ cup.

Hot Fudge Sauce

½ cup cocoa
1 cup sugar
1 cup light corn syrup
½ cup half-and-half

3 tablespoons butter or margarine
¼ teaspoon salt
1 teaspoon vanilla extract

Combine first 6 ingredients in a saucepan; bring to a boil, and boil 5 minutes. Remove from heat, and stir in vanilla. Serve over ice cream. Yield: 2 cups.

Note: Store remaining sauce in an airtight container in the refrigerator.

Friday Dinner

Cream of Spinach Soup
Shrimp Stroganoff
Lemon Pudding
Sauvignon Blanc

The recipe for Cream of Spinach Soup makes two extra large servings. Any leftover can be stored in the refrigerator in a tightly covered container or packaged and frozen. To serve, reheat over medium heat and garnish.

Cream of Spinach Soup

1 (10-ounce) package frozen
   chopped spinach
2 tablespoons butter or margarine,
   melted
2 tablespoons all-purpose flour
2 cups water

¾ cup nonfat dry milk solids
½ teaspoon instant minced onion
Salt and pepper to taste
Hot sauce or sherry to taste
Commercial sour cream or ground
   nutmeg

Prepare spinach according to package directions; drain well. Combine spinach with remaining ingredients except sour cream or nutmeg in container of an electric blender; process until smooth. Pour mixture into a medium saucepan, and cook over low heat, stirring constantly, until smooth and thickened. Serve warm. Garnish with sour cream or nutmeg. Yield: about 3 cups.

Shrimp Stroganoff

½ pound raw shrimp, peeled and
   deveined
1 small onion, finely chopped
2 tablespoons butter or margarine
1 (2½-ounce) can sliced
   mushrooms, drained

1½ teaspoons all-purpose flour
⅛ teaspoon salt
Dash of pepper
½ cup commercial sour cream
1½ cups hot cooked rice

Sauté shrimp and onion in butter in a large skillet for 10 minutes or until shrimp are tender; add mushrooms, and cook over low heat 5 minutes. Sprinkle with flour, salt, and pepper; stir in sour cream, and cook gently for 10 minutes. (Do not allow mixture to boil.) Serve over rice. Yield: 2 servings.

Lemon Pudding

½ cup sugar
2 tablespoons all-purpose flour
Pinch of salt
Grated rind of 1 lemon
Juice of 1 lemon

1 egg, separated
¾ cup milk
2 teaspoons butter or margarine, melted

Combine sugar, flour, salt, lemon rind, and juice in a large mixing bowl; mix well. Stir in beaten egg yolk, milk, and butter. Beat egg white (at room temperature) until stiff but not dry; fold into lemon mixture. Pour into a greased 1-quart casserole. Bake at 325° for 30 to 40 minutes or until edges are lightly browned. Yield: 2 servings.

Saturday Brunch

Potato-Sprout Omelet
Spinach Salad
Bacon-Cornmeal Muffins
Baked Pears
Champagne or Coffee

For a leisurely weekend, this menu is hard to beat. Prepare and cook the Bacon-Cornmeal Muffins; then lower the oven temperature and cook the Baked Pears while serving the main part of the meal.

Potato-Sprout Omelet

1 medium potato, cut into ½-inch cubes
2 tablespoons chopped onion
2 to 4 tablespoons vegetable oil
2 eggs
⅓ cup small-curd cottage cheese

2 tablespoons milk
Salt and pepper
1 cup alfalfa sprouts
Avocado slices
Cherry tomatoes
Fresh parsley

Cook potato in boiling salted water until just tender; drain. Brown potato and onion in hot oil in a 10-inch omelet pan or heavy skillet over medium heat. Combine eggs, cottage cheese, and milk; mix just until blended. Pour over potato. Reduce heat to low; cover and cook about 5 to 8 minutes or until set. Season with salt and pepper to taste. Place alfalfa sprouts on half of omelet; carefully fold omelet in half. Garnish with avocado slices, cherry tomatoes, and parsley. Yield: 2 servings.

Spinach Salad

⅓ pound fresh spinach
¼ pound fresh mushrooms, sliced
⅓ cup vegetable oil
2 teaspoons wine vinegar

½ teaspoon sugar
2 tablespoons lemon or orange juice
1 orange, peeled and thinly sliced
¼ cup sliced almonds

Remove stems from spinach; wash leaves thoroughly, and pat dry. Tear leaves into bite-size pieces. Combine spinach and mushrooms in a large bowl, and set aside.

Combine oil, wine vinegar, sugar, and juice; mix well. Toss spinach and mushrooms with dressing until well coated. Arrange orange slices and almond slices on top. Yield: 2 servings.

Bacon-Cornmeal Muffins

6 slices bacon
½ cup self-rising flour
½ cup self-rising cornmeal

2 tablespoons sugar
1 egg, well beaten
½ cup milk

Cook bacon until crisp; drain and crumble, reserving ¼ cup drippings. Combine flour, cornmeal, and sugar. Add egg, milk, and reserved bacon drippings; stir until moistened. Stir in crumbled bacon. Spoon batter into greased muffin pans, filling two-thirds full; bake at 425° for 20 to 25 minutes. Yield: about 6 muffins.

Baked Pears

1 (8½-ounce) can pear halves,
   drained
6 gingersnaps, finely crushed

2 tablespoons sugar
2 tablespoons butter or margarine,
   melted

Place pear halves in a shallow baking dish. Combine remaining ingredients; sprinkle over pears. Bake at 300° for 20 minutes; serve warm. Yield: 2 servings.

Saturday Sandwich Supper

Wine-Sauced Chicken Livers
Asparagus-Beet Salad
Easy Peach Cobbler
Zinfandel

This meal can be a real treat after a day filled with errands. If you enjoy chicken livers, you are sure to like this new way to serve them.

Wine-Sauced Chicken Livers

¾ pound chicken livers
Soy sauce
2 tablespoons butter or margarine,
   divided
1 medium onion, sliced

All-purpose flour
Salt and pepper
½ cup dry white wine
1 English muffin, split and toasted

Drain chicken livers and pat dry. Place livers on a plate. Sprinkle with soy sauce, turning to coat. Set aside.

Melt 1 tablespoon butter in skillet; add onion and sauté until tender. Remove onion and set aside.

Sprinkle livers lightly with flour, salt, and pepper. Melt 1 tablespoon butter in a skillet. Add chicken livers; cook over low heat until lightly browned and tender. Add onion and wine to chicken livers. Stir well; cover and cook 2 to 3 minutes. Spoon chicken livers over toasted English muffin. Yield: 2 servings.

Asparagus-Beet Salad

1 small head lettuce or assorted
   salad greens
1 (10½-ounce) can asparagus
   spears, drained

1 (8¼-ounce) can Harvard or
   pickled beets, drained and diced
Salad dressing of choice
Croutons

Tear lettuce into bite-size pieces. Combine lettuce, asparagus, and beets in a salad bowl. Add dressing, and toss lightly. To serve, arrange ingredients on salad plate. Garnish with croutons. Yield: 2 servings.

Easy Peach Cobbler

1½ teaspoons cornstarch
1 tablespoon cold water
1 (8¾-ounce) can sliced peaches,
   undrained
½ cup biscuit mix

2 teaspoons sugar
2 tablespoons milk
1 tablespoon vegetable oil
Vanilla ice cream

Dissolve cornstarch in cold water; add to peaches, and cook over medium heat about 5 minutes or until mixture is thickened and bubbly. Pour into a 1-quart baking dish. Combine biscuit mix and sugar; add milk and vegetable oil, stirring to form a soft dough. Drop dough by spoonfuls on top of peaches. Bake at 400° for 20 minutes or until golden brown. Serve hot with ice cream. Yield: 2 servings.

Note: Canned apricots, cherries, or apples may be substituted for peaches.

SPECIAL
DINNERS

These menus are just that: special menus planned around some of the occasions, times, events, or seasons when a celebration with an extra-special meal is in order. These menus range from the simple picnic-style grill dinner to the more elegant candlelight dinner. And what better way to welcome a season than by serving the fresh vegetables available? For taste and economy try our two vegetable dinners using winter vegetables in one and summer vegetables in another.

We suggest an appropriate wine for each of the menus, but if your favorite differs from our suggestion, don't hesitate to serve it. One basic recommendation on which all wine authorities agree is that there is no "one" right wine for any food. Your personal preference in wine and food combinations will dictate the best choice for you.

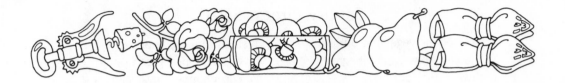

Dinner from the Sea

Barbecued Shrimp
Savory Green Salad
Commercial French Bread
Coffee Pecan Pie
Chardonnay

A menu like this is hard to beat for ease of preparation. Because everything can be prepared in advance, it is a relaxing but special meal to serve following a hectic day. Be sure to supply extra individual bowls to hold the discarded shrimp shells.

Barbecued Shrimp

1¼ to 1½ pounds fresh shrimp, unpeeled
3 stalks celery with leaves, very coarsely chopped
1 clove garlic, chopped
2 lemons, cut in half

½ cup butter or margarine, cut into cubes
2 tablespoons cracked black pepper
1 tablespoon Worcestershire sauce
1½ teaspoons salt
½ teaspoon hot sauce

Wash shrimp thoroughly and place in a very large, shallow pan. Add celery and garlic. Squeeze lemon juice over top and reserve lemon halves. Dot shrimp with butter, and sprinkle with remaining ingredients.

Place shrimp under broiler until butter melts and shrimp start to turn pink (about 5 minutes), stirring several times. When all shrimp are slightly pink, reduce temperature to 350° and bake for 15 to 20 minutes or until done, stirring often. Do not overcook or shrimp will become mushy. Taste for doneness. Garnish with reserved lemon halves. Yield: 2 generous servings.

Note: Flavor improves if shrimp are cooked ahead of time and then reheated, but do not overcook.

Savory Green Salad

2 tablespoons vegetable oil
1½ tablespoons wine vinegar
1 clove garlic, crushed
¼ teaspoon salt
¼ teaspoon pepper
¼ teaspoon dried thyme leaves

1 small tomato, chopped
½ cup chopped green onion
½ cup chopped fresh parsley
3 cups torn lettuce
½ cup croutons

Combine first 6 ingredients, and let stand several hours to allow flavors to blend. Add tomato, onion, and parsley; mix until well coated. Add lettuce, and toss well. Sprinkle with croutons just before serving. Yield: 2 servings.

Coffee Pecan Pie

1 egg, separated
¼ teaspoon salt
¼ cup sugar
1½ cups finely chopped pecans
1 tablespoon instant coffee granules

¼ cup boiling water
2¼ cups miniature marshmallows
½ teaspoon almond extract
2 cups whipping cream, divided
Grated chocolate

Combine egg white (at room temperature) and salt; beat until stiff but not dry. Gradually beat in sugar; fold in pecans. Spread into a well-greased 8-inch piepan. Prick with fork. Bake at 400° for 12 minutes; cool.

Dissolve coffee in boiling water, and add marshmallows; place over medium heat until marshmallows melt. Beat egg yolk; slowly add marshmallow mixture, beating constantly. Beat until mixture begins to set, and stir in almond extract.

Whip 1 cup whipping cream; fold into filling. Spoon into crust; chill. Whip remaining cream, and spread over top. Garnish with grated chocolate. Yield: one 8-inch pie.

Page 81: *Savory Green Salad and French bread make the Barbecued Shrimp a complete meal in this Dinner from the Sea.*

Page 82: *If you want dinner to be a celebration, serve Pecan-Stuffed Cornish Hens (page 89).*

Elegant Dinner for Two

Gazpacho
Fruit-Glazed Pork Chops with Rice
Fresh Spinach Salad
Commercial Breadsticks
Lemon Poached Pears
White Zinfandel

Serve this menu when a good supply of fresh tomatoes is available. The Gazpacho recipe makes six servings, but any unused portions of this refreshing soup can be refrigerated in a tightly covered container and stored for several days.

Fruit-Glazed Pork Chops are special because of the fruit topping. The recipe makes a double batch; the extra portions can be covered and refrigerated, or packaged and frozen, ready to heat to serve later.

Gazpacho

1 (10¾-ounce) can tomato soup, undiluted
1½ cups tomato juice
1¼ cups water
½ to 1 cup chopped cucumber
½ to 1 cup chopped tomatoes
½ cup chopped green pepper
½ cup chopped Spanish onion
2 tablespoons olive oil
2 tablespoons wine vinegar
1 tablespoon commercial Italian dressing
1 tablespoon lemon or lime juice
1 clove garlic, minced
¼ teaspoon salt
¼ teaspoon pepper
¼ teaspoon hot sauce
⅛ teaspoon garlic salt
Dash of Worcestershire sauce
Cucumber slices (optional)

Combine all ingredients except cucumber slices in a large bowl; chill at least 6 hours. Mix well before serving. Garnish each serving with cucumber slices, if desired. Yield: about 6 servings.

Note: Store remaining Gazpacho in an airtight container in refrigerator.

Fruit-Glazed Pork Chops with Rice

4 (1¼-inch-thick) butterfly pork
    chops
¾ cup (4 ounces) mixed dried fruit,
    peaches, apricots, apples, prunes
1 (1-ounce) package golden raisins
1½ cups orange juice

½ cup cream sherry
½ teaspoon dry mustard
¼ teaspoon ground ginger
1 tablespoon cornstarch
2 tablespoons cold water
Hot cooked rice

Place pork chops on rack in broiler pan. Broil at moderate temperature 3 to 5 inches from heat until done, about 20 to 25 minutes, turning once.

Combine dried fruit, raisins, orange juice, sherry, mustard, and ginger in a medium saucepan. Bring to a boil. Cover, reduce heat, and simmer 10 to 15 minutes or until fruit is tender and plump.

Combine cornstarch and cold water in small bowl. Stir into fruit mixture. Cook over medium heat, stirring constantly, until mixture is thickened and bubbly. Cook 1 minute longer. Serve pork chops over hot rice and spoon sauce over or around broiled chops, as desired. Yield: 4 servings.

To freeze: Place remaining cooked chops and sauce in a moisture-vapor proof freezer container. Seal, label, and date.

To reheat: Place frozen chops and sauce in a baking dish. Add 2 tablespoons water. Heat, covered, at 375° for 30 to 45 minutes or until thoroughly heated.

Fresh Spinach Salad

⅓ pound fresh spinach
¼ cup sliced water chestnuts
3 slices bacon, cooked and
    crumbled
⅓ cup vegetable oil
¼ cup sugar

⅛ teaspoon dry mustard
⅛ teaspoon onion juice
¼ teaspoon salt
3 tablespoons cider vinegar
Salt and pepper to taste
Sieved egg yolk

Remove stems from spinach; wash leaves thoroughly, and pat dry. Tear into bite-size pieces. Combine spinach, water chestnuts, and bacon in a large bowl; set aside.

Combine oil, sugar, mustard, onion juice, and salt in container of an electric blender; blend well. Remove lid; slowly add vinegar while blender is running.

Toss spinach mixture with dressing until well coated. Season with salt and pepper, and garnish with sieved egg yolk. Yield: 2 servings.

Lemon Poached Pears

2 fresh, ripe winter pears
1 cup water
¼ cup sugar
2 teaspoons lemon juice

½ teaspoon vanilla extract
¼ cup sliced almonds, toasted
Grated semisweet chocolate

Peel pears and core from blossom end, leaving stems intact. Combine water, sugar, lemon juice, and vanilla in a medium saucepan. Bring to a boil. Boil 5 minutes; add pears. Cover and simmer gently 12 to 15 minutes, or until pears are tender, basting occasionally with syrup. Cool pears in syrup.

To serve, place each pear in an individual dessert dish; sprinkle with sliced almonds and grated chocolate. Yield: 2 servings.

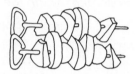

Dinner from the Grill

Curry Dip with Fresh Raw Vegetables
Steak and Mushroom Kabobs
Grilled Italian Tomatoes
Grilled Squash and Onion
Cornmeal Muffins
Pots de Crème
Zinfandel

Cooking on the grill has gained in popularity during recent years and is especially appealing for nice evenings. The menu which follows includes steak, a popular food for grilling, and vegetables, which are often overlooked when grilling.

Read the recipes carefully to establish a time schedule. The steak requires marinating time, and the squash requires a fairly long cooking time. Start the grill early to allow the squash and onion time to cook.

Curry Dip with Fresh Raw Vegetables

1 cup mayonnaise
¼ cup finely chopped onion
1 teaspoon lemon or lime juice

1 teaspoon curry powder
¼ teaspoon salt

Combine all ingredients, mixing well. Chill several hours before serving. Serve with raw vegetables. Yield: about 1 cup.

Steak and Mushroom Kabobs

1 (1-pound) sirloin steak
6 large mushroom caps

Rosemary Marinade

Cut steak into 1½-inch cubes. Marinate steak and mushrooms in Rosemary Marinade in refrigerator for 4 hours. Alternate steak and mushrooms on skewers. Grill over hot coals 3 to 5 minutes on each side or until desired doneness, basting frequently with marinade. Yield: 2 servings.

Rosemary Marinade:

¼ cup dry red wine
¼ cup vegetable oil
1½ teaspoons vinegar
1 tablespoon catsup
½ teaspoon Worcestershire sauce
1 small clove garlic, chopped

½ teaspoon sugar
¼ teaspoon dried rosemary leaves, crushed
¼ teaspoon dried marjoram leaves
¼ teaspoon salt

Combine all ingredients, mixing well. Yield: about ⅔ cup.

Grilled Italian Tomatoes

1 large tomato
1 tablespoon commercial Italian dressing
½ teaspoon dried basil leaves

Salt and pepper to taste
1½ tablespoons butter or margarine, melted
⅓ cup breadcrumbs

Cut tomato in half crosswise; sprinkle each with half the Italian dressing, basil, salt, and pepper. Combine butter and breadcrumbs; spoon over tomato halves.

Place tomato halves on heavy-duty aluminum foil. Seal foil, leaving a small amount of space for steam to escape. Cook over hot coals 10 minutes. Yield: 2 servings.

Grilled Squash and Onion

2 medium-size yellow squash, cut into ½-inch slices
1 medium onion, cut into ½-inch slices

Garlic salt
Salt and pepper to taste
1 tablespoon butter or margarine

Alternate squash and onion slices in rows on a large sheet of aluminum foil. Sprinkle vegetables with seasonings; dot with butter.

Fold foil securely to seal; place on grill and cook over moderate heat about 45 minutes or until tender. Yield: 2 servings.

Cornmeal Muffins

½ cup yellow cornmeal
½ cup all-purpose flour
2 tablespoons sugar
1 teaspoon baking powder
½ teaspoon soda

¼ teaspoon salt
1 egg, beaten
½ cup commercial sour cream
2 tablespoons vegetable oil
2 tablespoons milk

Combine first 6 ingredients. Stir together egg, sour cream, oil, and milk; add to dry ingredients, mixing well. Fill lightly greased muffin pans two-thirds full. Bake at 425° for 15 or 20 minutes or until golden brown. Yield: 6 to 9 muffins.

Pots de Creme

1 (4-ounce) package sweet baking
  chocolate
1 tablespoon sugar
½ cup whipping cream

2 egg yolks
½ teaspoon vanilla extract
Whipped cream
Chocolate Curls (optional)

Melt chocolate over hot water in top of double boiler. Stir in sugar. Gradually add whipping cream, stirring until smooth. Remove from heat.

Beat yolks well with a wire whisk. Gradually stir about one-fourth of chocolate mixture into yolks; add to remaining chocolate mixture, stirring constantly. Stir in vanilla. Spoon into cordial glasses or demitasse cups. Refrigerate. Garnish with whipped cream and chocolate curls, if desired. Yield: 4 servings.

Chocolate Curls:

4 (1-ounce) squares semisweet
  chocolate

Melt squares over hot water in a double boiler. (This amount is needed for length and width of chocolate strip. Excess may be reused.) Pour chocolate out in a stream onto a waxed paper-lined cookie sheet. Spread chocolate with a spatula into a 3-inch-wide strip. (Vary length of curls by altering width of strip.) Smooth top of strip with spatula. Chill until chocolate partially cools and feels slightly tacky but is not firm. (If chocolate is too hard, curls will break; if too soft, chocolate will not curl.)

Gently pull a vegetable peeler across length of chocolate until curls form, letting chocolate curl up on top of peeler. If chocolate becomes too firm, remelt and repeat process. Transfer curls to a tray by inserting a wooden pick in end of curl. (Curls will melt from heat of hand.) Chill curls until ready to use.

Note: Remaining curls may be frozen in an airtight container.

Keep staples—such as sugar, flour, and spices—in tightly covered containers at room temperature. Staples that are frequently replenished should be rotated so that the oldest is always used first.

Dinner for a Special Time

Oysters Rockefeller
Pecan-Stuffed Cornish Hens
Sautéed Broccoli
Baked Tomatoes
Rich Biscuits
Strawberries with Mint
Chardonnay

What foods could be more appropriate to serve in celebration of birthdays, promotions, or other special times than Oysters Rockefeller, Cornish hens, and strawberries?

If you have only one oven, first bake the hens; then put the prepared oysters in the oven during the last part of cooking time. Cover the hens with foil to keep them warm while serving the oysters.

The tomatoes and Rich Biscuits can be baked while the appetizer is being served.

Oysters Rockefeller

Rock salt
2 tablespoons finely chopped
   scallions or green onion
2 tablespoons finely chopped celery
3 tablespoons butter or margarine
3 cups chopped fresh spinach
1½ tablespoons finely chopped
   parsley
Pinch of garlic powder
¼ teaspoon salt

Pinch of pepper
3 tablespoons fine dry breadcrumbs
1 dozen oysters on the half shell,
   drained
2 tablespoons dry sherry
Lemon juice
Hot sauce
3 slices bacon, cooked and
   crumbled
1 tablespoon chopped pimiento

Sprinkle a thin layer of rock salt in a 12-inch pizza plate or piepan.

Sauté scallions and celery in butter until tender. Stir in spinach, parsley, garlic powder, salt, and pepper. Cook, uncovered, 10 minutes, stirring occasionally. Remove from heat; add breadcrumbs, stirring well.

Arrange oysters (in shells) over salt. Brush each oyster with sherry, and sprinkle with a few drops of lemon juice and hot sauce; top with spinach mixture. Garnish with bacon and chopped pimiento. Bake at 350° for 15 minutes. Place under broiler (about 5 inches from source of heat) for 1 minute. Yield: 2 servings.

Pecan-Stuffed Cornish Hens

2 (1- to 1½-pound) Cornish hens
Salt and pepper
Pecan Dressing
¼ cup butter or margarine, melted

2 tablespoons apricot-, peach-, or
  plum-flavored brandy
Celery leaves

Remove giblets from hens; reserve for another use. Rinse hens with cold water, and pat dry. Sprinkle cavity of each with salt and pepper. Secure neck skin to back with wooden pick; lift wingtips up and over back so they are tucked under hen.

Lightly stuff cavity of hens with Pecan Dressing; close cavity, and secure with wooden picks. Tie leg ends to tail with cord or string. Brush hens with half of butter, and sprinkle generously with pepper. Combine remaining butter with brandy; set aside.

Place hens, breast side up, in a large shallow baking pan. Arrange any remaining dressing around hens in baking pan. Bake at 350° for 1 to 1½ hours, depending on size of hens; baste every 10 minutes with brandy mixture. Garnish with celery leaves. Yield: 2 servings.

Pecan Dressing:

⅓ cup unsweetened apple juice
2 tablespoons apricot-, peach-, or
  plum-flavored brandy

2 tablespoons butter or margarine
1 cup cornbread stuffing mix
2 tablespoons chopped pecans

Combine apple juice, brandy, and butter in a large saucepan; cook over medium heat, stirring occasionally, until butter melts. Add stuffing mix and pecans, stirring lightly. Yield: enough dressing for 2 Cornish hens.

Note: Small portions of leftover meat or fowl may be frozen until there is enough for a pot pie, curry, or rice casserole.

Sauteed Broccoli

¼ cup butter or margarine
1 (10-ounce) package frozen
  broccoli spears, thawed and
  coarsely chopped
1 (4-ounce) can sliced mushrooms,
  drained

3 tablespoons sliced almonds
  (optional)
Salt and pepper to taste

Melt butter in a skillet, and add remaining ingredients. Sauté 10 minutes, stirring often. Yield: 2 servings.

Baked Tomatoes

2 tomatoes
Onion salt

2 teaspoons grated Parmesan cheese
2 teaspoons chopped parsley

Cut tomatoes in half crosswise, and sprinkle with onion salt, cheese, and parsley. Bake at 400° for 10 to 15 minutes. Yield: 2 servings.

Rich Biscuits

2 packages dry yeast
2 tablespoons warm water
  (105° to 115°)
5 cups self-rising flour
¼ cup sugar

1 cup shortening
2 cups buttermilk
½ to ¾ cup butter or margarine,
  melted

Dissolve yeast in water (mixture will be thick).

Sift together flour and sugar in a large bowl; cut in shortening until mixture resembles coarse meal. Add buttermilk and yeast mixture, stirring well.

Turn dough out onto a well-floured surface. Roll out to ¼-inch thickness. Cut with a 2¼-inch cutter. With dull edge of knife, make a crease just off center on each round. Brush biscuits with some of the melted butter. Fold over so top overlaps slightly; press edges together. Dip biscuits in remaining butter, and place on an ungreased baking sheet. Bake at 400° for 15 minutes or until golden brown. Yield: 3 dozen biscuits.

Note: Dough can be stored in an airtight container in refrigerator for 1 week.

Strawberries with Mint

2 cups fresh strawberries
1 tablespoon chopped fresh mint
½ teaspoon grated orange rind

¼ cup orange juice
¼ cup powdered sugar
Whipped cream (optional)

Cap strawberries; rinse and drain. Combine strawberries, mint, orange rind, and orange juice; toss gently. Sprinkle with sugar; chill at least 1 hour. Garnish with whipped cream, if desired. Yield: 2 servings.

During the week, keep a shopping list handy to write down items as you need them. This will eliminate unnecessary trips to the store. Before your weekly shopping trip, make a complete shopping list. If the list is arranged according to the layout of the store, you will save time and steps.

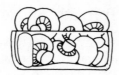

Winter Vegetable Dinner

Calico Cheese Soup
Spinach Sauté
Spicy Honeyed Squash
Brown Rice with Mushrooms
Baked Pears with Sherry
Coffee Refresher
Sauvignon Blanc

Cheese soup topped with croutons is a good source of protein and completes the Winter Vegetable Dinner. The Coffee Refresher and Baked Pears with Sherry provide a grand finale to this simple menu.

Calico Cheese Soup

¼ cup finely chopped carrots
¼ cup finely chopped celery
Boiling water
1 tablespoon minced onion
2 tablespoons butter or margarine
1½ tablespoons all-purpose flour

1 cup milk, scalded
1 cup chicken broth
1 cup (4 ounces) shredded Cheddar
  cheese
Garlic Parmesan Croutons

Place carrots and celery in boiling salted water to cover; cover and cook until crisp-tender. Drain and set aside.

Sauté onion in butter until tender. Stir in flour, milk, and chicken broth, blending well. Cook, stirring constantly, until slightly thickened. Add cheese; stir until melted. Add vegetable mixture; cook 10 minutes. Top with Garlic Parmesan Croutons. Yield: 2½ to 3 cups.

Garlic Parmesan Croutons:

½ clove garlic
¼ cup vegetable oil

2 cups bread cubes
¼ cup grated Parmesan cheese

Soak garlic in oil for 2 to 3 hours. Arrange bread cubes on a baking tray. Toast cubes at 325° until golden brown. Remove garlic from oil. Combine oil and Parmesan cheese; add croutons and toss. Serve over hot soup, or cool and serve with salad or other foods. Yield: 2 cups.

Spinach Saute

½ pound fresh spinach
1 medium tomato, peeled and cut
  into thin wedges

1 clove garlic, crushed
2 tablespoons vegetable oil
Salt and pepper to taste

Wash spinach thoroughly and drain. Sauté tomato and garlic in oil in a large skillet. Add spinach; cover and cook over low heat 15 minutes, stirring once or twice. Add salt and pepper to taste. Cook, uncovered, 5 to 10 minutes longer, stirring occasionally. Yield: 2 servings.

Spicy Honeyed Squash

1 medium acorn squash
1½ tablespoons butter or margarine,
  melted
Dash of ground cinnamon

⅛ teaspoon salt
⅛ teaspoon ground ginger
2 tablespoons honey

Wash squash; cut into ¾-inch slices, and remove seeds and membrane. Place slices in a 9-inch square pan. Add ½ inch of water to pan. Bake at 375° for 30 to 35 minutes.

Remove squash from oven; drain liquid from pan. Combine remaining ingredients; pour mixture over squash. Bake 15 additional minutes or until tender, basting frequently. Yield: 2 servings.

Brown Rice with Mushrooms

½ cup uncooked brown rice
3 slices bacon
2 tablespoons slivered almonds
¼ cup sliced green onion, divided

⅓ cup thinly sliced celery
½ cup sliced mushrooms
1 teaspoon soy sauce

Cook rice according to package directions. Fry bacon until crisp; drain well, reserving drippings. Crumble bacon, and set aside.

Sauté almonds, 3 tablespoons green onion, celery, and mushrooms in 2 tablespoons bacon drippings until almonds are golden brown (about 5 minutes). Set aside.

Heat 2 teaspoons drippings in a large skillet; add rice, and toss until lightly browned. Stir in vegetable mixture and soy sauce. Transfer to a serving dish, and top with remaining onion and crumbled bacon. Yield: 2 servings.

Baked Pears with Sherry

2 large pears, halved and cored
2 tablespoons slivered almonds,
  toasted
2 teaspoons butter or margarine,
  melted

⅛ teaspoon almond extract
Sugar to taste
⅓ cup cream sherry
Sweetened whipped cream

Place pears in a 9-inch square baking dish. Combine almonds, butter, and almond extract; spoon a small amount into cavity of each pear half. Sprinkle sugar over pears; add sherry. Bake at 350° for 30 minutes. Serve hot or cold with sweetened whipped cream. Yield: 2 servings.

Coffee Refresher

1 pint coffee ice cream   2 tablespoons crème de cacao
2 tablespoons brandy

Combine all ingredients in container of an electric blender; process until smooth. Pour into small cups or glasses; serve immediately. Yield: about 1¾ cups.

A special topping for cooked vegetables or casseroles can be made by tossing ½ cup herb-seasoned stuffing mix, crushed with 2 tablespoons melted butter or margarine; top dish with this mixture and sprinkle with 1 cup shredded cheese.

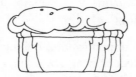

Summer Vegetable Dinner

Stuffed Zucchini
Stewed Corn
Sweet-and-Sour Cucumbers
Cheese-Topped Cornbread
Deep-Dish Blackberry Cobbler
Gamay

Prepare the cucumbers; refrigerate to chill. Bake the Stuffed Zucchini and cornbread at the same time. Either bake the cobbler in advance or bake it after the squash and bread are cooked. We think you will enjoy the extra cobbler served warmed or chilled.

Stuffed Zucchini

2 (6- to 8-inch) zucchini
1 small onion, finely chopped
2 tablespoons butter or margarine
1 (15-ounce) can red kidney beans,
    slightly mashed
1 cup (4 ounces) shredded sharp
    Cheddar cheese

¾ cup spaghetti sauce, divided
¼ teaspoon dried oregano leaves
¼ teaspoon dried basil leaves
¼ teaspoon salt
⅛ teaspoon pepper
¼ cup grated Parmesan cheese

Wash zucchini thoroughly; cook in boiling salted water 5 minutes. Cut zucchini in half lengthwise; remove seeds and membrane. Set shells aside.

Sauté onion in butter until tender. Combine onion, kidney beans, Cheddar cheese, ½ cup spaghetti sauce, oregano, basil, salt, and pepper; mix well.

Arrange zucchini shells in a lightly greased 9-inch square baking dish. Spoon bean mixture into zucchini. Top each with 1 tablespoon of remaining spaghetti sauce and 1 tablespoon Parmesan cheese. Cover and bake at 375° for 15 to 20 minutes or until thoroughly heated. Yield: 2 servings.

Stewed Corn

1¼ to 1½ cups fresh corn cut from
    cob
2 tablespoons butter or margarine
1 tablespoon bacon drippings

¼ cup boiling water
¼ teaspoon salt
Dash of pepper

Combine corn, butter, bacon drippings, and boiling water; cook over high heat 5 minutes, stirring constantly. Reduce heat; cover and cook an additional 15 minutes, stirring occasionally. Stir in salt and pepper. Yield: about 2 servings.

Sweet-and-Sour Cucumbers

1 cup sugar
⅓ cup vinegar
Salt and pepper to taste

1 medium cucumber, peeled and
    sliced

Combine sugar, vinegar, salt, and pepper in a small saucepan; heat until sugar is dissolved, stirring constantly. Cool. Pour vinegar mixture over cucumber. Cover and chill. Yield: 2 servings.

Note: As the cucumber is eaten, more can be added to the liquid. For variety, you can also add tomato wedges and green pepper chunks.

Keep small packages of leftovers from getting lost in the freezer by placing them in a large nylon-mesh or plastic bag.

Cheese-Topped Cornbread

2 cups chopped onion
¼ cup butter or margarine
1 (8-ounce) carton commercial sour
   cream
1 cup (4 ounces) shredded Cheddar
   cheese, divided
1½ cups self-rising cornmeal

2 tablespoons sugar (optional)
¼ teaspoon dillweed
2 eggs, beaten
1 (8¾-ounce) can cream-style corn
¼ cup milk
¼ cup vegetable oil
Dash of hot sauce

Sauté onion in butter in large skillet until tender; remove from heat. Stir in sour cream and ½ cup cheese; set aside.

Combine cornmeal, sugar, and dillweed; set aside.

Stir together eggs, corn, milk, oil, and hot sauce; add to cornmeal mixture, stirring well. Spoon into a lightly greased 9-inch square pan. Spread sour cream mixture over batter; sprinkle with remaining ½ cup cheese. Bake at 375° for 30 to 35 minutes. Cool slightly; cut into 3-inch squares. Yield: 9 servings.

Deep-Dish Blackberry Cobbler

4 cups fresh blackberries or 2
   (16-ounce) packages frozen
   blackberries, thawed
1 cup sugar
2 tablespoons all-purpose flour

2 tablespoons lemon juice
⅛ teaspoon salt
Triple-Crust Pastry
1½ tablespoons butter or margarine,
   divided

Combine berries, sugar, flour, lemon juice, and salt; stir well.

Prepare pastry, and divide dough in half. Roll half of dough to ⅛-inch thickness to fit sides and bottom of a lightly greased 2-quart baking dish. Spoon half of berry mixture into pastry-lined dish; dot with half of butter.

Divide remaining dough in half. Roll one portion of dough into a rectangle; place over berries, making a few slits in pastry. Top with remaining berry mixture, and dot with remaining butter.

Roll out remaining portion of dough to fit top of baking dish. Cover dish, and seal pastry edges. Make slits along the top. Bake at 450° for 10 minutes; reduce heat to 350°, and bake 45 minutes longer or until bubbly and golden brown. Serve warm. Yield: 6 servings.

Triple-Crust Pastry:

2 cups all-purpose flour
¾ teaspoon salt

⅔ cup shortening
3 tablespoons ice water

Combine flour and salt; cut in shortening until mixture resembles coarse meal. Sprinkle water over mixture, and stir with a fork; shape dough into a ball. Yield: crust for 1 cobbler.

Candlelight Dinner

Cream Cheese Ball
Mustard Cognac Beef Stew
Cracked Wheat Salad
Chilled Winter Fruit
Cabernet Sauvignon

A candlelight setting seems to enhance the flavor of Mustard Cognac Beef Stew. The Cracked Wheat Salad is different and provides a nice contrast in taste to the stew.

Cream Cheese Ball

1 (8-ounce) package cream cheese, softened
1 tablespoon commercial sour cream
1 teaspoon minced fresh marjoram
1 clove garlic, crushed
Cracked peppercorns or lemon pepper

Combine cream cheese, sour cream, marjoram, and garlic in a small mixing bowl; beat until fluffy and well blended. Form mixture into a ball, and coat with pepper. Chill 2 to 3 hours; serve with crackers. Yield: one 3-inch cheese ball.

Note: Instead of forming cheese mixture into a ball, it may be placed in a small crock and topped with pepper.

Mustard Cognac Beef Stew

4 (2- × 1- × ⅓-inch) slices salt pork
2 large onions, sliced
1½ pounds lean beef chuck, cut into 1-inch cubes
All-purpose flour
Butter or margarine
⅓ cup cognac
2 to 3 cups beef broth
1½ tablespoons Dijon mustard
3 large carrots, cut into 1-inch pieces
Salt and pepper to taste
1 tablespoon butter or margarine
½ pound small fresh mushrooms, sliced
⅓ cup red wine

Dice salt pork into small cubes. Cook in a large skillet over medium heat until golden brown. Remove with a slotted spoon; place in a Dutch oven. Add onion to pork drippings in skillet; sauté until onion is golden. Transfer onion to Dutch oven.

Dredge beef cubes in flour. Brown beef cubes, a few pieces at a time, in skillet over medium heat. Add butter, if needed. Add browned beef cubes to salt pork and onion in Dutch oven. Add cognac to skillet; stir to loosen brown drippings and cook until liquid is reduced slightly. Stir in 2 cups beef broth and mustard. Add to other ingredients in Dutch oven. Cover and simmer over low heat about 1½ hours or until meat is tender. Add additional beef broth, if necessary. Add carrots, salt, and pepper. Continue cooking 15 to 20 minutes or until carrots are fork-tender.

Melt 1 tablespoon butter in a medium skillet. Add mushroom slices; sauté over medium heat until lightly browned. Add red wine and bring to a boil. Stir mushroom-wine mixture into stew. Cover and simmer 5 minutes. Yield: 4 servings.

To Freeze: Cool any leftover stew and package in a freezer container with a tight-fitting lid. Label, date, and place in freezer for later use.

Cracked Wheat Salad

2 cups boiling water
⅓ cup cracked wheat
½ cup chopped parsley
1 medium tomato, chopped
2 tablespoons minced green onion
3 tablespoons lemon juice

3 tablespoons olive or vegetable oil
¼ teaspoon salt
Dash of pepper
Spinach or lettuce leaves
5 to 6 ripe olives, sliced
Parsley

Pour boiling water over cracked wheat in a medium bowl. Cover and let stand for 1 hour or until wheat has expanded and is light and fluffy. Drain well and return wheat to bowl. Add parsley, tomato, and onion; toss well.

Combine lemon juice, oil, salt, and pepper in a jar. Screw lid tightly and shake well. Pour dressing over wheat-vegetable mixture. Stir lightly to mix. Cover and refrigerate at least 1 hour. Serve on spinach leaves, and garnish with ripe olives and parsley. Yield: 2 servings.

Chilled Winter Fruit

1 large grapefruit
⅓ cup sugar
3 tablespoons orange marmalade

1 cup fresh cranberries
1 medium banana

Peel, section, and seed grapefruit, reserving juice. Add enough water to juice to measure ⅓ cup.

Combine juice, sugar, and marmalade in a medium saucepan; bring to a boil, stirring occasionally. Add cranberries; boil 5 to 8 minutes or until skins pop. Cool. Stir in grapefruit; cover and chill. Slice banana, and stir into chilled grapefruit mixture just before serving. Serve in individual compotes. Yield: 2 servings.

ETHNIC FAVORITES

These menus, based on authentic ethnic favorites, incorporate traditional ways of preparing and serving. All the recipes have been developed for simplicity and ease of preparation in the smaller quantities needed when cooking for two, and they call for ingredients or foods which are readily available to American cooks.

Whether you are an experienced cook or a beginner, these menus will create new interest in meal planning and preparation because they suggest new uses for food already familiar to many. For example, the French menu features chicken and several other popular foods, but we suggest some techniques which you may not use often in preparing them.

For lighter meals, choose either of the Oriental menus. They are based on traditional ways of serving. Remember to allow time for the relaxed, unhurried serving which makes Oriental meals so pleasant.

If your choice is for heavier, more elaborate foods, you will enjoy the Italian or Middle Eastern menus. Since both of these are more extensive in keeping with tradition in these countries, you will probably want to prepare them when you have more time for cooking.

To make any of these menus more interesting use accessories and serving utensils typical of the country or region, remembering that presentation is particularly important when serving an ethnic meal.

German-Style Dinner

Sausage and Cabbage
Nippy Beets
Hot German Potato Salad
Beer Muffins
Spiced Baked Apples
German Beer or White Riesling

This hearty, robust meal is a perfect choice for cool fall or winter days. The typical sausage and cabbage dish is served with beets, which add color and flavor. Beer, of course, is the ideal beverage.

Sausage and Cabbage

¼ medium cabbage, coarsely
   shredded
¼ cup chopped green pepper
Salt and pepper to taste

2 tablespoons water
½ pound German or Polish sausage,
   cut into 1-inch slices

Combine cabbage and green pepper in a medium skillet; season with salt and pepper. Add water, and heat until water begins to boil. Reduce heat, and place sausage on top of cabbage mixture. Cover and simmer about 15 minutes. Yield: 2 servings.

Nippy Beets

2 tablespoons butter or margarine
1 tablespoon cornstarch
1 tablespoon sugar
¼ teaspoon salt
2 tablespoons lemon juice

⅔ cup water
2 teaspoons prepared horseradish
8 to 10 small beets, cooked and
   peeled, or 1 (16-ounce) can
   whole beets, drained

Melt butter in a medium saucepan. Combine cornstarch, sugar, and salt; blend into butter. Stir in lemon juice and water; cook until thickened. Stir in horseradish, and pour over hot beets. Yield: 2 servings.

Hot German Potato Salad

2 medium potatoes
2 teaspoons instant minced onion
1 teaspoon all-purpose flour
1 teaspoon sugar
½ teaspoon salt
¼ teaspoon freshly ground pepper

½ teaspoon celery seeds
2 slices bacon
3 tablespoons vinegar
2 tablespoons sliced radishes
1 tablespoon chopped fresh parsley

Cook potatoes in boiling salted water about 30 minutes or until tender. Drain well, and cool slightly. Peel and cut potatoes into ½-inch cubes; place potatoes in the center of heavy-duty foil.

Combine onion, flour, sugar, salt, pepper, and celery seeds; sprinkle over potatoes.

Fry bacon until crisp; remove from pan, and drain on paper towels. Drain off bacon drippings, reserving 2 tablespoons in pan. Stir vinegar into drippings; pour over potatoes. Crumble bacon, and sprinkle over the potato cubes.

Wrap foil tightly, and place potato bundles on a cookie sheet. Bake at 400° for 1 hour. Add radishes and parsley; toss. Serve warm. Yield: 2 servings.

Beer Muffins

1 cup biscuit mix
1 teaspoon sugar
Dash of salt

¼ cup plus 2 tablespoons beer (at
   room temperature)

Combine all ingredients, mixing well. Spoon batter into greased muffin pans, filling two-thirds full. Bake at 425° for 10 to 12 minutes. Yield: about 4 muffins.

Spiced Baked Apples

2 large baking apples, peeled and
   cored
2 tablespoons sugar
½ teaspoon ground cinnamon

½ teaspoon ground nutmeg
2 teaspoons butter or margarine
⅓ cup apple juice
Red food coloring (optional)

Place apples in a shallow 1-quart casserole; pour 1 tablespoon sugar into cavity of each apple. Sprinkle each with ¼ teaspoon cinnamon and ¼ teaspoon nutmeg; top each with 1 teaspoon butter.

Heat apple juice to boiling; add red food coloring, if desired. Pour juice into casserole. Bake, uncovered, at 400° for 50 to 60 minutes or until tender, basting occasionally with juice. Yield: 2 servings.

Cupcake pans should be greased well on the bottom and very lightly on the sides.

Classic French Dinner

Crusty Onion Soup
Chicken in Wine Sauce
Braised Celery and Carrots
Asparagus Salad Vinaigrette
Lemon Custard in Meringue Cups
Fumé Blanc

Croutons and cheese make the crusty-topped soup an elegant first course to precede this classic Chicken in Wine Sauce. Lemon Custard in Meringue Cups is an elegant, but easy to prepare, dessert.

Crusty Onion Soup

1 medium onion, very thinly sliced
1 tablespoon butter or margarine
2 cups beef broth
¼ cup water

Salt and pepper to taste
¼ cup Madeira wine (optional)
Parmesan Croutons
¼ cup shredded Swiss cheese

Sauté onion in butter in a large skillet, covered, until onion is tender (about 5 minutes). Uncover and continue cooking onion until well browned; stir occasionally. Stir in broth and water; cover and simmer 30 minutes. Add salt and pepper; stir in wine, if desired.

Ladle soup into individual ovenproof dishes; place a Parmesan Crouton on each serving, and sprinkle with Swiss cheese. Bake at 400° for 15 minutes or until cheese is melted and golden brown. Yield: 2 servings.

Parmesan Croutons:

1 to 2 (1-inch-thick) slices French
  bread, cut in half
2 tablespoons butter or margarine,
  melted

2 tablespoons grated Parmesan
  cheese

Brush both sides of bread with butter; sprinkle with Parmesan cheese. Place on a cookie sheet, and bake at 350° for 20 minutes or until crisp and brown. Yield: 2 to 4 large croutons.

Chicken in Wine Sauce

1 whole chicken breast, split, skinned, and boned
Salt
Ground nutmeg
2 tablespoons butter or margarine
2 tablespoons minced onion
¼ pound fresh mushrooms, quartered
⅔ cup dry white wine
¼ cup cashews (optional)
1 teaspoon cornstarch
2 teaspoons dry white wine

Sprinkle chicken with salt and nutmeg; brown each side in butter in a heavy skillet. Add onion, mushrooms, and ⅔ cup wine; add cashews, if desired. Bring to a boil; reduce heat, cover, and simmer 15 minutes. Remove chicken.

Combine cornstarch and 2 teaspoons wine; mix well and stir into skillet. Cook, stirring constantly, until thickened. Serve chicken and sauce over hot braised vegetables. Yield: 2 servings.

Braised Celery and Carrots

2 tablespoons butter or margarine
2 celery hearts, split lengthwise into fourths
2 to 4 large carrots, peeled and cut into matchstick pieces
¼ cup chicken broth
¼ teaspoon salt
¼ teaspoon freshly ground pepper
1 tablespoon chopped parsley

Melt butter in a large heavy skillet or saucepan. Add celery and carrots. Stir to combine, and coat with butter. Add chicken broth, salt, and pepper. Cover and cook over medium heat about 20 to 25 minutes or until vegetables can be pierced with a fork. Carefully turn celery hearts and carrots once during cooking. Remove vegetables to a warm serving platter. Sprinkle with parsley. Yield: 2 servings.

Asparagus Salad Vinaigrette

1 (10-ounce) package frozen asparagus spears
¼ cup vegetable oil
3 tablespoons vinegar
1 tablespoon chopped dill pickle
1 teaspoon finely chopped onion
1 tablespoon minced parsley
¼ teaspoon salt
⅛ teaspoon pepper
Pinch of tarragon
Lettuce leaves
Pimiento strips

Cook asparagus just until tender, following package directions; drain and chill. Combine oil, vinegar, pickle, onion, parsley, and seasonings; chill at least 1 hour.

Arrange chilled asparagus on bed of lettuce. Garnish with pimiento strips, and serve with dressing. Yield: 2 generous servings.

Lemon Custard in Meringue Cups

1 egg white
¼ teaspoon vinegar
3 drops vanilla extract
Pinch of salt

⅓ cup sugar
Lemon Custard
Whipped cream (optional)

Combine egg white (at room temperature), vinegar, vanilla, and salt; beat until frothy. Gradually add sugar, 1 tablespoon at a time, beating until stiff peaks form (do not underbeat). Spoon into 2 equal portions on unglazed brown paper (do not use recycled paper). Using back of spoon, shape into circles about 4 inches in diameter; shape each circle into a shell (sides should be about 1½ inches high). Bake at 300° for 45 minutes. Cool away from drafts. Spoon Lemon Custard into shells. Garnish with whipped cream, if desired. Yield: 2 servings.

Lemon Custard:

⅓ cup sugar
1 tablespoon cornstarch
Dash of salt
½ cup boiling water

1 egg yolk
2 teaspoons grated lemon rind
1½ tablespoons lemon juice

Combine sugar, cornstarch, and salt in a heavy saucepan; stir well. Add water, and cook over low heat, stirring constantly, until thickened.

Combine egg yolk, lemon rind, and lemon juice; beat well. Gradually stir about one-fourth of hot mixture into yolks; add to remaining hot mixture, stirring constantly. Cook custard, stirring constantly, about 5 minutes or until smooth and thickened. Chill. Yield: ¾ cup.

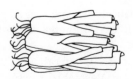

Special Mexican Meal

Chili con Queso
Vegetable Tostadas
Beef Enchiladas
Rum Baked Bananas
Mexican Beer or Splits of Red Wine

Keep frozen tortillas, found in most supermarkets, on hand, and you can create popular Mexican favorites anytime. Serve Rum Baked Bananas with or without vanilla ice cream.

Chili con Queso

1 (10-ounce) can tomatoes and
  green chiles
1 (4-ounce) can chopped green
  chiles
1 tablespoon cornstarch
1 medium onion, diced
1 clove garlic, minced

½ teaspoon salt
½ teaspoon black pepper
¼ to ½ teaspoon crushed red
  pepper
1 cup diced Colby cheese
Tortilla chips

Drain tomatoes and chopped green chiles, reserving liquid. Set vegetables aside.
  Combine reserved liquid and cornstarch in a 1-quart saucepan; cook over medium
heat, stirring constantly, until thickened. Stir in tomatoes, chiles, onion, garlic, and
seasonings. Cook, stirring constantly, until onion is tender. Stir in cheese; cook over
low heat until melted. Serve warm with tortilla chips. Yield: 2¼ cups.

Vegetable Tostadas

1 medium zucchini, thinly sliced
  (1½ cups)
1 medium onion, chopped
1 (2½-ounce) can sliced
  mushrooms, undrained
½ cup chopped celery
2 tablespoons chopped green
  pepper

¼ teaspoon salt
4 corn tortillas
2 tablespoons vegetable oil
1 cup (4 ounces) shredded Cheddar
  cheese
½ cup commercial sour cream
1 medium tomato, chopped
Hot sauce

Combine zucchini, onion, mushrooms, celery, green pepper, and salt in a 1½-quart
saucepan; cover and simmer 8 to 10 minutes or until crisp-tender. Drain well, and
set aside.
  Cook tortillas in hot oil until crisp. Drain on paper towels. Place tortillas on baking
sheet; top each with about ½ cup vegetable mixture. Sprinkle with cheese. Bake at
350° for 3 to 5 minutes or until cheese melts. Top each tostada with 2 tablespoons
sour cream; sprinkle with tomato and hot sauce to taste. Serve immediately. Yield: 2
to 4 servings.

Beef Enchiladas

1 (8-ounce) can tomato sauce
¼ cup chopped green pepper
1 tablespoon diced green chiles
1 teaspoon chili powder
Dash of cumin
4 flour tortillas
½ pound lean ground beef

⅔ cup shredded Monterey Jack
  cheese, divided
¼ cup chopped green onion
¼ cup commercial sour cream
1 tablespoon chopped parsley
½ teaspoon salt
Dash of pepper

Combine tomato sauce, green pepper, chiles, chili powder, and cumin in a medium saucepan. Simmer 10 to 12 minutes. Set aside.

Wrap tortillas tightly in foil; bake at 325° for 15 minutes.

Cook ground beef in a medium skillet until lightly browned; drain well. Stir in ½ cup cheese, green onion, sour cream, parsley, salt, and pepper. Spoon about ¼ cup of meat mixture off center of each tortilla. Fold edge nearest filling up and over filling just until mixture is covered. Fold in other side of tortilla to center; roll-up. Repeat with remaining ingredients.

Arrange in a 9-inch baking dish. Pour tomato sauce over enchiladas. Sprinkle with remaining cheese. Bake, uncovered, at 350° about 20 minutes or until hot and bubbly. Yield: 2 servings.

Rum Baked Bananas

2 firm bananas
Grated rind and juice of 1 lemon
2 tablespoons brown sugar

2 tablespoons butter or margarine, melted
1 to 2 tablespoons rum

Cut bananas in half lengthwise; place cut side down in a buttered baking dish. Brush bananas with lemon juice; sprinkle with grated lemon rind and brown sugar. Combine butter and rum; drizzle over bananas. Bake at 350° for 15 to 20 minutes. Serve plain or with ice cream. Yield: 2 servings.

Japanese Dinner for Two

Vegetable Tempura with Sauces
Japanese Batayaki
Clear Soup
Winter and Spring Fruits
Sake or Sauvignon Blanc

In a typical Japanese meal, small portions of several foods will be served, so allow time for enjoyment and pleasure. Because the presentation and arrangement will be important to this meal, care should be taken to cut the food artistically and arrange it on platters for the diners to enjoy.

For ease in serving, perform all the slicing and chopping, arrange the vegetables, prepare the tempura batter, and arrange the meat and vegetables for the batayaki before cooking. Then cook the tempura and serve. After savoring the tempura, cook and serve the batayaki, which is the term used in Japan to describe "meat cooked in butter."

The soup is traditionally served in the middle or at the end of the meal. To serve sake properly, warm it to about 100°. Each person should be served with a tiny serving pitcher, called a tokkuri, and a tiny cup, or sakzuki.

Because Japanese dinners usually end with a very light dessert of fruit, beautifully arranged, we suggest tangerines and strawberries which are winter and spring fruits.

Vegetable Tempura with Sauces

Tempura Vegetables:

Broccoli	Turnips
Carrots	Yellow Squash
Cauliflower	Zucchini
Okra	

Tempura Batter:

¼ cup all-purpose flour	1 egg white, lightly beaten
¼ cup cornmeal	½ cup ice water
1 tablespoon cornstarch	Fresh vegetables
½ teaspoon baking powder	Peanut oil
¼ teaspoon salt	

Combine dry ingredients; add egg white and water. Stir until well blended, but do not beat. (Batter should be lumpy.)

Dip well-chilled vegetables into batter, a few pieces at a time. Drop into deep oil heated to 375°, and fry until golden. Drain on tempura rack or paper towels. Serve immediately. Yield: about ¾ cup batter.

Basic Tempura Sauce:

¼ cup soy sauce	⅛ teaspoon monosodium glutamate
¼ cup sweet cooking rice wine	(optional)
⅔ cup water	

Combine all ingredients, stirring well; bring to a boil. Serve hot. Yield: about 1 cup.

Mustard-Sour Cream Sauce:

⅓ cup commercial sour cream	1 teaspoon dry sherry
⅓ cup plain yogurt	½ teaspoon hot sauce
3 tablespoons Dijon mustard	¼ teaspoon Worcestershire sauce
2 teaspoons prepared horseradish	

Combine all ingredients, stirring well. Chill until serving time. Yield: about 1 cup.

Tips for Tempura:

Vegetables should be cut well in advance and chilled thoroughly before cooking. Be sure they are completely dry.

Cut fibrous vegetables like carrots and broccoli stems on the diagonal to expose more surface area and ensure more even cooking. Other vegetables can be cut in slices, slivers, or wedges, depending on personal preference.

Use ice water in the tempura batter.

To be sure the oil temperature is 375°, use a deep fat thermometer or toss a bread cube into the hot oil. If it sinks to the bottom and immediately comes to the top and turns golden brown, the oil is ready.

Cook just a few pieces of food at a time. Drain on tempura rack or paper towels; serve immediately.

Japanese Batayaki

¼ cup butter or margarine, divided
6 to 8 whole green onions
12 whole fresh mushrooms
1 green pepper, cut into strips

1 large onion, cut into chunks
1 (½-pound) sirloin steak, cut into thin strips
Dipping Sauce

Melt 2 tablespoons butter in a large skillet over medium heat. Add vegetables; stir-fry about 5 minutes or until tender. Slide vegetables to one side of skillet. Add remaining butter and meat. Cook 3 to 5 minutes. Serve with Dipping Sauce. Yield: 2 servings.

Dipping Sauce:

½ cup soy sauce
Juice of ½ lemon

1 green onion, finely chopped
¼ teaspoon prepared horseradish

Combine ingredients, and serve at room temperature. Yield: about ½ cup.

Clear Soup

1½ cups water
1½ teaspoons chicken-flavored bouillon granules
½ teaspoon soy sauce

2 mushrooms, thinly sliced
1 green onion top, cut into long slivers
2 thin strips of lemon rind

Combine water, bouillon, and soy sauce in a medium saucepan. Heat to boiling. Stir well; pour into serving bowls. Top each serving with mushroom slices, onion pieces, and lemon rind. Yield: 2 servings.

Winter and Spring Fruits

3 to 4 fresh tangerines or oranges, peeled, seeded, and sectioned

1 cup fresh strawberry slices
¼ cup sweet white wine

Combine tangerine sections and strawberry slices in a glass serving bowl. Pour wine over fruit and toss gently. Cover tightly and refrigerate 2 to 3 hours. Yield: 2 servings.

Traditional Middle Eastern Dinner

Egg and Lemon Soup
Spinach Phyllo Cheese Pie
Shish Kabobs
Persian Pilaf
Lemon Yogurt Bars
Zinfandel or Pinot Noir

Our version of a Middle Eastern Dinner is simplified, yet contains such traditional ingredients as lamb, parsley, spinach, yogurt, and lemon.

The Spinach Phyllo Cheese Pie makes a hearty appetizer or side dish, but any leftovers can be served at another time. The phyllo sheets are available in supermarket frozen food cases.

Egg and Lemon Soup

1 (10¾-ounce) can chicken broth
1 cup water
2 tablespoons uncooked rice

1 egg
1 tablespoon lemon juice
1 tablespoon finely chopped parsley

Combine chicken broth, water, and rice in a medium saucepan. Stir well; bring to a boil. Cover; reduce heat and simmer about 15 to 18 minutes or until rice is tender.

Beat egg and lemon juice together. Stir about ¼ cup of the hot rice broth into the egg; add to remaining broth mixture. Cook and stir, without boiling, about 2 minutes, or until slightly thickened. Garnish with parsley. Yield: 2 servings.

Spinach Phyllo Cheese Pie

2 (10-ounce) packages frozen
  spinach, thawed
¼ cup chopped green onion
2 tablespoons olive oil
1 teaspoon salt
½ teaspoon pepper
3 eggs, beaten
1 tablespoon all-purpose flour

1 cup feta cheese, crumbled
¼ cup small-curd cottage cheese
2 tablespoons grated Parmesan
  cheese
10 sheets commercial phyllo pastry
¾ cup butter or margarine, melted
Ground cinnamon

Drain spinach thoroughly to remove all liquid. Combine the spinach and the next 9 ingredients.

Lay out phyllo pastry and cover 5 sheets with plastic wrap to keep from drying out. Lightly butter 5 sheets of pastry with a pastry brush. Fold each in half, short ends together, and arrange in bottom and up sides of a 9-inch square baking dish. Spread spinach mixture smoothly over phyllo; sprinkle lightly with cinnamon. Fold any overhanging phyllo over the spinach mixture.

Remove the plastic film, and spread the remaining phyllo sheets with butter; fold in half and arrange over spinach mixture. Brush pastry with butter and pinch edges together. Make one cut the vertical and horizontal length through the top crust only. Bake at 400° for 35 to 45 minutes or until crust is puffed and golden brown. Finish cutting into squares and place on a wire rack to cool so that the bottom crust stays crisp. Serve at room temperature. Yield: 4 servings.

Note: For appetizer servings, before baking make two full cuts each way through the top crust only. After baking, cut into squares. Yield: 9 appetizer servings.

Shish Kabobs

¼ cup commercial oil and vinegar salad dressing
2 tablespoons lemon juice
½ teaspoon dried oregano leaves
Pinch of dried rosemary leaves
⅛ teaspoon salt
Dash of pepper
1 pound boneless lamb, cut into 2-inch cubes
Salt to taste

Combine salad dressing, lemon juice, oregano, rosemary, ⅛ teaspoon salt, and pepper; add meat. Cover, and marinate 4 to 8 hours in refrigerator, turning meat several times.

Remove meat from marinade and place on skewers; salt to taste. Grill 20 to 25 minutes over medium heat, basting with marinade and turning occasionally. Yield: 2 servings.

Persian Pilaf

⅓ cup chopped onion
1 teaspoon butter or margarine
⅓ cup uncooked regular rice
½ cup chicken broth
3 tablespoons half-and-half
¼ cup raisins
¼ teaspoon salt
⅛ teaspoon ground nutmeg
Toasted almond slices (optional)

Sauté onion in butter in a large skillet until tender. Add rice; cook 1 minute. Stir in broth, half-and-half, raisins, and seasonings. Bring mixture to a boil, and cover. Reduce heat, and simmer 20 minutes or until rice is tender and liquid is absorbed. Fluff with fork. Garnish with toasted almonds, if desired. Yield: 2 servings.

Lemon Yogurt Bars

1 cup whole wheat flour
½ cup all-purpose flour
1 teaspoon soda
½ teaspoon baking powder
½ teaspoon salt
½ teaspoon grated lemon rind
½ cup lemon yogurt
½ cup raisins

½ cup finely grated carrots
⅓ cup honey
1 egg, lightly beaten
3 tablespoons vegetable oil
2 tablespoons milk
¼ cup chopped nuts (optional)
Creamy Lemon Frosting

Combine first 6 ingredients in a large bowl, stirring well. Combine yogurt, raisins, carrots, honey, egg, oil, milk, and nuts, if desired; add to dry ingredients, stirring until moistened. Spread batter in a greased 8-inch square baking pan. Bake at 350° for 25 to 30 minutes. Cool. Top with Creamy Lemon Frosting. Cut into bars. Yield: about 1 dozen.

Creamy Lemon Frosting:

½ (3-ounce) package cream cheese, softened
1 tablespoon butter or margarine, softened

½ teaspoon grated lemon rind
½ teaspoon lemon juice
1 cup sifted powdered sugar

Combine cream cheese and butter, creaming until fluffy. Add lemon rind and juice; mix thoroughly. Gradually add powdered sugar, beating until light and fluffy. Yield: ½ cup.

Veal Dinner Italiano

Parmesan Mushrooms
Lemon-Sauced Veal
Risotta
Marinated Bean Salad
Caraway Crisps
Italian Custard with Fruit
Barbera or Zinfandel

This Italian dinner features one of the country's more elegant dishes, veal served in a butter-lemon sauce. The Italian Custard with Fruit is adapted from zabaglione, a traditional Italian custard.

Parmesan Mushrooms

½ pound fresh mushrooms
1 small onion, minced
2 tablespoons chopped fresh parsley
3 tablespoons butter or margarine

½ to ¾ cup breadcrumbs
¼ to ⅓ cup grated Parmesan
cheese
Salt and pepper to taste

Wash mushrooms; pat dry. Remove stems and chop. Place caps in a buttered baking dish.

Sauté stems, onion, and parsley in butter. Add remaining ingredients; stir well. Stuff caps with mixture; bake at 350° for 15 minutes. Yield: 1½ dozen.

Lemon-Sauced Veal

1 (½-pound) veal round steak,
about ½ inch thick
2 tablespoons all-purpose flour
3 tablespoons butter or margarine,
divided

1 tablespoon vegetable oil
1½ tablespoons lemon juice
1 teaspoon finely chopped parsley
Salt and pepper

Cut veal into serving-size pieces. Pound to about ¼-inch thickness. Dredge with flour; shake off excess.

Heat 2 tablespoons butter and oil in a large skillet. Cook veal until brown, about 3 to 5 minutes on each side. Remove veal to a heated platter; keep warm.

Add remaining 1 tablespoon butter to skillet and melt, stirring to scrape drippings from bottom of skillet. Stir in lemon juice and parsley. Pour over veal; sprinkle lightly with salt and pepper. Yield: 2 servings.

Risotta

¼ cup chopped onion
2 tablespoons butter or margarine
½ cup uncooked regular rice
1 cup boiling water
¼ teaspoon salt

1 teaspoon chicken-flavored
bouillon granules
3 tablespoons chopped parsley
Grated Parmesan cheese

Combine onion, butter, and rice in a small saucepan. Cook over medium heat, stirring constantly, until onion is tender and rice is lightly browned. Stir in water, salt, bouillon granules, and parsley. Cover and cook 12 to 15 minutes. Stir gently with a fork. Cover and cook 5 minutes longer or until all liquid is absorbed. Sprinkle with Parmesan cheese. Yield: 2 servings.

Marinated Bean Salad

1 (10-ounce) package frozen
  French-style green beans
¼ cup Vinaigrette Dressing
Lettuce leaves

1 tomato, cut into wedges
½ small red onion, thinly sliced
Ripe olives
Grated Parmesan cheese

Cook beans according to package directions; drain well. Place beans in a medium bowl, pour Vinaigrette Dressing over warm beans, and toss to combine. Cover and refrigerate several hours or overnight.

When ready to serve, arrange lettuce leaves on plates. Arrange green beans, tomato wedges, onion rings, and ripe olives over beans. Sprinkle with Parmesan cheese. Yield: 2 servings.

Vinaigrette Dressing:

¼ cup olive or vegetable oil
1½ tablespoons wine vinegar
1 clove garlic, chopped

¼ teaspoon prepared mustard
Dash of pepper

Combine all ingredients, and mix well. Yield: about ⅓ cup.

Note: Store remaining dressing in tightly covered container in refrigerator.

Caraway Crisps

1 cup all-purpose flour
1 teaspoon salt
¼ cup shortening
½ cup (2 ounces) shredded Cheddar
  cheese

2 to 3 tablespoons water
Milk
Caraway seeds

Combine flour and salt; cut in shortening until mixture resembles coarse meal. Add cheese, mixing well. Add water gradually to mixture; mix until a dry, crumbly dough is formed.

Turn dough out onto a floured surface, and knead several times. Roll out to ¼-inch thickness and cut into 1¼-inch diamond-shaped pieces. Brush with milk, and sprinkle with caraway seeds. Bake at 425° for 12 to 15 minutes or until browned. Yield: about 2½ dozen.

Italian Custard with Fruit

2 egg yolks
1 tablespoon sugar
3 tablespoons Grand Marnier
3 tablespoons whipping cream,
  whipped

1 pint fresh strawberries, washed
  and hulled, or 2 cups fresh peach
  slices
Mint (optional)

Place egg yolks in top of a double boiler; beat with an electric mixer at medium speed until thick and lemon colored. Gradually add sugar, beating until soft peaks form.

Place egg yolk mixture over simmering water; beat in Grand Marnier. Continue cooking and beating until mixture is fluffy. Remove from heat and beat until cool. Fold in whipped cream.

Divide strawberries or peaches equally between 2 glass dessert dishes. Spoon sauce over top. Garnish with mint, if desired. Yield: 2 servings.

Chinese Pork Chop Dinner

Broiled Chicken Wings
Chinese Pork Chops
Steamed Spinach
Hot Cooked Rice
Chilled Burgundy Orange Slices
Gamay Rosé

Chinese meals are cooked very quickly and are served in small portions. The pork chops are cut into thin slices, coated with the traditional soy sauce, and served with steamed vegetables and rice.

Broiled Chicken Wings

½ pound chicken wings
1½ tablespoons lemon juice
1½ tablespoons soy sauce
Dash of onion powder

Salt and pepper to taste
1½ teaspoons honey
1½ teaspoons catsup

Remove tips from wings; cut wings into 2 pieces, and place in a shallow dish. Combine lemon juice, soy sauce, and onion powder; pour over chicken. Cover and marinate wings in refrigerator several hours or overnight.

Drain chicken wings, reserving 1 tablespoon marinade; place wings on a foil-lined broiler pan. Sprinkle with salt and pepper. Combine reserved marinade, honey, and catsup, stirring well; brush half of mixture on chicken wings. Broil 6 to 7 inches from heat for 7 minutes. Turn and brush with remaining sauce; broil 7 additional minutes. Yield: about 9 pieces.

Chinese Pork Chops

4 (½-inch-thick) pork chops
1 tablespoon soy sauce
Sugar
1 egg, beaten

2 tablespoons vegetable oil
3 tablespoons dry white wine
Steamed spinach or cabbage

Remove bones from pork chops and pound to ¼-inch thickness. Sprinkle both sides of each slice with soy sauce and a pinch of sugar. Place slices on a large plate. Pour beaten egg over pork slices; toss with fork to combine and coat.

Heat oil in a large skillet or wok until very hot. Add coated pork slices. Cook about 2 to 3 minutes, turning to brown both sides. Add wine; cover and cook about 2 to 3 minutes. Serve with steamed spinach or cabbage. Yield: 2 servings.

Steamed Spinach

½ pound fresh spinach leaves

Arrange washed spinach leaves in steamer basket over ½ inch of water. Cover; bring to a boil. Cook 3 to 5 minutes or until desired degree of doneness. Yield: 2 servings.

Chilled Burgundy
Orange Slices

2 large oranges
½ cup Burgundy or other dry red
  wine
1 tablespoon wine vinegar

1 (2-inch) stick cinnamon
8 whole cloves
⅓ cup sugar

Peel oranges and cut into crosswise slices about ⅜ inch thick; set aside. Combine wine, vinegar, seasonings, and sugar; simmer 10 minutes. Pour over orange slices. Cover and let stand until cool. Yield: about 2 servings.

Save lemon and orange rinds. Store in the freezer, and grate as needed for pies, cakes, breads, and cookies. Or the rinds can be candied for holiday uses.

ALL-OCCASION ENTERTAINING

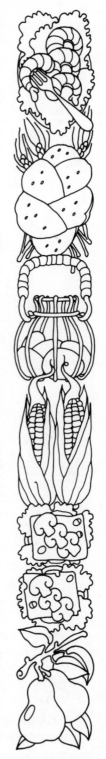

Entertaining, even for the experienced cook, can often be an intimidating event. The secret to successful entertaining by anyone, regardless of experience, is careful planning and thoughtful preparation. For your first parties, you may wish to choose an informal event and then tackle more spectacular or lavish events after you acquire skills and confidence.

If time is limited, you will want to choose a simple menu, perhaps something which can be cooked on the grill, or try one of our brunches or lunches which are somewhat less elaborate than a dinner meal. For these, as well as for multi-course meals, utilize all available space for serving. Set up cocktails and appetizers in the hallway, foyer, or on portable trays or tables. Serve the main meal buffet style, using the breakfast table, a chest or trunk normally used for storage, or even a cleared kitchen counter.

And remember that not all entertaining must be done at home. Consider using other space, like a public park, a beach, or a simple, rustic wooded setting. If you have a special hobby, such as sailing, skiing, or swimming, which would be of interest to your guests, plan to entertain around it and invite your guests to participate.

Our entertaining menus include a wide variety of foods that can be served at different times and for different occasions. There are simple, easy-to-prepare picnics and more elaborate dinner parties. Your final choice will be determined by your personal interest, time, energy, the money and space available—and the result you hope to achieve.

New Year's Day Buffet

Beef and Pork Tenderloin Sandwiches
Braunschweiger-Onion Spread
Crunchy Cheese Spread
Whole Wheat, Rye, and White Breads
Mustard and Mayonnaise
Pickled Black-Eyed Peas
Marinated Cherry Tomatoes
Special Bean Salad
Cheese Wafers
Sausage Balls
Red Apples and Fresh Pears
with Gouda and Swiss Cheese
Fruitcake
Pound Cake
Christmas Cookies
Pecan Pralines
Champagne

If you have never planned or attended a New Year's Day Party, you have missed one of the great occasions. Almost everyone will relish the thought of the change of pace in activities.

Plan to have at least two television sets available and food which can be served easily without a lot of fuss. That way your football enthusiasts will be able to relax and enjoy the day.

Our recipes include sandwiches served with an assortment of fillings and spreads. For ease as well as luck we suggest a different black-eyed pea recipe that is made at least a day before.

Desserts are simple ones. Fruit, cake slices, Pecan Pralines, and Christmas Cookies are easy to prepare and serve. And almost all party-goers will appreciate champagne or another beverage of your choice.

Beef and Pork Tenderloin Sandwiches

1 (6- to 7-pound) beef tenderloin,
   trimmed
2 (⅔-pound) pork tenderloins,
   trimmed
Marinade (recipe follows)
Vegetable oil

Party rye bread
Endive
Mayonnaise (optional)
Commercial barbecue sauce
   (optional)
Prepared horseradish (optional)

Place tenderloins in a large pan or dish; pour marinade over top, and cover tightly. Refrigerate overnight, turning meat several times; drain.

Place beef tenderloin, fat side up, on a rack in a shallow roasting pan; rub with 1 tablespoon vegetable oil. Bake at 450° for 15 minutes. Turn oven off; do not open door. Let roast remain in oven 45 minutes (roast will be medium rare). Remove from oven.

Place pork tenderloins, fat side up, on rack in a shallow roasting pan; rub with 1 teaspoon oil. Bake at 325° for 1 hour or until well done.

Slice tenderloins, and place on a serving platter. Serve on party rye bread with endive; top each sandwich with mayonnaise, barbecue sauce, or horseradish, if desired. Yield: about 24 servings.

Note: If tenderloins are cooked the day before serving, cover and place in refrigerator until ready to slice.

Marinade:

½ cup port wine
½ cup brandy
½ teaspoon dried tarragon leaves
½ teaspoon dried thyme

2 bay leaves
1¼ teaspoons salt
½ teaspoon pepper
½ teaspoon dry mustard

Combine all ingredients in a small bowl, mixing well. Yield: 1 cup.

Braunschweiger-Onion Spread

1 (16-ounce) carton commercial
   sour cream
2 (1⅜-ounce) envelopes dry onion
   soup mix
2 (3-ounce) packages cream cheese,
   softened

2 teaspoons steak sauce
4 drops hot sauce
2 (8-ounce) packages sliced
   braunschweiger, cut into small
   cubes

Combine sour cream and soup mix; stir well and set aside for 15 minutes.

Beat cream cheese until fluffy in a medium bowl. Add sour cream mixture, steak sauce, and hot sauce; mix well. Add braunschweiger; stir gently. Chill. Serve with rye bread, crackers, or chips. Yield: 4⅔ cups.

Crunchy Cheese Spread

2 cups (8 ounces) shredded sharp
   Cheddar cheese
½ cup chopped apple
½ cup chopped walnuts
½ cup chopped celery
½ cup shredded carrots
⅓ cup mayonnaise

2 tablespoons chopped raisins
2 tablespoons chopped dates
2 tablespoons chopped green
   pepper
1 tablespoon wheat germ
1 teaspoon lemon juice
1 teaspoon Worcestershire sauce

Combine all ingredients, mixing well. Serve the spread with whole wheat bread or
crackers. Yield: 4 cups.

Pickled Black-Eyed Peas

6 (15-ounce) cans black-eyed peas,
   drained
1¾ to 2 cups vegetable oil
¾ cup wine vinegar

3 cloves garlic
¾ cup thinly sliced onion
1¼ teaspoons salt
½ teaspoon pepper

Combine all ingredients; cover and chill 24 hours. Remove garlic. Chill in refrigerator for 2 days to 2 weeks before serving. Yield: 18 to 24 servings.

Marinated Cherry Tomatoes

3 pints cherry tomatoes, cut into
   halves
3 bunches green onions, sliced
3 cups vegetable oil
1 cup vinegar

1½ teaspoons dried basil leaves
1½ teaspoons dried oregano leaves
1½ teaspoons salt
¾ teaspoon pepper

Place tomatoes in a bowl; sprinkle with onion. Combine remaining ingredients in a
jar; shake well, and pour over vegetables. Cover and chill 3 to 4 hours. Yield: 18 to
24 servings.

Special Bean Salad

2 (30-ounce) cans kidney beans,
   drained
2 large cabbages, shredded
½ cup chopped onion
2 teaspoons celery seeds

2 teaspoons salt
¾ cup vinegar
2 cups mayonnaise
4 to 6 hard-cooked eggs, sliced

Set aside 1 cup beans. Combine remaining beans, cabbage, and onion; add celery
seeds, salt, vinegar, and mayonnaise. Toss thoroughly. Chill. Garnish with reserved
beans and eggs. Yield: 16 to 24 servings.

Cheese Wafers

½ cup butter or margarine, softened
1 cup (4 ounces) shredded sharp
   Cheddar cheese
1 cup all-purpose flour

Dash of salt
½ teaspoon red pepper
⅛ teaspoon paprika
Powdered sugar (optional)

Cream butter and cheese; add flour, salt, red pepper, and paprika, mixing well. Chill. Shape dough into a roll, 1 inch in diameter; wrap in foil. Refrigerate 24 hours.

Slice roll ¼ inch thick, and place on ungreased baking sheets. Bake at 350° for 15 minutes; cool. Sift a small amount of powdered sugar over wafers before removing from baking sheet, if desired. Yield: about 4 dozen.

Note: Dough may be shaped into a roll and frozen. Cheese Wafers also freeze well after baking.

Sausage Balls

1 pound hot bulk sausage
2 cups (8 ounces) shredded sharp
   Cheddar cheese

2 cups biscuit mix
2 tablespoons grated onion
1 tablespoon poultry seasoning

Combine all ingredients, mixing well. Roll into walnut-size balls. Place on ungreased baking sheets and bake at 400° for 15 minutes. Drain on absorbent paper. Serve hot. Yield: about 4 dozen.

Fruitcake

1 cup butter or margarine, softened
1 cup sugar
5 eggs
1½ teaspoons vanilla extract
1 teaspoon almond extract
3 cups all-purpose flour, divided
2 teaspoons baking powder
¼ cup orange juice
1 tablespoon lemon juice
7½ cups chopped pecans

¼ pound chopped candied orange
   peel
1 pound candied pineapple,
   chopped
¼ pound chopped candied lemon
   peel
¼ pound chopped candied citron
1 pound candied cherries, chopped
1 (15-ounce) package golden raisins
Candied cherries (optional)

Combine butter and sugar, creaming until light and fluffy. Add eggs, one at a time, beating well after each addition; stir in flavorings. Combine 2 cups flour and baking powder; add to creamed mixture alternately with orange and lemon juice.

Dredge pecans, chopped fruits, and raisins in remaining flour; stir to coat well. Stir mixture into batter. Spoon into a greased and waxed paper-lined 10-inch tubepan; bake at 250° for 3 hours or until cake tests done. Remove from oven. Cool cake about 10 minutes before removing from pan. Garnish with candied cherries, if desired. Chill before slicing. Yield: one 10-inch cake.

Pound Cake

3 cups sugar
1 pound butter or margarine,
  softened
6 eggs (at room temperature)

4 cups all-purpose flour
¾ cup milk
1 teaspoon almond extract
1 teaspoon vanilla extract

Combine sugar and butter; cream until light and fluffy. Add eggs, one at a time, beating well after each addition. Add flour to creamed mixture alternately with milk, beating well after each addition. Gently stir in flavorings.

Pour batter into a well-greased and floured 10-inch tube pan. Bake at 300° for 1 hour and 40 minutes or until cake tests done. Cool in pan for 10 minutes before removing. Yield: one 10-inch cake.

Christmas Cookies

1 cup butter or margarine, softened
1 (3-ounce) package cream cheese,
  softened
1 cup sugar

1 egg yolk
2½ cups all-purpose flour
1 teaspoon vanilla extract
Candied cherries or pecan halves

Cream butter and cream cheese; gradually add sugar, beating until light and fluffy. Add egg yolk, beating well. Add flour and vanilla; mix until blended. Chill dough at least 1 hour.

Shape dough into 1-inch balls, and place on greased cookie sheets. Gently press a candied cherry or pecan half into each cookie. Bake at 325° for 12 to 15 minutes. Yield: about 7 dozen.

Pecan Pralines

2 cups sugar
1 teaspoon soda
1 cup buttermilk
⅛ teaspoon salt

2 tablespoons butter or margarine
1 tablespoon light corn syrup
2½ cups pecan halves

Combine sugar, soda, buttermilk, and salt in a heavy 4-quart saucepan; cook over medium heat to 210° (about 5 minutes), stirring constantly. Add butter, syrup, and pecans; continue cooking until candy reaches 234° (soft ball stage), about 5 minutes more, stirring constantly.

Remove from heat; beat with a wooden spoon for 2 to 3 minutes, just until mixture begins to thicken. Working rapidly, drop by tablespoonfuls onto lightly buttered waxed paper; let cool. Wrap pralines in waxed paper and store in airtight container. Yield: about 18 (3-inch) pralines.

Note: If more pralines are desired, make separate batches rather than double or triple the recipe.

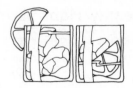

Spring Brunch

Bloody Marys
Orange Blossom Flips
Creamy Ham Sauce
Cottage Cheese Cornbread
Tangy Vegetable Toss
Peaches and Cream Parfait
Champagne or Riesling
Coffee

Serve this brunch when special houseguests have arrived for the weekend. Either a patio or deck make the perfect setting. A choice of pre-brunch drinks is offered, or, if you prefer, plan wine or champagne for the entire meal.

Bloody Marys

1½ cups tomato juice
¼ cup vodka
2 teaspoons Worcestershire sauce
2 teaspoons lemon juice

2 dashes of hot sauce
2 dashes of celery salt
Coarsely ground pepper to taste
Celery stalks

Combine first 7 ingredients, mixing well. Pour over ice cubes; garnish each serving with a stalk of celery. Yield: about 2 cups.
   Note: This recipe can be increased to serve any size group.

Orange Blossom Flips

1 (6-ounce) can frozen orange juice
   concentrate, undiluted
1 cup half-and-half
¾ cup cream sherry

1 egg
Dash of salt
2 ice cubes

Combine all ingredients in container of an electric blender; process until smooth and frothy. Yield: about 2½ cups.

Creamy Ham Sauce

2 tablespoons butter or margarine
2 tablespoons all-purpose flour
1 cup chicken broth
½ cup half-and-half

1 egg, slightly beaten
2 cups cubed ham
1 tablespoon minced parsley

Melt butter in a heavy saucepan over medium heat. Add flour; cook 1 minute, stirring constantly. Gradually add chicken broth and half-and-half; cook over medium heat, stirring constantly, until thickened and creamy.

Blend ¾ cup of sauce into beaten egg. Add egg mixture to hot sauce mixture. Stir in ham and parsley; continue cooking over medium heat until thoroughly heated, stirring constantly. Keep warm. Serve over Cottage Cheese Cornbread or other bread of your choice. Yield: 4 servings.

Cottage Cheese Cornbread

1 cup self-rising cornmeal mix
1 egg, beaten
½ cup buttermilk

½ cup small-curd cottage cheese
1 tablespoon butter or margarine

Combine cornmeal mix, egg, buttermilk, and cottage cheese; mix well.

Melt butter in an 8-inch piepan at 450°. Add batter. Bake 20 to 25 minutes or until cornbread is golden brown. Serve warm. Yield: 4 servings.

Tangy Vegetable Toss

6 ripe tomatoes, quartered
1 green pepper, cut into strips
1 medium onion, sliced and
   separated into rings
1 cucumber, cut into ¼-inch slices
¾ cup white wine vinegar
¼ cup water

1½ teaspoons mustard seeds
1½ teaspoons celery salt
½ teaspoon salt
1½ tablespoons sugar
¼ teaspoon black pepper
Dash of red pepper

Combine vegetables in a medium-size bowl, and set aside.

Combine remaining ingredients, mixing well. Bring to a boil; cook, stirring constantly, 1 minute. Pour hot mixture over vegetables, tossing lightly. Chill. Yield: 4 to 6 servings.

Peaches and Cream Parfait

½ teaspoon ascorbic-citric mixture
2 cups sliced fresh peaches
¼ cup butter or margarine, softened
¾ cup sifted powdered sugar
1 egg, slightly beaten

1 cup whipping cream, whipped
½ cup vanilla wafer crumbs
¼ cup finely chopped crystallized
   ginger

Prepare ascorbic-citric mixture according to package directions; sprinkle over peaches, mixing well. Set aside.

Cream butter and sugar; add egg, beating well. Cook egg mixture in top of a double boiler, stirring constantly, until thickened and mixture coats a metal spoon. Cool.

Fold egg mixture into whipped cream. Alternate layers of whipped cream mixture, cookie crumbs, peaches, and ginger in parfait glasses. Chill 2 hours. Yield: 4 servings.

Make Dinner a Party

Chilled Pea Soup
Blanc de Noir
Crabmeat-Stuffed Steak
Twice Baked Potatoes
Marinated Tomatoes
Chocolate Roulage
Cabernet Sauvignon

We think this dinner is special enough to become a party. Serve dry sherry or Blanc de Noir wine with the soup. While guests are enjoying this first course, broil or grill the steak. Cabernet Sauvignon is the wine suggested to accompany the main dish. And for a fitting finale, serve Chocolate Roulage.

Chilled Pea Soup

1 teaspoon beef-flavored bouillon granules	½ cup commercial sour cream
½ cup hot water	¼ teaspoon onion salt
1 (17-ounce) can small English peas, undrained	¼ teaspoon salt
	Dash of pepper
	Paprika

Dissolve bouillon in hot water; set aside.

Place peas in container of electric blender; blend until smooth. Add bouillon; blend well. Add sour cream, onion salt, salt, and pepper; blend until smooth. Chill for 1 to 2 hours. Sprinkle each serving with paprika. Yield: about 3 cups.

Crabmeat-Stuffed Steak

½ cup chopped onion
1 clove garlic, minced
2 tablespoons butter or margarine
1 (4-ounce) can sliced mushrooms, drained

½ pound fresh or frozen crabmeat
1 tablespoon Worcestershire sauce
1 (1½-inch-thick) porterhouse or sirloin steak

Sauté onion and garlic in butter until onion is tender. Add mushrooms, crabmeat, and Worcestershire sauce; mix well, and set aside.

Trim excess fat from steak. Cut a deep pocket into side of steak. Stuff pocket with crabmeat mixture; seal with skewers or wooden picks.

Broil steak 3 to 4 inches from heat for 5 to 6 minutes on each side or until desired degree of doneness. Yield: 4 servings.

Twice Baked Potatoes

4 medium baking potatoes
⅓ cup commercial sour cream
½ cup cubed process American cheese
1½ tablespoons butter or margarine

2 teaspoons fresh chives
2 teaspoons minced onion
½ teaspoon salt
¼ teaspoon pepper

Wash potatoes; bake at 400° for 1 hour or until done. Allow potatoes to cool to touch. Slice skin away from top of each potato. Carefully scoop out pulp, leaving shells intact; mash pulp.

Place sour cream over low heat until warm. Remove from heat; add potato pulp and remaining ingredients, mixing well. Stuff shells with potato mixture. Bake at 425° for 15 minutes. Serve hot. Yield: 4 servings.

Marinated Tomatoes

½ cup vegetable oil
2 tablespoons vinegar
2 tablespoons lemon juice
½ teaspoon salt
¼ teaspoon dry mustard

4 medium tomatoes, cut into ¾-inch slices
1 medium onion, sliced
Chopped parsley

Combine oil, vinegar, lemon juice, salt, and mustard in a small mixing bowl, stirring well. Place tomatoes and onion slices in a medium bowl. Pour dressing over vegetables and sprinkle with parsley. Cover bowl, and refrigerate 8 hours. Yield: 4 to 6 servings.

Whenever possible, buy most foods by weight or cost per serving rather than by volume or package size.

Chocolate Roulage

Vegetable oil
1 (6-ounce) package semisweet
  chocolate morsels
5 eggs, separated
1¼ cups sugar, divided
1 teaspoon vanilla extract
2 teaspoons cocoa

1 cup whipping cream
2 tablespoons powdered sugar
2 to 3 tablespoons green crème de
  menthe
Additional powdered sugar
Whole strawberries

Grease bottom and sides of a 15- × 10- × 1-inch jellyroll pan with oil; line with waxed paper, and grease waxed paper with oil.

Place chocolate morsels in top of a double boiler; bring water to a boil. Reduce heat to low; cook, stirring occasionally, until chocolate melts.

Place egg yolks in a large bowl; beat until foamy at high speed of electric mixer. Gradually add ¾ cup sugar, beating until mixture is thick and lemon colored. (The mixture will look much like cake batter.)

Gradually stir about one-fourth of hot chocolate mixture into yolk mixture; fold in remaining chocolate mixture.

Beat egg whites (at room temperature) at high speed of electric mixer until foamy. Gradually add ½ cup sugar, beating until stiff peaks form. Fold egg whites into chocolate mixture; gently fold in vanilla.

Pour chocolate mixture into jellyroll pan, spreading evenly. Bake on center rack of oven at 350° for 15 to 18 minutes; do not overbake (surface will shine when done). Immediately cover top with a damp linen towel or 2 layers of damp paper towels; place on a wire rack, and let cool 20 minutes. Carefully remove towel. Loosen edges with a metal spatula, and sift cocoa over top.

Place 2 lengths of waxed paper (longer than jellyroll pan) on a smooth, slightly damp surface; overlap edge of paper nearest you over second sheet. Quickly invert jellyroll pan onto waxed paper, with long side nearest you; remove pan, and carefully peel paper from chocolate roll.

Beat whipping cream until foamy; gradually add 2 tablespoons powdered sugar and crème de menthe, beating until soft peaks form.

Spoon whipped cream mixture over chocolate roll, spreading it so that there is more on the side facing you (mixture will spread out as you roll); leave a 1-inch margin on all sides.

Starting at long side, carefully roll jellyroll fashion; use the waxed paper to help support the roulage as you roll. Secure the waxed paper around the roulage; smooth and shape it with your hands.

Carefully slide roulage onto a large cookie sheet, seam side down; store in refrigerator until serving time. Before serving, sift additional powdered sugar over roulage; carefully transfer to serving dish, using the waxed paper to lift and slide it. Trim away excess waxed paper. Garnish with whole strawberries. Yield: 12 to 14 servings.

Note: The roulage is very fragile and may crack or break during rolling.

Tailgate Picnic

Chicken-Pineapple Salad
Marinated Green Beans
Crunchy Vegetables
Ham-Filled Biscuits
Cream Cheese Brownies
Jugs of White, Rosé, and Red Wine

A tailgate picnic can be a special occasion if you pack your food carefully. You will need a small ice chest, nonbreakable containers with tight-fitting lids, and, of course, a picnic basket. Pack foods made with eggs, milk, mayonnaise, and other perishable ingredients in plastic containers and place in the ice chest. Pack tablecloths, napkins, plates, knives and forks, beverages, tumblers, and other equipment in a basket or tote bag. Include slotted serving spoons for vegetables with liquids, such as the Marinated Green Beans.

Chicken-Pineapple Salad

3 cups diced cooked chicken
1 (20-ounce) can pineapple chunks, drained
3 tablespoons instant minced onion
3 tablespoons water
2 tablespoons butter or margarine, melted
1¼ teaspoons curry powder
⅓ cup mayonnaise

1 tablespoon lemon juice
½ teaspoon salt
Dash of red pepper
½ cup coarsely chopped pecans
⅓ cup golden raisins
1 apple, diced
Lettuce leaves (optional)
Flaked coconut (optional)

Combine chicken and pineapple; chill thoroughly.

Soak onion in water for 10 minutes. Combine onion, butter, and curry powder; cook 3 to 5 minutes over low heat, stirring occasionally. Cool. Combine onion mixture, mayonnaise, lemon juice, salt, and red pepper in a large bowl; mix well. Stir in chicken mixture, pecans, raisins, and apple; chill. Spoon onto lettuce and garnish with coconut, if desired. Yield: 6 servings.

Marinated Green Beans

1 cup sugar
1 cup vinegar
1 tablespoon vegetable oil
½ cup water

2 (16-ounce) cans French-style or
  whole green beans, drained
2 medium onions, thinly sliced and
  separated into rings

Combine sugar, vinegar, oil, and water in a medium saucepan. Boil for 2 minutes. Combine beans and onion rings; add hot marinade. Set aside to cool. Refrigerate and marinate at least overnight. Yield: 6 to 8 servings.

Crunchy Vegetables

1 pound fresh broccoli
1 small head cauliflower
2 carrots, sliced
1 zucchini, sliced
2 small onions, sliced and separated
  into rings

⅔ cup mayonnaise or salad dressing
⅓ cup vegetable oil
⅓ cup apple cider vinegar
¼ cup sugar
1 tablespoon salt

Trim off large leaves of broccoli. Remove tough end of lower stalks, and wash broccoli thoroughly. Cut into bite-size pieces.

Wash cauliflower, and remove green leaves. Separate cauliflower into flowerets, slicing large flowerets into bite-size pieces.

Combine vegetables in a large bowl. Combine remaining ingredients; stir well. Add mayonnaise mixture, tossing to coat vegetables. Chill salad several hours before serving. Yield: 6 to 8 servings.

Ham-Filled Biscuits

4½ cups all-purpose flour
1 tablespoon sugar
1 teaspoon soda
1 tablespoon baking powder
1½ teaspoons salt
1 cup shortening

2 packages dry yeast
¼ cup warm water (105° to 115°)
2 cups buttermilk
Butter or margarine, melted
Sliced ham

Combine first 5 ingredients; mix well. Cut in shortening. Dissolve yeast in water; add yeast mixture and buttermilk to flour mixture, mixing well.

Turn dough out on a floured surface, and knead until smooth and elastic (about 8 to 10 minutes). Roll dough to ¼-inch thickness, and brush with melted butter. Cut with a 2-inch biscuit cutter, and place ½ inch apart on a greased baking sheet; top each with a second biscuit. Bake at 400° for 12 to 15 minutes. Fill with sliced ham. Yield: about 3 dozen.

Note: Dough may be refrigerated up to 1 week before rolling out.

Cream Cheese Brownies

1 (4-ounce) package sweet baking chocolate
5 tablespoons butter or margarine, divided
1 (3-ounce) package cream cheese, softened
1 cup sugar, divided
3 eggs, divided
1 tablespoon all-purpose flour
1½ teaspoons vanilla extract, divided
½ cup all-purpose flour
½ teaspoon baking powder
¼ teaspoon salt
¼ teaspoon almond extract
½ cup chopped pecans

Melt chocolate and 3 tablespoons butter over low heat, stirring frequently; set aside to cool.

Soften remaining 2 tablespoons butter. Add cream cheese, creaming until light. Gradually add ¼ cup sugar, beating until fluffy. Stir in 1 egg, 1 tablespoon flour, and ½ teaspoon vanilla. Set aside.

Beat 2 eggs until lemon colored. Gradually add remaining ¾ cup sugar, beating until thick. Combine ½ cup flour, baking powder, and salt; add to egg mixture, mixing well. Stir in cooled chocolate, 1 teaspoon vanilla, almond extract, and pecans. Pour half of chocolate batter into a greased 8-inch square pan. Spread with cheese mixture; top with remaining chocolate batter. Cut through mixture in pan with a knife to create a marbled effect. Bake at 350° for 35 to 40 minutes. Cool; cut into 2-inch squares. Yield: 16 brownies.

Brunch for Four

Wine Spritzers
Spiced Apples in Wine
Sausage Quiche
Broiled Tomatoes
Lemon Muffins
Coffee

This hearty brunch is best served when the pace is leisurely to allow time for the quiche to bake. Wine Spritzers, a refreshing beverage, are easy to make with your favorite jug wine, such as a California Chablis.

Wine Spritzers

2 cups Chablis or other dry white
  wine
2 cups club soda

4 lemon wedges
4 lime slices

Combine wine and club soda; mix gently. Pour over ice in 4 wine goblets or glasses. Arrange a lemon wedge and lime slice on small wooden skewers or picks; garnish each serving. Yield: 4 servings.

Spiced Apples in Wine

5 large apples
1 cup red wine
¼ cup plus 2 tablespoons sugar
2 whole cloves
1 (2-inch) stick cinnamon

2 (2-inch) strips lemon rind
¼ cup raisins
1 teaspoon cornstarch
2 teaspoons water
1 tablespoon port wine

Peel and core apples; cut into thick slices. Heat red wine, sugar, cloves, cinnamon stick, and lemon rind in a saucepan. Add apple slices; cover and cook until tender. Transfer apples to a shallow 1-quart baking dish. Add raisins to sauce in saucepan; simmer 5 minutes. Combine cornstarch and water; stir into sauce. Cook until slightly thickened; remove cloves, cinnamon, and rind. Pour sauce over apples. Carefully stir in port wine. Chill. Yield: 4 servings.

Sausage Quiche

Pastry for 9-inch quiche dish or
  pieplate
1 pound hot bulk pork sausage
1 (4-ounce) can sliced mushrooms,
  drained
½ cup chopped onion
¼ cup chopped green pepper
1 teaspoon minced parsley

½ teaspoon whole basil leaves
Dash of garlic powder
⅛ teaspoon salt
1½ cups (6 ounces) shredded
  Cheddar cheese
1 cup milk
2 eggs
Paprika

Line a 9-inch quiche dish or pieplate with pastry; trim excess pastry around edges. Place a piece of buttered aluminum foil, buttered side down, over pastry; press into pastry shell. (This keeps the sides of shell from collapsing.) Cover foil with a layer of dried peas or beans. Bake at 400° for 10 minutes; remove peas and foil. Prick shell, and bake 3 to 5 additional minutes or until lightly browned. Cool.

Cook sausage until browned; drain. Combine sausage with next 7 ingredients, mixing well. Spoon into quiche shell; top with cheese.

Combine milk and eggs, beating just until foamy. Pour evenly over cheese; sprinkle with paprika. Bake at 325° for 50 minutes or until cheese is lightly browned and quiche is set. Yield: one 9-inch quiche.

Broiled Tomatoes

¾ cup herb-seasoned stuffing mix
1 tablespoon butter or margarine,
  melted

¼ cup grated Parmesan cheese
Dijon mustard
4 tomatoes, halved

Combine stuffing mix, butter, and cheese; mix well.

Spread mustard over surface of tomatoes. Spoon stuffing mixture over mustard. Broil 4 inches from heat about 7 minutes or until topping is lightly browned. Yield: 4 servings.

Lemon Muffins

1 cup all-purpose flour
1 teaspoon baking powder
¼ teaspoon salt
½ cup butter or margarine, softened
½ cup sugar

2 eggs, separated
3 tablespoons lemon juice
1 tablespoon grated lemon rind
2 tablespoons sugar
¼ teaspoon ground cinnamon

Combine flour, baking powder, and salt; set aside.

Beat butter until creamy; gradually add ½ cup sugar, and beat until light and fluffy. Beat egg yolks, and beat into creamed mixture. Add dry ingredients to creamed mixture alternately with lemon juice, mixing just until combined (do not overmix).

Beat egg whites (at room temperature) until stiff; gently stir in lemon rind. Fold into muffin mixture. Spoon batter into greased muffin pans, filling two-thirds full. Combine 2 tablespoons sugar and cinnamon; top each muffin with ½ teaspoon sugar mixture. Bake at 375° for 20 to 25 minutes or until done. Yield: about 1 dozen.

Page 131: *Sure to be a favorite ethnic menu is the Japanese Dinner for Two featuring Vegetable Tempura with Sauces, Batayaki, and Clear Soup. Menu begins on page 105.*

Page 132: *If you are looking for an elegant, crowd-pleasing dessert, serve Chocolate Roulage (page 125) filled with crème de menthe-flavored whipped cream.*

Patio Wine-Tasting Party

Fish Course
Hot Seafood Salad
Dark Rye Rounds
French Bread
Chardonnay or Sauvignon Blanc
Meat Course
Baked Zucchini and Sausage
Smoked Turkey
Zinfandel or Petit Sirah
Cheese Course
Fontina, Gorgonzola, and Muenster Cheeses
Spinach Soufflé Roll
Cabernet Sauvignon or Merlot
Dessert Course
Fresh Strawberries and Fresh Green Grapes
with Brown Sugar and Sour Cream
Meringue Icebox Cookies
Muscat

Our wine-tasting menu is planned for eight and includes recipes for four courses. Select one bottle of wine for each course and an extra one for the meat and cheese courses. Remember when serving more than one wine to use a fresh glass with each course, preferably glasses of different sizes and shapes.

With the increase in the variety of wines available, a Patio Wine-Tasting Party is a fun, simple way to entertain guests. Our menu wines are all California, because they are so widely available, but other American or European wines of your choice are just as appropriate.

Our suggestions are based on the "classic" combinations often recommended, but there is no such thing as the "right" or "wrong" wine-food combination. *Whatever you enjoy is probably the right choice for you and your guests. For the fish course, we suggest one of two white California wines, either Chardonnay or Sauvignon Blanc. Both are best served well chilled. Zinfandel, a wine unique to California, is our suggestion for the meat course. For the cheese course we recommend Cabernet Sauvignon or Merlot.*

An assortment of desserts is served with a Muscat wine recommendation. It may be new to you, but try it with cheese and a fruit dessert. You and your guests will appreciate this elegantly simple combination which can be served anytime.

Hot Seafood Salad

¾ pound scallops, coarsely
  chopped (about 1 cup)
¾ pound small shrimp, peeled and
  deveined (about 1 cup)
1½ cups dry white wine
2 cups (5½ ounces) sliced fresh
  mushrooms
1 tablespoon butter or margarine
1 (8-ounce) carton commercial sour
  cream
1 cup chopped celery

¼ cup sliced almonds, toasted
¼ cup crumbled blue cheese
¼ cup chopped green pepper
2 tablespoons minced onion
1 to 2 tablespoons lemon juice
1 teaspoon salt
½ cup seasoned dry breadcrumbs
2 tablespoons butter or margarine,
  melted
Lemon wedges

Rinse scallops and shrimp. Combine scallops, shrimp, and wine in a saucepan; simmer 3 minutes. Drain.

Sauté mushrooms in 1 tablespoon butter 2 to 3 minutes or just until tender. Combine scallops, shrimp, mushrooms, sour cream, celery, almonds, cheese, green pepper, onion, lemon juice, and salt; stir well. Spoon scallop mixture into 8 (10-ounce) custard cups or other individual serving dishes. Combine breadcrumbs and remaining butter, stirring well. Sprinkle breadcrumbs over scallop mixture. Bake at 300° for 10 to 15 minutes. Garnish with lemon wedges. Yield: 8 servings.

French Bread

3 cups warm water (105° to 115°)
1⅛ teaspoons dry yeast
Pinch of sugar
About 10 cups unbleached
  all-purpose flour

2 tablespoons sugar
1 tablespoon plus 1½ teaspoons salt

Combine water, yeast, and a pinch of sugar in a medium bowl; set aside.

Combine 10 cups flour, 2 tablespoons sugar, and salt in a large mixing bowl; stir well. Spoon about one-third of flour mixture into bowl of food processor. Pour one-third of yeast mixture through chute; process with steel blade until dough forms a ball. Turn dough out onto a floured surface. Repeat process with remaining flour mixture and yeast mixture, using one-third of each at a time.

Press the 3 balls of dough together; knead until smooth and elastic (dough will be very stiff). Place in a well-greased bowl, turning once to grease top. Cover and let rise in a warm place (85°), free from drafts, until doubled in bulk. Punch down; cover and let rise until doubled in bulk.

Turn dough out on a floured surface, and divide into 3 equal portions; shape each portion into a 14- to 16-inch loaf. Place 2 loaves on 1 greased baking sheet and remaining loaf on another. Cover and let rise until doubled in bulk. Cut ¼-inch-deep slashes in top of each loaf, using a sharp knife or razor blade.

Place a loafpan of boiling water on lower shelf of oven. Place 1 baking sheet of bread on lower shelf of oven, and bake at 400° for 30 minutes; move bread to upper shelf, and bake an additional 5 minutes. Repeat baking process with remaining baking sheet of bread. Allow to cool on wire racks. Yield: 3 loaves.

Note: Conventional mixing procedures may be used to make bread. Place yeast mixture in a large bowl, and gradually stir in flour mixture; proceed by following the remaining directions.

Baked Zucchini and Sausage

2 pounds medium zucchini
2 eggs, beaten
2 tablespoons water
1 cup soft breadcrumbs
¼ cup plus 2 tablespoons vegetable oil, divided
1½ pounds Italian sausage
¼ cup butter or margarine
½ cup chopped onion
¼ cup all-purpose flour
1 (14½-ounce) can chicken broth
½ cup half-and-half
½ cup grated Parmesan cheese

Wash zucchini and remove ends; cut diagonally into ½-inch slices. Combine eggs and water, mixing well. Dip zucchini slices in egg mixture; coat with breadcrumbs. Pour 2 tablespoons oil in a skillet; brown one-third of zucchini slices over low heat. Repeat with remaining oil and zucchini. Place zucchini along edges of a greased 13- × 9- × 2-inch baking dish.

Place sausage in a skillet; cook over low heat about 20 minutes or until done, turning often to brown evenly. Drain off excess drippings. Place sausage in center of casserole.

Melt butter in a saucepan over medium heat; add onion, and sauté 1 minute. Stir in flour; remove from heat. Gradually add chicken broth, stirring constantly. Return to heat; cook until smooth and thickened, stirring constantly. Stir in half-and-half and cheese. Pour sauce over zucchini and sausage. Cover with foil. Bake at 375° for 30 minutes. Yield: 8 servings.

Smoked Turkey

1 (8- to 12-pound) turkey   Vegetable oil
Seasoned salt

Rinse turkey, and pat dry; rub with seasoned salt and vegetable oil.

Prepare charcoal fire in smoker, and let burn 10 to 15 minutes; add 6 to 8 pieces of hickory to fire. Place water pan in smoker, and fill with water.

Place turkey on grill, and cover with lid. Allow turkey to cook 8 to 10 hours (do not open smoker). Turkey is done when drumsticks move easily in joint. Yield: 16 to 20 servings.

Note: Use the following timetable for roasting turkey. Times are based on an oven temperature of 325°. The turkey will be done when a meat thermometer inserted in the thickest part of the thigh registers 185°.

Ready-To-Cook Weight	Approximate Roasting Time
6 to 8 pounds	3 to 3½ hours
8 to 12 pounds	3½ to 4½ hours
12 to 16 pounds	4½ to 5½ hours

Note: Add ½ hour to total roasting time if turkey is stuffed.

Spinach Souffle Roll

Vegetable oil   ¼ cup grated Parmesan cheese
¼ cup plus 2 tablespoons   7 eggs, separated
   all-purpose flour   ¼ teaspoon cream of tartar
¼ teaspoon salt   ¼ teaspoon salt
Dash of red pepper   Additional grated Parmesan cheese
⅓ cup butter or margarine   Spinach-Mushroom Filling
1¼ cups milk   4 ounces sliced Cheddar cheese,
¾ cup (3 ounces) shredded Cheddar   cut diagonally
   cheese   Fresh spinach (optional)

Grease bottom and sides of a 15- × 10- × 1-inch jellyroll pan with oil. Line with waxed paper, allowing paper to extend beyond ends of pan; grease waxed paper with oil.

Combine flour, ¼ teaspoon salt, and red pepper; stir well. Melt butter in a large, heavy saucepan over low heat; add flour mixture, stirring with a wire whisk until smooth. Cook 1 minute, stirring constantly with whisk. Gradually add milk; cook over medium heat, stirring constantly with whisk, until very thick and mixture leaves sides of pan. Remove from heat; beat in ¾ cup Cheddar and ¼ cup Parmesan cheese.

Place egg yolks in a large bowl; beat at high speed of an electric mixer until thick and lemon colored. Gradually stir in one-fourth of hot cheese mixture; add remaining cheese mixture, beating well.

Combine egg whites (at room temperature) and cream of tartar; beat at high speed of electric mixer until foamy. Add ¼ teaspoon salt, and beat until stiff peaks form. Fold one-third of egg whites into cheese mixture; then carefully fold in remaining egg whites. Pour cheese mixture into jellyroll pan, spreading evenly. Bake on center rack of oven at 350° for 15 minutes or until puffed and firm to the touch. (Do not allow to overcook.)

Loosen edges of soufflé with a metal spatula, but do not remove from pan; place on wire rack. Let cool 15 minutes. Place 2 lengths of waxed paper (longer than jellyroll pan) on a smooth, slightly damp surface; overlap edge of paper nearest you over second sheet. Sprinkle additional Parmesan cheese over the waxed paper.

Quickly invert jellyroll pan onto waxed paper, with long side nearest you; remove pan, and carefully peel waxed paper from soufflé. Spoon Spinach-Mushroom Filling over surface, spreading to edges. Starting at long side, carefully roll the soufflé jellyroll fashion; use the waxed paper to help support the soufflé as you roll. Using your hands, gently smooth and shape the roll. Carefully slide the roll, seam side down, onto a large ovenproof platter or cookie sheet. Arrange cheese slices on top. Place 3 inches from heat, and broil until cheese melts and is lightly browned. If desired, garnish with fresh spinach. Yield: 8 servings.

Spinach-Mushroom Filling:

2 (10-ounce) packages frozen chopped spinach
¼ cup finely chopped onion
¼ cup butter or margarine
½ cup diced fresh mushrooms
¾ cup (3 ounces) shredded Cheddar cheese

¼ cup grated Parmesan cheese
½ cup commercial sour cream
¼ teaspoon salt
¼ teaspoon ground nutmeg

Cook spinach according to package directions; drain and press dry.

Sauté onion in butter until transparent. Add mushrooms, and sauté 3 minutes. Stir in remaining ingredients. Yield: about 1¾ cups.

Note: The soufflé is very fragile and may crack or break during rolling.

Meringue Icebox Cookies

½ (11-ounce) package piecrust mix
1 egg white, beaten stiff
⅓ cup sugar

⅓ cup finely chopped pecans
½ teaspoon lemon extract

Prepare piecrust mix as directed on package. Turn piecrust out onto a lightly floured board; roll into an 18- × 12-inch rectangle. Combine remaining ingredients, blending well; spread on pastry to within ½ inch of the edge. Roll up lengthwise, jellyroll fashion; chill.

Cut into ¼-inch slices with a serrated knife. Bake on a lightly greased and floured cookie sheet at 325° for 15 to 18 minutes or until golden brown. Remove at once to a cooling rack. Yield: about 2 dozen.

Buffet Dinner for Eight

Special Broiled Oysters
Gingered Orange Pork Roast
Steamed Broccoli
Cauliflower Salad
Oatmeal Muffins
Almond Pumpkin Charlotte
Gewürztraminer or Gamay

Serve this dinner buffet style, particularly if space is limited, setting up an extra table if needed for dining. Include the Almond Pumpkin Charlotte on the buffet, placing it on a pedestal plate.

Special Broiled Oysters

2 dozen unshucked oysters
4 slices bacon
¼ cup finely chopped onion
3 tablespoons finely chopped green pepper

2 teaspoons butter or margarine
2 teaspoons crumbled Roquefort cheese
1¼ teaspoons Worcestershire sauce

Wash and rinse oysters thoroughly in cold water. Shuck oysters, reserving the deep half of shells; place oysters in colander to drain. Set aside.

Cut bacon slices in half lengthwise; cut each half into thirds crosswise. Set aside.

Place oysters in half shells; arrange on a rack in a broiling pan. Place a piece of bacon over each oyster. Combine onion and green pepper; spoon over each oyster.

Melt butter in a small saucepan. Add cheese and Worcestershire sauce; cook over low heat until cheese is melted, stirring constantly. Spoon sauce over oysters. Broil 4 inches from heat 10 minutes. Yield: 24 appetizer servings.

Gingered Orange Pork Roast

1 (4- to 5-pound) boneless pork loin roast, rolled and tied
1½ teaspoons ground ginger, divided

¼ cup frozen orange juice concentrate, thawed and undiluted
¼ cup honey

Rub surface of roast with 1 teaspoon ginger. Place roast in shallow roasting pan. Insert meat thermometer in center of thickest part of roast. Bake, uncovered, at 325° about 2½ hours or until meat thermometer registers 170°.

Combine orange juice concentrate, honey, and remaining ½ teaspoon ginger in a small saucepan. Bring to a boil; boil 1 minute. Brush sauce over roast several times during the last 30 minutes of cooking. Let roast stand about 15 minutes before slicing. Yield: 8 to 10 servings.

Steamed Broccoli

2 to 3 pounds fresh broccoli
Water

Salt and pepper to taste
Pimiento strips

Trim off large leaves of broccoli. Remove tough ends of lower stalks, and wash broccoli thoroughly. Make lengthwise slits in thick stalks. Arrange broccoli in steaming rack with stalks to center of rack. Steam 10 to 15 minutes or to desired degree of doneness. Season broccoli to taste with salt and pepper. Arrange broccoli on a serving plate. Garnish with strips of pimiento. Yield: 8 servings.

Cauliflower Salad

2 cups diced raw cauliflower
¼ cup chopped celery
3 hard-cooked eggs, chopped
¼ cup chopped green pepper
¼ cup chopped sweet pickle

½ teaspoon salt
¼ teaspoon white pepper
½ cup mayonnaise
½ medium head lettuce, torn into
  bite-size pieces

Combine all ingredients in a large salad bowl; toss lightly. Chill well. Yield: about 8 servings.

Oatmeal Muffins

1 cup cornmeal
½ cup regular oats, uncooked
½ cup all-purpose flour
1 tablespoon wheat germ
¼ cup sugar

2½ teaspoons baking powder
1 teaspoon salt
1 cup buttermilk
½ cup vegetable oil
2 eggs, beaten

Combine first 4 ingredients in a large bowl; stir in sugar, baking powder, and salt. Add buttermilk, oil, and eggs, stirring just until moistened (batter will be lumpy). Fill well-greased muffin pans two-thirds full. Bake at 375° for 20 to 25 minutes. Yield: 20 to 24 muffins.

Almond Pumpkin Charlotte

2 envelopes unflavored gelatin
⅔ cup milk
⅓ cup dark rum
4 eggs, separated
⅔ cup firmly packed brown sugar, divided
1 (16-ounce) can pumpkin
2 teaspoons grated orange rind

½ teaspoon pumpkin pie spice
1 cup whipping cream, whipped
½ cup blanched, slivered almonds toasted
Gingersnap-Lady Finger Crust
Rum Cream
Sugared Almonds

Combine gelatin, milk, rum, egg yolks, and ⅓ cup of sugar in a 2-quart saucepan. Stir over low heat 5 to 10 minutes to make a soft custard; remove from heat. Stir in pumpkin, orange rind, and pumpkin pie spice.

Beat egg whites (at room temperature) in a large bowl to form soft peaks. Gradually beat in remaining ⅓ cup of sugar to form stiff peaks. Gently fold pumpkin mixture and whipped cream into egg white mixture. Fold in almonds. Pour into prepared Gingersnap-Lady Finger Crust. Cover and chill at least 6 hours or up to 3 days. To serve, remove sides of pan. Pipe rosettes of Rum Cream on top of charlotte. Sprinkle Sugared Almonds over cream. Yield: 10 to 12 servings.

Gingersnap-Lady Finger Crust:

¼ cup light corn syrup
3 tablespoons dark rum
1½ (3-ounce) packages lady fingers, split

⅔ cup finely crushed gingersnap crumbs

Combine corn syrup and rum in a small bowl. Brush lady fingers on both sides with rum mixture. Dip in crumbs to coat both sides. Line sides and bottom of a 9-inch springform pan with lady fingers, rounded sides out. Yield: one 9-inch crust.

Rum Cream:

½ cup whipping cream
1 tablespoon powdered sugar

1½ tablespoons dark rum

Beat whipping cream to form soft peaks. Beat in powdered sugar and dark rum; continue beating to form stiff peaks. Yield: about 1 cup.

Sugared Almonds:

¼ cup blanched, slivered almonds
1 tablespoon sugar

¼ teaspoon pumpkin pie spice

Combine blanched slivered almonds, sugar, and pumpkin pie spice in small skillet. Stir occasionally over low heat until sugar melts and coats almonds. Pour mixture onto cookie sheet to cool. Separate into almond pieces. Yield: ¼ cup.

Pans used for pastry never need greasing. The pastry shell or crumb crust will not stick to the sides.

RECIPES FOR TWO

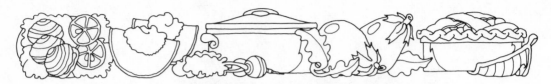

APPETIZERS AND SANDWICHES

Bacon-Wrapped Bananas

2 slices bacon
2 small firm bananas
Lemon juice

Cook bacon until transparent. Brush bananas with lemon juice. Wrap bacon around bananas, securing with wooden picks. Place in a shallow baking dish. Bake at 375° for 25 minutes turning once. Yield: 2 servings.

Marinated Cocktail Broccoli

¾ pound fresh broccoli
¾ cup olive oil
2 tablespoons wine vinegar
⅛ to ¼ teaspoon garlic powder
Pepper to taste

Wash broccoli, and cut off flowerets; reserve stems for use in another recipe. Combine remaining ingredients, and pour over flowerets. Marinate 24 hours before serving. Yield: 2 to 4 appetizer servings.

Cheese Rounds

1 cup (4 ounces) shredded sharp
   Cheddar cheese, at room temperature
½ cup butter or margarine, softened
1¼ cups all-purpose flour
1 teaspoon minced onion
¼ teaspoon salt

Combine cheese and butter; beat until light and fluffy. Add remaining ingredients, stirring well. Turn dough out on a floured surface; knead 4 to 6 times. Chill dough 4 to 6 hours.

Roll dough to ¼-inch thickness on a floured surface; cut with a 2-inch biscuit cutter. Place on a lightly greased cookie sheet. Bake at 400° for 12 to 15 minutes. Cool on wire racks. Yield: about 1½ dozen.

Nachos

1 (6-ounce) bag tortilla chips
1 to 2 cups (4 to 8 ounces) shredded
   Cheddar cheese
5 to 6 jalapeño peppers, sliced into
   rings

Place chips on a cookie sheet or ovenproof platter. Top each with 1 to 2 teaspoons cheese and a slice of jalapeño pepper.

Bake at 400° for 2 to 3 minutes or until cheese melts. Serve immediately. Yield: 4 to 6 servings.

Roasted Chestnuts

Wash chestnuts; cut a long slit through shell on each side of nut with a sharp knife. Place chestnuts in a single layer in a baking pan; bake at 300° for 1 hour. Cool; remove shell and inner skin from nuts.

Boiled Chestnuts

Wash chestnuts; cut a long slit through shell on each side of nut with a sharp knife. Place chestnuts in a large saucepan, and cover with water. Bring water to a boil; reduce heat and simmer 30 minutes. Drain and cool; remove shell and inner skin from nuts.

Toasted Buttered Pecans

½ pound pecan halves (about 2 cups)
1½ teaspoons seasoned salt
2 tablespoons butter or margarine

Spread pecans evenly in a shallow baking pan. Sprinkle with seasoned salt, and dot with butter. Bake at 325° for 25 minutes, stirring frequently. Yield: 2 cups.

Anchovy Dip for Artichokes

½ cup butter or margarine
¼ cup peanut oil
1 (2-ounce) can anchovy fillets, drained and chopped

Combine all ingredients in a small saucepan, and cook over low heat until butter melts. Transfer to a chafing dish set over low heat; serve with cooked artichokes. Yield: about ¾ cups.

Sour Cream Clam Dip

1 (6½-ounce) can minced clams
1½ cups commercial sour cream
1 teaspoon onion salt
¼ teaspoon salt
¼ teaspoon Worcestershire sauce

Drain clams, reserving 2 tablespoons liquid. Combine clams, reserved clam liquid, and remaining ingredients; stir well. Chill 3 to 4 hours. Serve with crackers. Yield: 1½ cups.

Easy Cheese Dip

½ pound process cheese spread, cubed
⅓ cup picante sauce

Melt cubed cheese in top of a double boiler; stir in picante sauce. Serve hot with corn chips or tortilla chips. Yield: 1 cup.

Horseradish Dip

1 (8-ounce) carton commercial sour cream
3 tablespoons mayonnaise
2 to 3 teaspoons prepared horseradish
4 slices bacon, cooked and crumbled
Dash of Worcestershire sauce
Salt to taste

Combine all ingredients, mixing well. Chill overnight. Serve with crisp raw vegetables. Yield: 1¼ cups.

Seafood Dip

¾ cup mayonnaise
½ cup catsup
3 tablespoons grated Parmesan cheese
1 teaspoon parsley flakes

Combine all ingredients; stir well and chill. Serve with boiled shrimp. Yield: about 1½ cups.

Easy Vegetable Dip

⅔ cup commercial sour cream
⅔ cup mayonnaise
1 tablespoon finely chopped parsley
1 tablespoon instant minced onion
1 tablespoon dried dillweed
¼ teaspoon dry mustard

Combine all ingredients; mix well. Chill. Serve as a dip for assorted fresh vegetables. Yield: about 1½ cups.

Vegetable Dip

½ cup mayonnaise
2 tablespoons chili sauce
2 tablespoons catsup
1 to 2 tablespoons grated onion
1 clove garlic, minced
¾ teaspoon dry mustard
½ teaspoon pepper
Dash of paprika
Dash of hot sauce

Combine all ingredients in a jar; mix well. Chill 3 to 4 hours. Serve with cold boiled shrimp or assorted raw vegetables. Yield: about 1 cup.

Note: May be served as salad dressing. Add 2 tablespoons vegetable oil to jar; shake well, and chill.

Onion Dip for Two

1 teaspoon chicken-flavored bouillon granules
1 tablespoon hot water
1 (3-ounce) package cream cheese, softened
1 tablespoon minced onion
1 tablespoon mayonnaise
Dash of garlic powder
Dash of pepper
Dash of hot sauce

Dissolve bouillon granules in water; add remaining ingredients, mixing well. Serve with fresh vegetables. Yield: about ½ cup.

Apple-Cream Cheese Spread

1 (3-ounce) package cream cheese, softened
1 tablespoon orange juice
2 teaspoons powdered sugar
½ cup peeled, grated apple

Combine first 3 ingredients; mix until smooth. Stir in apple. Chill. Use as a spread for banana bread or other fruit-nut bread. Yield: about 1 cup.

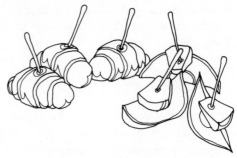

Blue Cheese Spread

1 (3-ounce) package cream cheese, softened
¼ cup crumbled blue cheese, at room temperature
2 tablespoons mayonnaise
¾ cup coarsely chopped pitted ripe olives
¼ cup minced celery

Combine cream cheese, blue cheese, and mayonnaise in a medium bowl; mix until smooth. Stir in olives and celery. Yield: about 1 cup.

Braunschweiger Spread

¼ cup finely chopped fresh mushrooms
1½ teaspoons butter or margarine
1 (4-ounce) roll braunschweiger, softened
1 tablespoon mayonnaise
¼ teaspoon Worcestershire sauce
Salt to taste

Sauté mushrooms in butter just until tender or about 1 to 2 minutes. Remove from heat, and add remaining ingredients; mix well. Serve with assorted crackers or rye bread. Yield: about ¾ cup.

Crunchy Chicken Filling

1 cup finely chopped cooked chicken
⅓ cup crushed pineapple, drained
¼ cup finely chopped celery
3 tablespoons finely chopped toasted
   almonds
3 tablespoons mayonnaise
¾ teaspoon sugar
¾ teaspoon vinegar
⅛ teaspoon salt
Dash of pepper

Combine all ingredients; stir well. Chill to allow flavors to blend. Serve on bread or, if desired, in patty shells. Yield: about 1¼ cups.

Chicken Spread

1 (5-ounce) can boned chicken,
   undrained
2 tablespoons whipping cream
¼ cup finely chopped almonds
2 tablespoons mayonnaise or salad
   dressing
½ teaspoon dry mustard

Combine all ingredients, blending well. Store in refrigerator. Use as sandwich spread or filling. Yield: about 1 cup.

Coffee-Cream Cheese Spread

1 (8-ounce) package cream cheese,
   softened
¼ cup butter or margarine, softened
1 tablespoon Kahlúa or other
   coffee-flavored liqueur
1 teaspoon sesame seeds, toasted

Combine cream cheese and butter; mix well. Stir in Kahlúa and sesame seeds. Serve with whole wheat wafers. Yield: about 1¼ cups.

Creamy Crabmeat Spread

1 (3-ounce) package cream cheese,
   softened
¼ cup mayonnaise
1 tablespoon catsup
1 (6½-ounce) can crabmeat, drained
   and flaked
1 tablespoon grated onion

Combine cream cheese, mayonnaise, and catsup; mix until smooth. Stir in crabmeat and onion. Serve with assorted crackers. Yield: 1 cup.

Shrimp-Cucumber Spread

2 tablespoons mayonnaise
1 (3-ounce) package cream cheese,
   softened
1 tablespoon catsup
1 teaspoon dry mustard
Dash of garlic powder
1 (4½-ounce) can broken shrimp,
   drained
¼ cup minced cucumber
1 teaspoon minced onion

Combine mayonnaise, cream cheese, catsup, mustard, and garlic powder in a medium bowl; mix until smooth. Add shrimp, cucumber, and onion; stir well. Serve on rye bread. Yield: about ¾ cup.

Ham-and-Egg Spread

1 cup ground cooked ham
2 tablespoons chopped pickle
½ teaspoon finely chopped pimiento
2 hard-cooked eggs, minced
¼ cup mayonnaise

Combine all ingredients, mixing well; chill. Use as a sandwich spread or filling. Yield: about 1¼ cups.

Egg Salad Sandwiches

2 hard-cooked eggs, chopped
¼ cup finely chopped celery
2 teaspoons chopped parsley
¾ teaspoon chopped pimiento
⅛ teaspoon salt
Dash of pepper
3 tablespoons mayonnaise or salad
  dressing
6 slices buttered toast
1 tomato, sliced
4 slices bacon, cooked
2 lettuce leaves

Combine chopped eggs, celery, parsley, pi-miento, salt, and pepper; add mayonnaise, and mix well. Spread 2 slices of toast with egg mixture; top each with another slice of toast. Arrange tomato slices, bacon, and lettuce on top of toast. Top with remaining toast. Cut each sandwich into quarters to serve, using wooden picks to hold layers together. Yield: 2 servings.

Ham and Swiss Cheese Sandwiches

2 tablespoons butter or margarine,
  softened
2 teaspoons finely chopped onion
2 teaspoons mustard with horseradish
¾ teaspoon poppy seeds or sesame
  seeds
2 hamburger buns
2 slices cooked ham
2 slices Swiss cheese

Combine butter, onion, mustard, and poppy seeds; mix well. Spread on both sides of hamburger buns. Place 1 ham slice and 1 cheese slice on bottom of each bun; cover with top bun. Wrap each sandwich in foil, and bake at 350° for 25 minutes. Yield: 2 servings.

Ham and Turkey Sandwiches

2 slices boiled or baked ham
2 slices cooked turkey or chicken
2 slices process American cheese
4 slices bread
½ cup milk
1 egg, beaten
⅛ teaspoon salt
Dash of pepper
2 tablespoons butter or margarine,
  melted
2 tablespoons vegetable oil

Place 1 slice ham, 1 slice turkey, and 1 slice cheese on each of 2 slices of bread; top with remaining bread.

Combine milk, egg, salt, and pepper. Dip each sandwich into egg mixture; brown on both sides in combination of butter and oil. Serve hot. Yield: 2 servings.

Cheese-Topped Turkey Sandwiches

⅔ cup finely chopped turkey
2 tablespoons mayonnaise
2 teaspoons prepared mustard
6 dill pickle slices
2 slices whole wheat bread, toasted
½ cup (2 ounces) shredded sharp
  Cheddar cheese
Garlic powder

Combine turkey, mayonnaise, and mustard. Place pickle slices on toast; top with turkey mixture. Sprinkle with cheese and garlic powder; broil sandwiches until cheese is bubbly. Yield: 2 servings.

Shred Cheddar or Swiss cheese and freeze; whenever you need some for cooking, just measure.

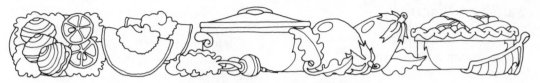

BREADS

Biscuits for Two

1 cup all-purpose flour
1½ teaspoons baking powder
½ teaspoon salt
1 tablespoon vegetable oil
½ cup milk

Combine dry ingredients in a small bowl. Mix oil and milk; pour into dry ingredients, and stir until almost smooth. Turn dough out on a lightly floured board or pastry cloth; knead lightly 5 or 6 times.

Roll dough to about ½-inch thickness; cut with a 2½-inch biscuit cutter, and place on a lightly greased baking sheet. Bake at 450° for 10 to 12 minutes or until golden brown. Yield: 6 biscuits.

Buttermilk Biscuits

1 cup all-purpose flour
2 teaspoons baking powder
¼ teaspoon salt
⅛ teaspoon soda
2 tablespoons shortening
½ cup buttermilk

Combine dry ingredients; cut in shortening until mixture resembles coarse meal. Add buttermilk, stirring until well mixed. Turn dough out on floured surface, and knead lightly 3 or 4 times.

Roll dough to ¼-inch thickness; cut into rounds with a 2½-inch biscuit cutter. Bake at 450° for 10 to 12 minutes or until golden brown. Yield: about 6 biscuits.

Easy Buttermilk Biscuits

1 cup self-rising flour
½ teaspoon baking powder
¼ cup shortening
½ cup buttermilk

Combine flour and baking powder; cut in shortening until mixture resembles coarse meal. Add buttermilk, mixing well. Turn dough out on floured surface; knead lightly 10 or 12 times.

Roll dough to ½-inch thickness; cut with a 3-inch biscuit cutter. Place on a lightly greased baking sheet; bake at 450° for 10 to 12 minutes or until lightly browned. Yield: about 6 biscuits.

Buttery Biscuits

1 cup all-purpose flour
2 teaspoons baking powder
1 teaspoon sugar
¼ teaspoon cream of tartar
¼ teaspoon salt
¼ cup butter or margarine
⅓ cup milk

Combine dry ingredients; cut in butter until mixture resembles coarse meal. Add milk, mixing well. (Dough will be soft.) Turn dough out on floured surface; knead 10 times.

Roll dough to ½-inch thickness; cut with a 2½-inch biscuit cutter. Place biscuits on a lightly greased baking sheet; bake at 450° for 10 to 12 minutes or until golden brown. Yield: about 6 biscuits.

Sausage Biscuits

¼ pound bulk sausage
2 tablespoons shortening
1 cup self-rising flour
⅓ cup plus 2 teaspoons buttermilk

Cook sausage until done in a small skillet over medium heat, stirring to crumble; drain well. Cut shortening into flour until mixture resembles coarse meal; stir in buttermilk with a fork just until blended. Stir in sausage.

Roll dough to ½-inch thickness on a lightly floured surface; cut out with a 2-inch biscuit cutter, and place biscuits on a lightly greased baking sheet. Bake at 450° for 10 to 12 minutes or until lightly browned. Yield: about 8 biscuits.

Cheeseburger Biscuits

⅓ pound ground beef
¼ cup finely chopped onion
2 tablespoons finely chopped celery
1 tablespoon vegetable oil
2 tablespoons tomato paste
¼ cup water
¼ teaspoon salt
⅛ teaspoon chili powder
¼ teaspoon Worcestershire sauce
2 tablespoons chopped pitted ripe olives
1½ cups biscuit mix
½ cup milk
1 (1-ounce) slice process American
   cheese, halved

Sauté beef, onion, and celery in oil until vegetables are tender. Add tomato paste, water, salt, chili powder, Worcestershire sauce, and olives, mixing well; simmer 10 minutes, stirring occasionally. Set aside.

Combine biscuit mix and milk, stirring until a soft dough is formed. (More biscuit mix may be added, if needed.)

Beat vigorously 30 seconds, and turn out on a lightly floured surface; knead about 10 times. Roll the dough to ½-inch thickness.

Cut into four 4-inch circles; place 2 dough circles on a greased baking sheet. Spoon one-half of the meat mixture onto each, leaving a ¼-inch border; top each with a cheese slice.

Place remaining dough circles on top, pressing the edges to seal. Bake at 375° for 25 minutes or until biscuits are golden brown. Yield: 2 servings.

Carrot Bread

1½ cups all-purpose flour
1 cup sugar
1 teaspoon soda
½ teaspoon ground cinnamon
⅔ cup vegetable oil
2 eggs
1 cup grated carrots

Combine all ingredients in a large mixing bowl; mix 2 minutes on medium speed of electric mixer. Spoon into a greased 9- × 5- × 3-inch loafpan. Bake at 350° for 55 minutes or until done. Cool 10 minutes in pan; remove to wire rack, and cool completely. Yield: 1 loaf.

Note: To make 3 mini-loaves, spoon batter into 3 greased and floured 6- × 3½- × 2-inch disposable loafpans. Bake at 350° for 40 to 45 minutes or until done. Yield: 3 mini-loaves.

Page 149: *Pack a lunch of Picnic Salad Rolls, Ham and Cheese Roll-Ups, a crisp apple, and Chocolate Chip-Peanut Squares. Menu begins on page 31.*

Page 150: *Breads to serve anytime include Prune-Orange Rolls (page 28), Lemon Muffins (page 130), Sour Cream Biscuits (page 62), or Braided Yeast Bread (page 156).*

Orange-Pecan Bread

4 to 5 oranges (rind only)
2 cups water, divided
1 teaspoon soda
1¾ to 2 cups sugar
3¼ cups all-purpose flour
1 tablespoon baking powder
⅛ teaspoon salt
2 eggs
2 tablespoons butter or margarine,
    melted
1 cup milk
1 cup chopped pecans

Peel oranges; scrape white membrane from rind. Finely chop rind. Combine 1 cup water, rind, and soda in a heavy saucepan; boil 5 minutes (watch carefully; mixture will foam). Drain well. Combine cooked rind, sugar, and 1 cup water in a saucepan. Boil until consistency of jelly (about 45 minutes), stirring occasionally; cool.

Combine flour, baking powder, and salt; set aside. Beat eggs and butter until frothy. Alternately add dry ingredients and milk to eggs, beginning and ending with dry ingredients. Stir just until all ingredients are moistened. Stir in orange rind mixture and pecans. Spoon batter into a well-greased 9- × 5- × 3-inch loafpan. Bake at 350° for 1 hour and 10 minutes or until bread tests done. Cool on wire rack. Yield: 1 loaf.

Special Banana Bread

1 cup whole wheat flour
¼ cup all-purpose flour
1½ teaspoons baking powder
½ teaspoon salt
⅓ cup butter or margarine, softened
⅔ cup sugar
1 egg
2 small bananas, mashed
¼ cup milk

Combine flour, baking powder, and salt.
Combine butter and sugar; cream mixture until light and fluffy. Add egg, and mix well.
Combine bananas and milk; add to creamed mixture alternately with dry ingredients, stirring only until just combined.
Pour batter into two greased and floured 6- × 3½- × 2-inch disposable loafpans. Bake at 350° for 40 to 45 minutes or until bread tests done. Cool 10 minutes in pan; remove to wire rack. Yield: 2 mini-loaves.

Lemon-Nut Bread

¾ cup butter or margarine, softened
1½ cups sugar
3 eggs
2¼ cups all-purpose flour
¼ teaspoon salt
¼ teaspoon soda
¼ cup buttermilk
Grated rind of 1 lemon
¾ cup chopped pecans
Juice of 2 lemons
¾ cup sifted powdered sugar

Combine butter and sugar, creaming until light and fluffy; add eggs, beating well. Combine dry ingredients. Add buttermilk and dry ingredients alternately to creamed mixture, beginning and ending with buttermilk; stir just until all ingredients are moistened. Stir in lemon rind and pecans.

Spoon batter into a greased and floured 9- × 5- × 3-inch loafpan. Bake at 325° for 1 hour and 15 minutes or until bread tests done. Cool 15 minutes; remove from pan.

Combine lemon juice and powdered sugar; stir well. Punch holes in top of warm bread with a wooden pick; pour on glaze. Cool on wire rack. Yield: 1 loaf.

Note: To make 3 mini-loaves, spoon batter into 3 greased and floured 6- × 3½- × 2-inch disposable loafpans. Bake at 325° for 45 to 50 minutes or until done. Yield: 3 mini-loaves.

Raisin-Nut Bread

1 cup sugar
2 eggs, beaten
¼ teaspoon salt
1 cup buttermilk
1 teaspoon soda
2 cups all-purpose flour
1 cup chopped pecans
1½ cups raisins
2 tablespoons butter or margarine,
 melted

Combine sugar, eggs, and salt. Combine buttermilk and soda; stir into sugar mixture. Add flour, and beat until smooth. Add pecans, raisins, and butter; mix well. Pour batter into a greased 9- × 5- × 3-inch loafpan. Bake at 325° for 1 hour and 15 minutes or until done. Cool on a wire rack. Yield: 1 loaf.

Note: To make 3 mini-loaves, spoon batter into 3 greased and floured 6- × 3½- × 2-inch disposable loafpans. Bake at 325° for 45 to 50 minutes or until done. Yield: 3 mini-loaves.

Zucchini Bread

1½ cups all-purpose flour
1 teaspoon soda
½ teaspoon salt
¼ teaspoon baking powder
¾ teaspoon ground cinnamon
⅓ cup finely chopped pecans
2 eggs
1 cup sugar
½ cup vegetable oil
1 teaspoon vanilla extract
1 cup coarsely shredded zucchini
½ cup crushed pineapple, well drained

Combine flour, soda, salt, baking powder, cinnamon, and pecans; set aside.

Beat eggs lightly in a large mixing bowl; add sugar, oil, and vanilla; beat until

creamy. Stir in zucchini and pineapple. Add dry ingredients, stirring only until dry ingredients are moistened.

Spoon batter into a well-greased and floured 9- × 5- × 3-inch loafpan. Bake at 350° for 1 hour or until done. Cool 10 minutes before removing from pan; turn out on rack and cool completely. Yield: 1 loaf.

Note: To make 3 mini-loaves, spoon batter into 3 greased and floured 6- × 3½- × 2-inch disposable loafpans. Bake at 350° for 45 to 50 minutes or until done. Yield: 3 mini-loaves.

Southern Spoonbread

1 cup boiling water
½ cup cornmeal
½ cup milk
1 egg
1 tablespoon butter or margarine,
 melted
2 tablespoons all-purpose flour
1½ teaspoons baking powder
½ teaspoon salt

Pour boiling water over cornmeal in a medium bowl. Beat in remaining ingredients in order listed. Pour batter into a greased 1-quart casserole.

Bake at 400° for 20 to 25 minutes or until mixture is firm. Serve hot. Yield: 2 generous servings.

Banana Muffins

¼ cup butter or margarine, softened
½ cup sugar
1 egg, beaten
2 small ripe bananas, mashed
⅔ cup all-purpose flour
¼ teaspoon soda

Combine butter and sugar; beat until light

and fluffy. Add egg, and beat well. Stir in bananas. Combine flour and soda; add to creamed mixture, stirring just enough to moisten the dry ingredients.

Fill well-greased muffin pans two-thirds full. Bake at 350° for 25 minutes or until done. Serve hot. Yield: about 8 muffins.

Spiced Apple Muffins

1 cup all-purpose flour
½ cup finely chopped apple
3 tablespoons sugar
2 teaspoons baking powder
½ teaspoon salt
½ teaspoon ground cinnamon
⅛ teaspoon ground nutmeg
⅓ to ½ cup milk
2 tablespoons shortening, melted
1 egg, beaten

Combine first 7 ingredients; make a well in center of mixture. Combine ⅓ cup milk, shortening, and egg; add to flour mixture, stirring just until moistened. Add additional milk, if needed.

Spoon batter into greased muffin pans, filling two-thirds full. Bake at 400° for 25 minutes or until golden brown. Yield: about 8 muffins.

Refrigerator Bran Muffins

½ cup boiling water
1½ cups bran cereal, divided
½ cup sugar
¼ cup shortening
1 egg
1¼ cups all-purpose flour
1¼ teaspoons soda
¼ teaspoon salt
1 cup buttermilk
⅓ cup raisins

Pour boiling water over ½ cup cereal; stir to moisten cereal, and set aside to cool. Cream sugar and shortening until light and fluffy; add egg, beating well.

Combine flour, soda, and salt; add to creamed mixture alternately with buttermilk; stir lightly. Blend in cereal and water mixture, remaining 1 cup cereal, and raisins. Cover and store in refrigerator up to five or six weeks, or until ready to use.

When ready to bake, spoon batter into greased muffin pans, filling two-thirds full. Bake at 400° for 20 minutes. Yield: 1 dozen.

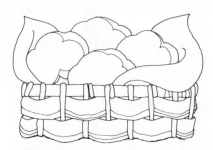

Cranberry-Bran Muffins

¾ cup all-purpose flour
2 teaspoons baking powder
¼ teaspoon salt
¼ cup sugar
½ cup coarsely chopped cranberries
1 egg, well beaten
½ cup milk
2 tablespoons butter or margarine, melted
½ cup bran cereal

Combine flour, baking powder, salt, and sugar. Combine ¼ cup flour mixture and chopped cranberries; stir mixture to coat cranberries well. Set cranberries aside.

Add egg, milk, and butter to remaining flour mixture; stir until moistened. Fold in cranberries and cereal. Spoon batter into greased muffin pans, filling two-thirds full. Bake at 425° for 20 to 25 minutes. Yield: about 8 muffins.

Orange Muffins

1 cup all-purpose flour
2 teaspoons baking powder
⅛ teaspoon salt
1½ tablespoons butter or margarine, melted
1 egg, beaten
½ cup milk
⅓ cup firmly packed light brown sugar
Grated rind and juice of 1 orange

Combine flour, baking powder, and salt. Add butter, egg, milk, and sugar; stir until moistened. Stir in orange rind and juice. Spoon batter into greased muffin pans, filling two-thirds full. Bake at 400° for 20 minutes. Yield: about 6 muffins.

Fruit Muffins

1 cup whole wheat flour
¾ cup unprocessed bran
½ cup peeled, chopped apple
¼ cup raisins
¼ cup sunflower seeds
1½ teaspoons grated orange rind
¾ teaspoon soda
¼ teaspoon salt
¼ teaspoon ground nutmeg
Juice of 1 orange
About ¾ cup buttermilk
1 egg, slightly beaten
¼ cup molasses
1 tablespoon vegetable oil

Combine first 9 ingredients in a large bowl; stir well. Make a well in center.

Combine orange juice and enough buttermilk to make 1 cup. Combine buttermilk mixture, egg, molasses, and oil in a small bowl. Add to dry ingredients, stirring just until moistened.

Fill greased muffin pans two-thirds full. Bake at 350° for 25 minutes or until done. Yield: about 6 to 8 muffins.

Coconut Muffins

2 cups all-purpose flour
3 tablespoons sugar
1 tablespoon baking powder
½ teaspoon salt
½ teaspoon ground ginger
¼ cup shortening
1 egg, beaten
⅓ cup molasses
¾ cup milk
1 cup flaked coconut

Combine flour, sugar, baking powder, salt, and ginger; cut in shortening with pastry blender until mixture resembles coarse meal. Add egg, molasses, milk, and coconut; stir with a fork until all flour is moistened. (Batter will be slightly lumpy.)

Spoon batter into greased muffin pans, filling two-thirds full. Bake at 400° for 20 minutes. Yield: about 10 muffins.

Upside-Down Muffins

¼ cup shortening
2 tablespoons sugar
1 egg
1 cup all-purpose flour
1½ teaspoons baking powder
¼ teaspoon salt
⅓ cup milk
¼ cup butter or margarine, melted
½ cup chopped pecans
3 tablespoons brown sugar
¼ teaspoon ground cinnamon

Cream shortening and sugar; add egg, beating until smooth and creamy. Combine flour, baking powder, and salt; add to creamed mixture alternately with milk, mixing well after each addition.

Place 1½ teaspoons butter and 1 tablespoon pecans in each of 8 well-greased muffin cups. Combine brown sugar and cinnamon; mix well. Place equal amounts of sugar mixture in each muffin cup.

Spoon batter into muffin cups, filling two-thirds full. Bake at 400° for 15 to 20 minutes. Remove from muffin cups immediately. Yield: 8 muffins.

Note: Spoon any remaining sugar mixture over warm muffins.

Blender Popovers

1 egg
½ cup milk
½ cup all-purpose flour
¼ teaspoon salt

Place egg and milk in container of electric blender; blend until bubbly. Add flour and salt; blend until smooth. Pour into well-greased muffin pans, filling one-half full. Bake at 450° for 20 minutes; reduce heat to 350°, and bake an additional 10 to 12 minutes or until golden brown. Yield: 4 or 5 popovers.

Coffee Dunkers

¾ cup butter or margarine, softened
1 (1-pound) package light brown sugar
3 eggs
4½ cups all-purpose flour

Cream butter and sugar until light and fluffy; add eggs, mixing well. Add flour, and mix well. Cover tightly and allow mixture to stand 3 to 4 hours at room temperature.

Form dough into 4½- × 1-inch logs. Bake at medium-high temperature in a lightly oiled waffle iron for 2 minutes. Let stand at room temperature until hardened. To serve, dunk in coffee, tea, or hot chocolate. Yield: 2 dozen.

Note: May be frozen if well wrapped; allow to harden after thawing.

Applesauce Pancakes

1 cup biscuit mix
½ cup milk
½ cup applesauce
1 egg
Spiced Apple Syrup

Combine biscuit mix, milk, applesauce, and egg in a medium mixing bowl; beat until smooth.

For each pancake, pour about ¼ cup batter onto a hot lightly greased griddle or skillet. Turn pancakes when tops are covered with bubbles and edges look cooked. Serve hot with butter and Spiced Apple Syrup. Yield: about 6 (4-inch) pancakes.

Spiced Apple Syrup:

½ cup applesauce
½ (10-ounce) jar apple jelly
¼ teaspoon ground cinnamon
Dash of ground cloves
Dash of salt

Combine all ingredients in a small saucepan. Cook over low heat, stirring occasionally, until jelly melts and mixture is blended. Yield: ¾ cup.

Sour Cream Pancakes

½ cup biscuit mix
½ teaspoon baking powder
1 egg, lightly beaten
½ cup commercial sour cream
3 to 5 tablespoons milk

Combine first 4 ingredients, mixing well. Add milk gradually, using enough to obtain desired consistency.

For each pancake, pour about ¼ cup batter onto a hot lightly greased griddle. Turn pancakes when tops are covered with bubbles and edges look cooked. Yield: about 4 (4-inch) pancakes.

Skillet Cinnamon Toast

2 tablespoons powdered sugar
2 teaspoons ground cinnamon
¼ cup butter or margarine, divided
2 (1-inch-thick) slices bread, quartered

Combine sugar and cinnamon; set aside. Melt 2 tablespoons butter in a skillet; add 4 bread sections, and cook until browned. Remove bread from skillet, and roll each piece in sugar mixture. Repeat procedure with remaining bread and butter. Yield: 2 servings.

French Breadsticks

3½ to 4 cups all-purpose flour, divided
2 teaspoons salt
2 teaspoons sugar
1 package dry yeast
1¼ cups warm water (105° to 115°)
Cornmeal
1 egg white
2 tablespoons water
Coarse salt (optional)

Combine 1¼ cups flour, salt, sugar, and yeast in a large mixing bowl. Add water and beat on low speed of electric mixer to combine; continue beating 3 minutes at high speed.

If using a heavy-duty mixer with dough hooks, add enough remaining flour to make a stiff dough. Knead with dough hooks until dough is smooth and elastic. To knead by hand, turn dough out onto a floured surface; knead in needed amount of remaining flour. Continue kneading until dough is smooth and elastic.

Place dough in a lightly greased bowl; turn to coat all sides. Cover and let rise in a warm place (85°), free from drafts, until doubled in bulk. Punch dough down; cover and let rise again.

Punch dough down; turn out on a lightly floured surface; knead several times or until

smooth. Divide dough into 24 equal pieces. Roll each piece into a pencil-like stick, ½ inch in diameter and 12 inches long. Place sticks 1 inch apart on a well-greased baking sheet sprinkled with cornmeal.

Combine egg white and water. Beat lightly. Brush sticks with mixture. Let rise in a warm place (85°), free from drafts, until doubled in bulk, about 50 minutes. Brush with egg white wash again. Sprinkle with coarse salt, if desired.

Place a pan of boiling water on bottom shelf of oven; place baking sheet on shelf above. Bake at 400° for 15 minutes; brush with egg white wash. Continue baking for 10 to 12 minutes or until breadsticks are golden brown. Yield: 24 sticks.

Braided Yeast Bread

2 packages dry yeast
½ cup warm water (105° to 115°)
½ cup butter or margarine, melted
1½ teaspoons salt
½ cup sugar
½ cup milk, scalded
3 eggs, slightly beaten
5 to 5½ cups unbleached flour
Melted shortening
1 egg yolk
2 tablespoons water

Dissolve yeast in ½ cup warm water; let stand 5 minutes.

Combine butter, salt, and sugar. Add milk, stirring until sugar dissolves; cool to 105° to 115°. Add yeast, 3 eggs, and 2 cups flour; mix well. Gradually stir in remaining flour.

Turn dough onto a floured board; knead 8 to 10 minutes. Divide dough in half; cut each half into thirds. Shape each third into an 8-inch rope. Place 3 ropes on a greased baking sheet; pinch ends together at one end to seal (do not stretch). Braid ropes; pinch loose ends to seal. Repeat with remaining dough. Brush with melted shortening.

Cover and let rise in a warm place (85°), free from drafts, 40 to 50 minutes or until doubled in bulk.

Combine egg yolk and 2 tablespoons water; brush on each loaf. Bake at 350° for 30 minutes or until bread tests done. Cool on wire rack. Yield: 2 loaves.

Basic White Bread

2¾ to 3 cups all-purpose flour, divided
1½ tablespoons sugar
1 teaspoon salt
1 package dry yeast
1 cup water
2 tablespoons vegetable oil
Melted butter

Combine 1 cup flour, sugar, salt, and yeast in large mixing bowl. Heat water and oil to very warm (120° to 130°); add to flour mixture. Blend mixture at low speed until moistened. Beat 3 minutes at medium speed. Stir in additional 1¾ cups to 2 cups flour until dough pulls cleanly away from sides of bowl.

Turn dough out on a floured surface, and knead 8 to 10 minutes or until smooth and elastic. Place dough in a well-greased bowl, turning to grease top. Cover and let rise in a warm place (85°), free from drafts, 1½ to 2 hours or until doubled in bulk.

Punch dough down several times to remove air bubbles. Cover with inverted bowl; let rest on counter 15 minutes. Roll dough into a 14- × 7-inch rectangle. Beginning at narrow edge, roll up dough; press firmly to eliminate air pockets. Pinch edges to seal. Place seam side down in a well-greased 9- × 5- × 3-inch loafpan.

Cover; let rise in warm place about 1 hour or until dough is about 1 inch above pan edges. Bake at 375° for 45 to 55 minutes or until deep golden brown and loaf sounds hollow when tapped. Remove from pan; brush with melted butter. Yield: 1 loaf.

Note: Dough may be divided and baked in two 6- × 3½- × 2-inch well-greased disposable loafpans. Bake 40 to 45 minutes or until deep golden brown.

Basic Whole Wheat Bread

1 cup whole wheat flour
3 cups unbleached flour
3 tablespoons sugar
2 teaspoons salt
1 package dry yeast
1 cup milk
⅓ cup water
2 tablespoons butter or margarine
Vegetable oil

Combine whole wheat and unbleached flour. Mix 1¼ cups flour mixture, sugar, salt, and yeast in a large mixing bowl.

Combine milk, water, and butter in a medium saucepan. Place over low heat until temperature of liquid reaches 120° to 130°.

Gradually add milk mixture to dry ingredients in mixing bowl; beat 2 minutes at medium speed, scraping bowl occasionally. Add 1 cup flour. Beat 2 minutes more; stir in enough additional flour to make a stiff dough.

Turn out onto lightly floured board; knead until smooth and elastic, about 8 to 10 minutes. Cover with plastic wrap and then a towel. Let dough rest 20 minutes.

Roll dough into a 14- × 9-inch rectangle. Shape into a loaf. Place into a greased 9- × 5- × 3-inch loaf pan. Brush loaf with oil. Cover with plastic wrap and refrigerate 2 to 24 hours.

When ready to bake, remove from refrigerator and uncover carefully. Pierce any air bubbles with a greased wooden pick. Let stand at room temperature 10 minutes. Bake at 400° about 40 minutes or until done. Remove from pan, and cool on wire rack. Yield: 1 loaf.

Sweet Roll Dough

⅔ cup milk
½ cup sugar
⅓ cup shortening
1¼ teaspoons salt
⅔ cup warm water (105° to 115°)
2 packages dry yeast
2 tablespoons sugar
3 eggs, beaten
About 6 cups all-purpose flour

Scald milk; add ½ cup sugar, shortening, and salt, stirring until sugar dissolves and shortening melts. Cool mixture to lukewarm.

Combine water, yeast, and 2 tablespoons sugar in a large bowl; let stand 5 minutes. Stir in milk mixture, eggs, and 3 cups flour; beat until mixture is smooth. Add remaining flour, 1 cup at a time, stirring well until a soft dough is formed.

Turn dough out on a floured surface, and knead until smooth and elastic (5 to 8 minutes). Place in a well-greased bowl, turning to grease top. Cover tightly, and let rise in a warm place (85°), free from drafts, 1½ hours or until doubled in bulk.

Punch dough down and divide in half. Proceed with directions for Honey Twist or Cinnamon Rolls. Yield: 2 coffee cakes or 3 dozen rolls.

Note: To freeze baked bread, cool and wrap with plastic wrap or freezer paper and place in freezer. To serve, unwrap and bake at 325° for 15 to 20 minutes or until heated through.

Honey Twist

½ cup chopped pecans
¼ cup sugar
¼ cup all-purpose flour
¼ cup butter or margarine, melted
¼ cup honey
½ recipe Sweet Roll Dough

Combine all ingredients except Sweet Roll Dough in a heavy ovenproof 9- or 10-inch skillet; stir well and set aside.

Turn dough out on a floured surface; shape dough into a long rope 1 inch in diameter. Coil rope in prepared skillet, beginning at center and working outward; leave a small space between sections of rope. Cover; let rise in a warm place (85°), free from drafts, about 45 minutes or until doubled in bulk.

Bake at 375° for 30 to 35 minutes or until cake sounds hollow when tapped. Invert coffee cake immediately onto a serving plate. Store cooled cake in an airtight container. Yield: 1 coffee cake.

Cinnamon Rolls

½ recipe Sweet Roll Dough
1½ tablespoons butter or margarine, softened
½ cup sugar
2 teaspoons ground cinnamon
Raisins (optional)
Chopped pecans (optional)

Turn dough out on a floured surface; roll dough into a 18- x 12-inch rectangle. Spread butter over dough, leaving a narrow margin on all sides. Combine sugar and cinnamon; sprinkle over butter. Sprinkle dough with raisins and nuts, if desired. Tightly roll up jellyroll fashion, beginning at long side. Pinch edge and ends to seal. Cut roll into 1-inch slices. Place slices, cut side down, in a greased 9-inch cakepan (fit will be tight).

Cover; let rise in a warm place (85°), free from drafts, 45 minutes or until doubled in bulk. Bake at 375° for 25 to 30 minutes. Store rolls in an airtight container. Yield: 1½ dozen.

Bread is done if it sounds hollow when tapped. It will be pulled away from sides of the pan and golden brown in color.

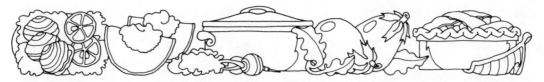

CHEESE AND EGG DISHES

Baked (Shirred) Eggs

Break and slip 2 eggs into a greased individual shallow baking dish or ramekin. Add 1 tablespoon of milk or half-and-half, if desired. Season with salt and pepper. Preheat oven. Bake eggs at 325° for 12 to 18 minutes or until desired degree of doneness. Serve in baking dish. Yield: 1 serving.

Soft-Cooked Eggs

Place unshelled eggs in a saucepan and add enough tap water to come at least 1 inch above eggs. Cover; bring water rapidly just to boiling. Turn off heat; if necessary, remove pan from burner to prevent further boiling. Let eggs stand in the hot water 2 to 4 minutes, depending on desired degree of doneness. Cool eggs promptly in cold water for several seconds to prevent further cooking and to make them easier to handle.

To serve, slice the shell through middle with a knife. With a teaspoon, scoop egg out of each half shell into individual serving dish. If egg cup is used, slice off large end of egg with knife and eat from shell.

Hard-Cooked Eggs

Put unshelled eggs in a saucepan and add enough tap water to come at least 1 inch above eggs. Cover; bring water rapidly just to boiling. Turn off heat; if necessary, remove pan from burner to prevent further boiling. Let eggs stand in the hot water 15 minutes for large eggs, adjusting time up or down by approximately 3 minutes for each

size larger or smaller. Cool immediately and thoroughly in cold water to prevent darkening of the yolks and to make shells easier to remove.

To remove shell, crackle it by tapping gently all over. Roll egg between hands to loosen shell; peel, starting at large end. Hold egg under running cold water or dip in a bowl of water to help ease off shell.

Deviled Ham-Stuffed Eggs

3 hard-cooked eggs
½ (2¼-ounce) can deviled ham
2 tablespoons grated carrot
1 tablespoon mayonnaise or salad dressing
⅛ teaspoon dry mustard
Paprika (optional)
Fresh parsley (optional)

Cut eggs in half lengthwise; remove yolks. Mash yolks; add ham, carrot, mayonnaise, and mustard. Stir well.

Fill egg halves with mixture; chill. Sprinkle with paprika or garnish with fresh parsley, if desired. Yield: 2 servings.

Fried Eggs

Heat 1 to 2 tablespoons butter in skillet until just hot enough to sizzle a drop of water. If you use a very large skillet, you will need more butter. Break and slip 2 eggs into skillet. Reduce heat immediately. Cook slowly to desired degree of doneness, spooning butter over eggs to baste or turning eggs to cook both sides. Yield: 1 serving.

Sunny-Side-Up Eggs

1 tablespoon butter or margarine
2 eggs
Salt and pepper
Lemon verbena (optional)

Melt butter in a heavy skillet, and heat until hot enough to sizzle a drop of water. Break each egg into a saucer; carefully slip each egg one at a time into skillet. Cook eggs over low heat until whites are firm and yolks are soft or to desired degree of doneness; season with salt and pepper. Garnish eggs with lemon verbena, if desired. Yield: 2 servings.

Poached Eggs

Lightly oil a saucepan. Add enough liquid (water, milk, or broth) to make 2 inches deep. Bring to a boil; reduce heat to simmer. Break eggs, one at a time, into a saucer; slip each egg into liquid, holding saucer close to water's surface. Simmer 3 to 5 minutes, depending on degree of doneness desired. When done, remove eggs with slotted pancake turner or spoon; drain on paper towel and trim edges, if desired.

Scrambled Eggs

2 eggs
2 tablespoons milk
¼ teaspoon salt
Dash of pepper
1 tablespoon butter or margarine

Beat eggs, milk, salt, and pepper together with fork, mixing thoroughly for uniform yellow color, or mixing slightly for white and yellow streaks. Heat butter in 8-inch skillet over medium heat until just hot enough to sizzle a drop of water. Pour in egg mixture. As mixture begins to set, gently pull eggs with edge of pancake turner across the bottom of the skillet, forming large soft curds.

Continue until eggs are thickened, but do not stir constantly. Eggs are done when thickened but still moist. Yield: 1 serving.

Sour Cream Scrambled Eggs

4 slices bacon, cut into small pieces
4 eggs
2 tablespoons commercial sour cream
2 tablespoons process American cheese spread
¼ teaspoon seasoned salt
Dash of pepper

Fry bacon in a large skillet; drain off all but 3 tablespoons drippings.

Combine remaining ingredients in container of electric blender; process on low speed until light and fluffy. Pour into skillet with bacon and hot drippings. Cook over low heat, stirring gently, until done. Serve immediately. Yield: about 2 servings.

Tortilla Egg Casserole

2 flour tortillas
3 eggs, scrambled
1 cup (4 ounces) shredded Cheddar cheese
⅓ pound bacon, cooked, drained, and crumbled
½ medium onion, finely chopped
⅓ cup Guacamole
6 ripe olives, sliced
Commercial sour cream
Commercial salsa

Wrap tortillas tightly in foil; bake at 350° for 15 minutes.

Layer eggs, cheese, bacon, onion, Guacamole, and olives evenly on each warm tortilla. Top with sour cream and salsa. Yield: 2 servings.

160   *Eggs*

Guacamole:

1 small ripe avocado, peeled, seeded,
   and chopped
Lemon juice
Salt and pepper to taste
Chili powder

Process avocado in container of electric blender until smooth (about 15 seconds). Add lemon juice and seasonings to taste. Process on low speed until mixed. Yield: about ⅔ cup.

Omelets

Omelets are a more elegant form of beaten eggs, cooked in an omelet pan or skillet and folded around a filling. Almost any food that strikes one's fancy is right for filling omelets.

The most familiar omelet is the plain or French omelet, in which the whole egg is beaten and cooked on top of the range in a minute or so. A lighter, fluffier version is the puffy omelet. For this omelet, the yolks and whites are beaten separately, then combined. The mixture cooks briefly on top of the range, and finishes cooking in the oven.

Plain Omelet Technique:

Combine eggs, 1 tablespoon water per egg, and salt and pepper to taste in a mixing bowl. Blend well. Heat butter (1 tablespoon per 2 eggs) in omelet pan or skillet over medium high heat until butter foams. Pour in egg mixture. Shake pan vigorously, or use a spatula to push cooked portions at edges toward center so that uncooked portions flow underneath. Slide pan back and forth over heat to keep mixture in motion.

While top is still moist and creamy looking, spoon desired filling over half of omelet. Cut partially through the center with edge of spatula. Fold unfilled side over filling. Slide omelet onto plate and serve immediately.

Puffy Omelet Technique:

A puffy omelet has a light, airy texture achieved by beating the whites and yolks separately. Beat egg whites (at room temperature) until stiff but not dry. Beat the yolks in a separate bowl with clean beaters until lemon colored. Add salt and pepper if desired. Use a rubber spatula or wire whisk to gently fold the egg yolks into the whites.

Pour this mixture into a heated, buttered omelet pan; gently smooth surface with knife or spatula. Cook over medium heat until puffed and lightly browned on bottom; then finish cooking in oven. Knife inserted in center should come out clean. The omelet may be folded or cut in half or wedges to serve.

Omelet Fillings:

⅓ to ½ cup yogurt or sour cream
   seasoned with choice of herbs
½ cup cottage cheese or shredded
   Cheddar, Muenster, mozzarella, or
   crumbled blue cheese
⅓ to ½ cup chopped cooked chicken,
   turkey, beef, pork, or lamb
2 slices cooked, crumbled bacon
½ cup fresh or cooked vegetables (green
   pepper, celery, mushrooms, onion,
   avocado, bean sprouts, water
   chestnuts)
⅓ to ½ cup olives
2 tablespoons jelly, jam, or preserves
   with toasted almonds or pecans

Yield: Any of the above yields enough filling for one 2-egg omelet.

Ham and Cheese Omelet

3 eggs, separated
½ teaspoon all-purpose flour
2 tablespoons milk
½ medium onion, chopped
1 tablespoon chopped fresh parsley
½ teaspoon salt
Dash of pepper
2 tablespoons butter or margarine, divided
2 slices cooked ham, cut into pieces
2 slices process American cheese

Beat egg whites (at room temperature) until stiff but not dry. Beat egg yolks until thick and lemon colored. Combine yolks, flour, milk, onion, parsley, salt, and pepper; mix well. Fold into egg whites.

For each omelet, melt 1 tablespoon of butter in an 8-inch skillet until just hot enough to sizzle a drop of water; pour in half of egg mixture. As mixture begins to cook, gently lift edges of omelet and tilt pan to allow the uncooked portion to flow underneath. When mixture is set and no longer flows freely, sprinkle half of ham on one side of omelet; cover ham with one slice of cheese. Fold omelet in half, and place on a warm platter. Repeat procedure with remaining ingredients. Yield: 2 servings.

Rolled Omelet Sandwich

2 eggs
1½ tablespoons water
1 teaspoon pickle relish
¼ teaspoon prepared mustard
Dash of salt
Dash of pepper
1 tablespoon butter or margarine
1 (¾- to 1-ounce) slice Swiss cheese
1 sandwich or hard roll, split and buttered
2 tomato slices

Combine eggs, water, pickle relish, mustard, salt, and pepper in a small bowl. Beat well with a fork.

Melt butter in an 8-inch skillet until just hot enough to sizzle a drop of water; pour in egg mixture. As mixture begins to cook, gently lift edges of omelet and tilt pan to allow uncooked portion to flow underneath. Slide pan back and forth to keep mixture in motion and sliding freely. While top is still moist, cover with cheese slice. Cook about 30 seconds longer or just until cheese begins to melt. Roll omelet around cheese slice. Turn omelet onto split roll. Top with tomato slices. Yield: 1 serving.

Note: To make 2 sandwiches, keep the first sandwich in warm oven while preparing the second one.

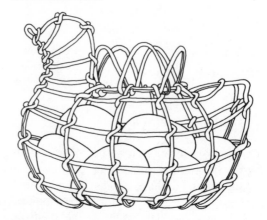

Wine Omelet

2 tablespoons chopped green onion
⅓ cup chopped onion
1⅔ cups sliced fresh mushrooms
3 tablespoons butter or margarine, divided
¼ to ⅓ cup dry white wine
3 eggs, well beaten
½ cup (2 ounces) shredded Swiss cheese, divided

Sauté onion and mushrooms in 1½ tablespoons butter in a small saucepan. Add wine; simmer until liquid is absorbed. Set aside onion and mushrooms, and keep warm.

Melt remaining 1½ tablespoons butter in a 6- or 7-inch omelet pan or heavy skillet and heat until just hot enough to sizzle a drop of water; rotate pan as butter melts to coat bottom of pan. Pour in beaten eggs. As eggs begin to cook, gently lift edges of omelet to allow uncooked portions to flow underneath. Slide pan back and forth over heat to keep mixture in motion.

When eggs are set and top is still moist and creamy, sprinkle cheese, reserving 1 tablespoon, over half of omelet. Spoon mushroom mixture over cheese. Fold unfilled side over filling; sprinkle with remaining cheese, and cover for a few seconds or until cheese melts. Slide omelet onto a warm plate, and serve immediately. Yield: 2 servings.

Roquefort and Apple Omelet

2 tart apples, peeled, cored, and sliced
3 tablespoons butter or margarine, divided
5 eggs, beaten
2 tablespoons milk
2 to 3 tablespoons grated Parmesan cheese
Salt and pepper to taste
¼ cup (2 ounces) crumbled Roquefort cheese

Sauté apples in 2 tablespoons butter for 1 minute in a heavy skillet; remove from skillet, and set aside.

Combine eggs, milk, Parmesan cheese, salt, and pepper; beat well.

Add 1 tablespoon butter to skillet, and heat until just hot enough to sizzle a drop of water. Pour in egg mixture. As mixture begins to cook, gently lift edges of omelet and tilt pan to allow uncooked portion to flow underneath. When omelet is set and no

longer flows freely, remove from heat. (It will be moist and creamy on top.)

Sprinkle Roquefort cheese and half of sautéed apple wedges on one side of omelet; fold in half. Transfer to a warm dish, and garnish with remaining apple wedges. Serve immediately. Yield: 2 servings.

Brandied Apricot Omelet

½ cup apricot preserves
2 teaspoons brandy
2 eggs, separated
2 tablespoons water
⅛ teaspoon salt
1 tablespoon butter or margarine
Rum Sauce

Combine preserves and brandy; set aside. Combine egg whites (at room temperature), water, and salt; beat until stiff but not dry. Beat egg yolks until thick and lemon colored; fold into egg whites.

Heat butter in an ovenproof 8- or 9-inch omelet pan or heavy skillet until hot enough to sizzle a drop of water. Pour in egg mixture, and gently smooth surface. Reduce heat and cook omelet about 5 minutes or until puffy and lightly browned on bottom, gently lifting omelet at edge to judge color.

Bake at 325° for 12 to 15 minutes or until knife inserted in center comes out clean. Tip skillet and loosen omelet with a spatula. Spoon preserve mixture over half of omelet; carefully fold omelet in half. Top with Rum Sauce. Yield: 2 servings.

Rum Sauce:

1 egg
½ cup sifted powdered sugar
½ cup whipping cream, whipped
2 teaspoons light rum

Beat egg until thick and lemon colored; gradually add sugar, beating well. Add whipped cream and rum, beating well. May be refrigerated several hours. Yield: about 1 cup.

Crepes

Crêpes are very thin pancakes which can be used for very simple leftover foods or combined with an almost unlimited number of fillings and sauces to make more elegant entrées or desserts.

To use baked crêpes immediately:

Simply stack crêpes, as they are baked, on a deep dinner plate, pieplate or other similar container. Keep crêpes covered with foil, plastic wrap, or a large pan or pot cover and store at room temperature.

To reheat, cover crêpes tightly with foil to prevent drying and bake at 250° for 5 to 10 minutes or until warm.

To refrigerate crêpes:

Place a sheet of foil, waxed paper, or plastic wrap between each crêpe. Cover tightly with plastic wrap or foil or seal in a plastic bag. Store flat in the refrigerator.

To freeze crêpes:

Layer crêpes in two serving portions with waxed paper, foil, or plastic wrap, as above. Place the stack of crêpes on a paper plate, in a pieplate or deep dinner plate, or in a round freezer container to protect them. (Crêpes become brittle when frozen and could break.) Cover tightly with plastic wrap or seal in a heavy-duty plastic bag or freezer container. Store flat in the freezer. Crêpes will keep in the freezer for several weeks.

To thaw crêpes:

Remove crêpes from freezer and let stand at room temperature for several hours or in refrigerator overnight. For faster thawing, unwrap crêpes and heat at 250°, carefully peeling crêpes apart as they thaw and become flexible. Crêpes can also be thawed in the microwave oven for 1 or 2 minutes.

Basic Crepes

1 cup all-purpose flour
¾ cup water
¾ cup milk
3 eggs
2 tablespoons butter or margarine, melted
¼ teaspoon salt

Combine all ingredients in container of an electric blender; blend 1 minute. Scrape down sides of blender container with rubber spatula; blend an additional 15 seconds or until smooth. Refrigerate batter 1 hour. (This allows flour particles to swell and soften so the crêpes are light in texture.)

Brush the bottom of an 8-inch crêpe pan with melted butter; place pan over medium heat until butter is just hot, not smoking.

Pour 3 to 4 tablespoons batter into pan; quickly tilt pan in all directions so that batter covers the pan in a thin film. Cook about 1 minute.

Lift edge of crêpe to test for doneness. Crêpe is ready for flipping when it can be shaken loose from pan. Flip crêpe, and cook about 30 seconds on other side. (This side is rarely more than spotty brown.)

Stack crêpes between layers of waxed paper to prevent sticking. Yield: about 1 dozen.

Note: To make crêpes with electric mixer, combine water, milk, eggs, and butter. Add flour and salt, and beat until smooth. Proceed as above.

Whole Wheat Crepes

1 cup whole wheat flour
2 eggs
½ cup milk
½ cup water
¼ teaspoon salt
2 tablespoons butter or margarine, melted

Combine all ingredients in container of electric blender; blend 30 seconds. Scrape down sides of container with a rubber spatula; blend 30 additional seconds or until smooth. Follow cooking directions for Basic Crêpes. Yield: about 1 dozen.

Dessert Crepes

3 eggs
1 cup milk
3 tablespoons butter or margarine, melted
¾ cup all-purpose flour
2 tablespoons sugar
½ teaspoon salt

Combine all ingredients in container of electric blender; blend 1 minute. Scrape down sides of blender container with rubber spatula; blend an additional 15 seconds or until smooth. Follow cooking directions for Basic Crêpes. Yield: about 1 dozen.

Mushroom Filling for Crepes

1 tablespoon chopped onion
2 tablespoons butter or margarine
1 egg, beaten
½ cup small-curd cottage cheese
1 (3-ounce) can sliced mushrooms, drained
Pinch of salt
⅛ teaspoon pepper
4 to 6 Basic or Whole Wheat Crêpes
Cream of mushroom soup

Sauté onion in butter until tender. Combine next 5 ingredients, mixing well; stir in onion mixture. Fill crêpes. Yield: 1 cup.

Baking Directions:

Spoon Mushroom Filling off-center on each crêpe. Roll crêpe over filling. Place seam side down in a 9-inch square baking dish.

Bake at 350° for 20 to 30 minutes. Remove from oven, and spoon cream of mushroom soup (or other topping) over crêpes. Return to oven for an additional 5 minutes. Yield: 2 servings.

Spinach Filling for Crepes

1 (10-ounce) package frozen chopped spinach
1 tablespoon chopped onion
2 tablespoons butter or margarine
¼ teaspoon salt
⅔ cup Béchamel Sauce, divided
4 to 6 Basic or Whole Wheat Crêpes

Cook spinach according to package directions; drain well. Sauté onion in butter until tender. Combine spinach, onion, salt, and ⅓ cup Béchamel Sauce, mixing well. Fill crêpes. Yield: about 1 cup.

Bechamel Sauce:

1 tablespoon butter or margarine
1½ tablespoons all-purpose flour
Pinch of salt
Dash of pepper
½ cup milk
2 tablespoons half-and-half
½ cup (2 ounces) shredded Swiss cheese

Melt butter in a heavy saucepan over low heat; blend in flour, salt, and pepper. Cook 1 minute. Gradually add milk and half-and-half; cook over medium heat, stirring constantly, until thickened and bubbly. Add cheese; stir until melted. Yield: ⅔ cup.

Baking Directions:

Spoon Spinach Filling down center of each crêpe. Roll up and arrange seam side down in a buttered 9-inch square baking dish. Top with remaining ⅓ cup Béchamel Sauce. Bake at 350° for 20 to 30 minutes or until thoroughly heated. Serve immediately. Yield: 2 servings.

Sausage Filling for Crepes

½ pound bulk pork sausage
2 tablespoons chopped onion
¼ cup shredded Cheddar cheese
½ (3-ounce) package cream cheese, softened
¼ teaspoon ground marjoram
4 to 6 Basic or Whole Wheat Crêpes
Topping

Sauté sausage and onion until brown; drain well. Stir in next 3 ingredients. Fill crepes as indicated below. Yield: about 1 cup.

Topping:

¼ cup commercial sour cream
2 tablespoons butter, softened

Combine sour cream and butter, beating well. Yield: ⅓ cup.

Baking Directions:

Spoon Sausage Filling off-center on each crêpe. Roll crêpe over filling. Place seam side down in a 9-inch square baking dish. Bake at 350° for 20 to 30 minutes. Remove from oven, and spoon Topping over crêpes. Return to oven for an additional 5 minutes. Yield: 2 servings.

Banana Nut Custard Filling for Crepes

3 tablespoons sugar
1 tablespoon cornstarch
Pinch of salt
1 cup milk
1 egg yolk
¼ cup chopped walnuts
¼ teaspoon vanilla extract
2 bananas
4 Dessert Crêpes
Quick Chocolate Nut Sauce

Combine sugar, cornstarch, and salt in small saucepan. Beat milk and egg yolk until blended. Gradually stir in small amount of milk mixture into dry ingredients, making a smooth paste. Gradually stir in remaining milk mixture. Cook over medium heat, stirring constantly, until mixture thickens and boils. Boil and stir 1 minute. Remove from heat. Stir in walnuts and vanilla. Cover with plastic wrap. Chill thoroughly. Fill crepes as indicated below. Yield: about 1¼ cups.

Quick Chocolate Nut Sauce:

⅓ cup chocolate syrup
¼ cup chopped walnuts

Combine chocolate syrup and walnuts. Serve over filled crêpes. Yield: ½ cup.

Serving Directions:

Slice banana; reserve a few slices for garnish. Arrange several slices in an overlapping row down center of each crêpe. Spoon about ¼ cup custard mixture down center of each crêpe. Fold 2 opposite sides of crêpe over filling. Arrange on serving platter. Spoon Quick Chocolate Nut Sauce over crêpes and garnish with reserved banana slices. Yield: 2 servings.

Strawberry Filling for Crepes

½ cup small-curd cottage cheese
½ cup vanilla yogurt
2 tablespoons powdered sugar
1½ cups fresh strawberries, halved
2 tablespoons sugar
4 Whole Wheat Crêpes

Put cottage cheese through a sieve or food mill. Combine cottage cheese, yogurt, and powdered sugar; set aside.

Combine strawberries and sugar. Spread the center of each crêpe with 1 tablespoon cheese filling and a few strawberries; roll up crêpes and place on a serving platter.

Spoon remaining cheese filling and strawberries on top of crêpes. Yield: 2 servings.

Spinach Frittata

¼ pound fresh mushrooms, sliced, or ½ can (4-ounce) sliced mushrooms
2 tablespoons finely chopped onion or 1½ teaspoons instant minced onion
1½ tablespoons butter or margarine
4 eggs
¼ teaspoon seasoned salt
Dash of pepper
½ cup cooked chopped spinach, well drained
3 tablespoons grated Parmesan cheese
Parsley (optional)
Red peppers (optional)

Sauté mushrooms and onion in butter in an 8-inch ovenproof skillet over medium heat until tender, but not brown (about 7 to 10 minutes). Beat eggs and seasonings. Stir in drained spinach. Pour over mushrooms and onion. Cook over low to medium heat until eggs are set, about 5 to 7 minutes. Sprinkle with cheese. Broil about 6 inches from heat for 2 to 3 minutes. Cut in wedges to serve. Garnish with parsley and peppers, if desired. Yield: 2 servings.

Note: If using canned mushrooms and instant minced onion, do not sauté in butter. Add mushrooms with liquid and instant minced onion to egg mixture. Cook as above.

Quiche

Quiche, an unsweetened open-faced custard pie, is good to serve either hot or cold as an entrée, appetizer, or snack. It is incredibly simple to make and requires only eggs, milk (or half-and-half), cheese, seasonings, any filling ingredients you want to add, and a baked pastry shell.

Our recipe for two individual pastry shells may be used for any quiche recipe. Split filling between two pastry shells and reduce cooking time by about 10 minutes or until fillings are firm.

Quiche Pastry Shells

1 cup all-purpose flour
¼ teaspoon salt
¼ cup cold butter or margarine
2½ to 3 tablespoons ice water

Combine flour and salt in a medium mixing bowl. Cut in butter with pastry blender until mixture resembles coarse meal. Sprinkle cold water by tablespoonfuls evenly over flour mixture. Stir with fork until ingredients are moistened. Shape dough into a ball.

Divide dough in half; roll each half out to ⅛-inch thickness on a lightly floured board. Arrange one pastry piece in each of two 5- × 1½-inch disposable tart pans. Flute edges; prick sides and bottoms. Place on baking sheet. Bake at 450° for 10 to 12 minutes. Cool slightly. Yield: two 5-inch pastry shells.

Broccoli Quiche

1 cup shredded Swiss cheese
1 cup cooked broccoli, well-drained
2 baked 5-inch Quiche Pastry Shells
2 eggs, beaten
¾ cup milk
¼ teaspoon salt
1 teaspoon Worcestershire sauce
2 tablespoons grated Parmesan cheese

Arrange one-half of Swiss cheese and broccoli in each of the baked pastry shells. Combine eggs, milk, salt, and Worcestershire sauce. Beat together until well-blended. Pour over cheese and broccoli in pastry shells. Sprinkle with Parmesan cheese. Place on baking sheet. Bake at 375° for 20 to 30 minutes or until set. Yield: two 5-inch quiches.

Ham and Cheese Quiche

½ cup diced cooked ham
2 baked 5-inch Quiche Pastry Shells
½ cup (2 ounces) shredded Cheddar
   cheese
Dash of ground nutmeg
2 eggs
½ cup half-and-half
¼ teaspoon salt
¼ teaspoon pepper
¼ teaspoon paprika
½ teaspoon parsley flakes

Divide ham between quiche shells; top each with cheese, and sprinkle with nutmeg.

Beat eggs until foamy; stir in half-and-half and seasonings. Pour over cheese in quiche shells. Bake at 350° for 20 to 30 minutes or until set. Yield: two 5-inch quiches.

Quiche Lorraine

3 to 4 slices bacon, cut into ½-inch
   pieces
2 tablespoons chopped green onion
2 baked 5-inch Quiche Pastry Shells
1 cup (4 ounces) shredded Swiss
   cheese, divided
2 eggs, beaten
¾ cup whipping cream
½ teaspoon salt
Dash of red pepper
Dash of white pepper
Ground nutmeg

Sauté bacon and onion in a skillet until browned; drain well. Sprinkle half of bacon mixture evenly in each pastry shell. Top with ¼ cup cheese, and set aside.

Combine remaining ingredients; mix well. Pour over cheese layers, and top with remaining cheese. Sprinkle lightly with nutmeg. Bake at 350° for 20 to 30 minutes or until set. Yield: two 5-inch quiches.

Cheese Souffle

3 eggs, separated
Dash of dry mustard
Pinch of ground thyme
Pinch of ground nutmeg
Pinch of red pepper
Dash of salt
Dash of pepper
1 tablespoon brandy (optional)
¼ cup ricotta cheese
⅓ cup grated Romano cheese
⅓ cup shredded Gruyère cheese
Breadcrumbs

Combine egg yolks and seasonings; add brandy, if desired. Beat until light and lemon colored. Stir in cheese.

Beat egg whites (at room temperature) until stiff but not dry; stir about one-fourth of egg whites into egg yolk mixture. Fold in remaining egg whites.

Lightly grease two 6-ounce ramekins and coat with breadcrumbs. Spoon mixture evenly into each. Bake at 400° for 20 minutes or until puffed and brown. Yield: 2 servings.

Individual Souffles

2 tablespoons butter or margarine
2 tablespoons all-purpose flour
⅛ teaspoon salt
Dash of red pepper
½ cup milk
1 cup (4 ounces) shredded Cheddar
   cheese
3 eggs, separated
⅛ teaspoon cream of tartar

Melt butter in a heavy saucepan. Blend in flour, salt, and pepper; cook 1 minute, stirring constantly. Gradually stir in milk; cook over medium heat, stirring constantly, until thickened and bubbly. Remove from heat.

Add cheese, stirring until melted.

Beat egg yolks until thick and lemon colored. Gradually stir about one-fourth of hot mixture into yolks; add to remaining hot mixture, stirring constantly.

Beat egg whites (at room temperature) until foamy; add cream of tartar. Continue beating until soft peaks form; gently fold into cheese sauce. Spoon mixture into two lightly greased 10-ounce soufflé dishes. Bake at 350° for 30 minutes. Serve immediately. Yield: 2 servings.

Macaroni and Cheese Souffle

¼ cup uncooked elbow macaroni
½ cup scalded milk
1 cup (4 ounces) shredded sharp
   Cheddar cheese, divided
½ cup soft breadcrumbs
2 tablespoons chopped pimiento
1½ tablespoons butter or margarine,
   melted
2 teaspoons chopped parsley
2 teaspoons grated onion
¼ teaspoon salt
2 eggs, separated
¼ teaspoon cream of tartar

Cook macaroni according to package directions; drain and set aside.

Combine milk and ¾ cup cheese, stirring until cheese melts. Add macaroni, breadcrumbs, pimiento, butter, parsley, onion, and salt. Beat egg yolks; stir into mixture.

Beat egg whites (at room temperature) and cream of tartar until stiff but not dry; fold into macaroni mixture. Spoon into a lightly greased 1-quart baking dish. Bake at 325° for 40 to 50 minutes or until set. Sprinkle with remaining cheese; return to oven, and bake 5 additional minutes or until cheese melts. Yield: 2 servings.

Enchiladas with Sour Cream

1 (10¾-ounce) can cream of mushroom
   soup, undiluted
½ cup commercial sour cream
½ (4-ounce) can chopped green chiles
⅛ teaspoon salt
⅛ teaspoon pepper
¼ teaspoon garlic powder
1 cup (4 ounces) shredded Cheddar
   cheese
½ cup chopped green onion
½ (8-ounce) package or 6 corn tortillas
Hot vegetable oil

Combine soup, sour cream, green chiles, and seasonings in a saucepan. Cook over medium heat, stirring often, until hot.

Combine cheese and onion, mixing well.

Cook each tortilla in hot oil for a few seconds or just until softened; drain on paper towels. Immediately spoon about 1½ tablespoons cheese mixture and 2 tablespoons soup mixture onto center of each. Roll up tightly, and place in a greased 9-inch square baking dish.

Spoon remaining soup mixture over top of enchiladas, and sprinkle with remaining cheese mixture. Bake at 350° for 20 to 30 minutes. Yield: 2 servings.

Green Noodles with Cheese

2 cups spinach noodles
3 tablespoons butter or margarine,
   melted
⅛ teaspoon garlic powder
3 tablespoons grated Parmesan cheese
3 tablespoons shredded Swiss cheese
Freshly ground black pepper

Cook noodles according to package directions; drain. Combine butter and garlic powder; add noodles, mixing well. Sprinkle with cheese and pepper. Yield: 2 servings.

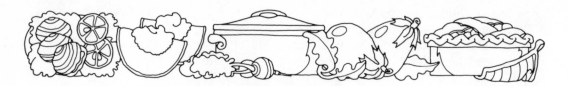

DESSERTS

Creative Desserts

Combine your favorite dessert items in the desired amounts and enjoy your own specialty. Choose either a simple glass plate, a pretty bowl, or a stemmed glass to add to the appeal. Allow time to chill fruits combined with liqueurs before serving.

Base	Topping
Vanilla Ice Cream	Chocolate, caramel, or fruit sauce; Chocolate Mint liqueur; Crème de Menthe; Drambuie; Cognac
with pound cake	Chocolate fudge sauce
with fresh strawberries, peaches, or kiwi slices	Drambuie
Chocolate Ice Cream	Caramel or chocolate sauce
with grated chocolate	Irish Cream liqueur
with fancy cookies	Praline liqueur
Coffee Ice Cream	Chocolate Mint liqueur
with grated chocolate	Chocolate Mint liqueur
Pound Cake	Dessert toppings (chocolate, caramel, fruit)
with ice cream	Vanilla or chocolate pudding
with fresh strawberries or peaches	Vanilla or chocolate pudding
Fresh Fruit	
Oranges	Kirsch
Strawberries or peaches	Champagne
Pineapple	Coconut Amaretto
Apple or pear slices	Grand Marnier
Green grapes	Sour cream and brown sugar

Rich Pound Cake

1 cup butter or margarine, softened
1¾ cups sugar
5 eggs
½ teaspoon almond extract
2 cups all-purpose flour

Cream butter and sugar until light and fluffy; add eggs, one at a time, beating well after each addition. Add almond extract. Stir in flour, mixing well.

Spoon batter into a greased and floured 9- × 5- × 3-inch loafpan. Bake at 350° for 1 hour and 10 minutes or until cake tests done. Cool in loafpan 10 minutes before removing to cake rack. Yield: one 9-inch loaf.

Pineapple Upside-Down Cake

2 tablespoons butter or margarine
¼ cup firmly packed brown sugar
½ cup crushed pineapple, drained
½ cup all-purpose flour
½ teaspoon baking powder
Pinch of salt
⅓ cup sugar
1 egg, slightly beaten
1 tablespoon butter or margarine, melted
½ teaspoon vanilla extract
⅓ cup milk

Combine 2 tablespoons butter and brown sugar. Divide mixture between two 10-ounce custard cups; spread evenly. Top butter mixture with crushed pineapple. Sift flour, baking powder, salt, and sugar in a mixing bowl. Combine egg, melted butter, vanilla, and milk, and stir into dry ingredients. Beat thoroughly.

Pour batter over pineapple. Bake at 350° for 25 to 30 minutes or until cake tests done. Remove from oven and immediately invert onto serving plates. Let stand with custard cups over cakes to allow sugar mixture to drain down and coat cake. Yield: 2 servings.

Variations: Fresh peach or apple slices may be substituted for pineapple. Increase sugar depending on the acidity of the fruit.

Frozen raspberries, blueberries, or peaches may also be substituted. Use less sugar if sweetened frozen fruit is used.

Carrot Loaf Cake

2 eggs, slightly beaten
1 cup sugar
⅔ cup vegetable oil
1 cup all-purpose flour
1 teaspoon baking powder
1 teaspoon soda
1 teaspoon ground cinnamon
½ teaspoon vanilla extract
1½ cups grated (about 2 large) carrots
½ cup chopped pecans
Dash of salt
Cream Cheese Frosting

Combine eggs, sugar, and oil in a large mixing bowl; mix well. Add dry ingredients, mixing well. Stir in vanilla, carrots, pecans, and salt.

Pour batter into a greased 8- × 4½- × 3-inch loafpan. Bake at 325° for 45 minutes or until cake tests done. Cool and frost with Cream Cheese Frosting. Cover and store in refrigerator. Yield: 1 loaf cake.

Cream Cheese Frosting:

¼ cup butter or margarine, softened
1 (3-ounce) package cream cheese, softened
½ teaspoon vanilla extract
2 cups sifted powdered sugar

Combine butter and cream cheese. Cream until smooth. Add vanilla and powdered sugar; beat until smooth. Yield: enough for one 8-inch loaf cake.

Mix Easy Yellow Cake

1 cup all-purpose flour
1½ teaspoons baking powder
½ teaspoon salt
¾ cup sugar
¼ cup butter, margarine, or shortening
¼ cup plus 3 tablespoons milk
1 egg
½ teaspoon vanilla extract

Sift together flour, baking powder, salt, and sugar; set aside. Beat butter in a medium mixing bowl just to soften.

Add flour mixture and milk to butter; mix until flour is dampened. Beat at medium speed 2 minutes. Add egg and vanilla; beat 1 minute longer.

Turn batter into a greased, waxed paper-lined 9-inch cakepan. Bake at 375° about 25 minutes or until a cake tester comes out clean when inserted in center of cake. Let cake cool in pan 5 minutes on wire rack. Loosen sides with a spatula; turn out on wire rack to finish cooling. Yield: one 9-inch layer.

Note: Use ½ cup milk if using shortening.

Sour Cream Chocolate Cake

4 (1-ounce) squares unsweetened chocolate
1 cup hot water
2 eggs, beaten
2 cups sugar
1 (8-ounce) carton commercial sour cream
2 teaspoons vanilla extract
2 cups all-purpose flour
1 teaspoon soda
½ teaspoon salt
Cocoa Frosting

Combine chocolate and hot water in a small saucepan; place over low heat, stirring until chocolate is melted. Remove from heat.

Combine eggs and sugar in a medium mixing bowl, mixing well; add sour cream, chocolate mixture, and vanilla. Mix well.

Combine dry ingredients; gradually add to chocolate mixture, mixing well. Pour into 2 greased and floured 8-inch cakepans. Place in a cold oven and set at 300°; bake about 55 minutes. Let layers cool before removing from pans. Spread with Cocoa Frosting. Yield: one 8-inch layer cake.

Cocoa Frosting:

2 cups sugar
¼ cup cocoa
½ cup butter or margarine
1 tablespoon light corn syrup
½ cup milk
1 cup chopped pecans
1 teaspoon vanilla extract

Combine sugar and cocoa in a small saucepan, mixing well. Add butter, corn syrup, and milk; bring to a boil, and boil 2 minutes. Remove from heat; cool until lukewarm. Beat until thick enough to spread. Stir in pecans and vanilla. Yield: enough for 8-inch layer cake.

Mix Easy Chocolate Cake

2 (1-ounce) squares unsweetened chocolate
½ cup hot water
1 cup all-purpose flour
1 cup sugar
½ teaspoon soda
¼ teaspoon baking powder
½ teaspoon salt
¼ cup vegetable shortening
¼ cup buttermilk
1 egg
½ teaspoon vanilla extract

Add chocolate squares to hot water in a small saucepan. Stir over low heat until chocolate is dissolved. Pour into mixing bowl.

Sift dry ingredients. Add to chocolate mixture. Add shortening. Beat at medium speed 1 minute, scraping bottom and sides of bowl.

Add buttermilk, egg, and vanilla. Beat at medium speed 1 minute longer. Pour into greased and waxed paper-lined 9-inch cake-pan. Bake at 350° for 30 to 35 minutes or until top springs back when lightly touched. Cool and frost with favorite frosting. Yield: one 9-inch layer.

Orange Cheesecake

15 graham cracker squares, crushed
2 tablespoons sugar
¼ teaspoon ground cinnamon
¼ cup butter or margarine, melted
2 eggs
½ cup sugar
1½ cups commercial sour cream
2 teaspoons vanilla extract
2 (8-ounce) packages cream cheese, softened and cut into 1-inch pieces
2 tablespoons butter or margarine, melted
1 (11-ounce) can mandarin oranges
¼ cup Cointreau or Triple Sec
½ cup orange juice
1½ tablespoons cornstarch
Mint leaves (optional)

Combine first 4 ingredients; press into a buttered 9-inch springform pan. Bake at 400° for 6 minutes. Cool.

Combine eggs, ½ cup sugar, sour cream, and vanilla in container of electric blender; blend for 15 seconds. Gradually add cream cheese, and continue blending. Add 2 tablespoons butter, blending until well mixed.

Pour cheese mixture into prepared crust. Bake at 325° for 35 minutes or until set in center. (Filling will be very soft but will firm up as cake cools.)

Drain mandarin oranges, reserving ½ cup liquid; set aside. Combine mandarin oranges and Cointreau; let sit 30 minutes.

Drain mandarin oranges, reserving Cointreau. Combine reserved ½ cup mandarin orange liquid, reserved Cointreau, orange juice, and cornstarch; stir well. Cook over low heat 5 minutes or until thickened; cool slightly. Arrange oranges on top of cheesecake; top with glaze. Chill 6 hours or overnight before serving. Garnish with mint, if desired. Yield: 8 servings.

Buttercream Frosting

2½ tablespoons butter or margarine, softened
1½ cups sifted powdered sugar
¾ teaspoon vanilla extract
3 tablespoons half-and-half or milk

Combine all ingredients in small mixing bowl. Beat at medium speed until smooth. Yield: enough frosting for one 9-inch layer.

Variations: For orange or lemon frosting, substitute ¾ tablespoon grated rind and 1½ tablespoons orange or lemon juice for vanilla and half-and-half.

For chocolate frosting, add 1½ (1-ounce) squares unsweetened chocolate, melted.

Easy Caramel Frosting

¼ cup butter or margarine
½ cup firmly packed brown sugar
2 tablespoons milk
About ¾ cup sifted powdered sugar

Melt butter in medium saucepan. Stir in brown sugar. Boil and stir over medium to low heat 2 minutes. Stir in milk. Bring to a boil, stirring constantly.

Cool to lukewarm. Gradually add ¾ cup powdered sugar. Beat until thick enough to spread, adding additional powdered sugar if needed. Yield: enough frosting for one 9-inch layer.

Chocolate Whipped Cream Topping

1 tablespoon cocoa
1 tablespoon sugar
Dash of salt
½ cup whipping cream

Combine cocoa, sugar, and salt. Add cream gradually, stirring to keep mixture smooth. Chill one hour; beat at high speed of electric mixer until mixture is stiff. Yield: enough topping for one 9-inch layer.

Fudge Frosting

1½ (1-ounce) squares unsweetened chocolate
1 tablespoon butter or margarine
1½ cups sifted powdered sugar, divided
3 tablespoons half-and-half or milk
Dash of salt
½ teaspoon vanilla extract

Melt chocolate and butter in medium saucepan over low heat; blend well. Add 1 cup sugar, half-and-half, and salt to chocolate mixture. Beat until smooth. Cook over medium heat, stirring constantly, until mixture bubbles completely around edge and boils gently. Remove from heat.

Gradually add remaining ½ cup sugar, beating until smooth after each addition. Stir in vanilla. If necessary, place over bowl of ice water and beat until thick enough to spread. Yield: enough frosting for one 9-inch layer.

Chocolate Nut Cupcakes

⅓ cup shortening
1 cup sugar
1 egg
2 cups all-purpose flour
½ teaspoon salt
2½ teaspoons baking powder
¾ cup milk
1 teaspoon vanilla extract
1 (6-ounce) package semisweet chocolate morsels
½ cup chopped walnuts
1 (16½-ounce) can milk chocolate frosting

Cream shortening and sugar until light and fluffy; add egg, beating well. Combine flour, salt, and baking powder; add to creamed mixture, and mix well. Add milk, vanilla, chocolate morsels, and nuts; mix well.

Spoon batter into lightly greased muffin pans, filling two-thirds full. Bake at 375° for 20 minutes. Remove from pan; cool. Frost with chocolate frosting. Yield: 1½ dozen.

Pumpkin Cupcakes

1 cup all-purpose flour
2 teaspoons baking powder
¼ teaspoon salt
½ teaspoon ground cinnamon
⅛ teaspoon ground cloves
¼ cup shortening
⅔ cup sugar
1 egg
½ cup cooked, mashed pumpkin
2 tablespoons milk
Lemon Glaze

Combine all ingredients except Lemon Glaze; mix well. Spoon into greased muffin pans, filling two-thirds full. Bake at 350° about 30 minutes. Cool 5 minutes; drizzle with Lemon Glaze. Yield: 1 dozen.

Lemon Glaze:

1½ tablespoons butter or margarine,
   melted
½ cup sifted powdered sugar
About 1 tablespoon lemon juice
⅛ teaspoon grated lemon rind

Combine butter and powdered sugar; add
lemon juice, stirring until smooth. Add more
lemon juice, if needed, to make proper consistency. Stir in lemon rind. Yield: enough
for 1 dozen cupcakes.

Banana Brownies

1 (6-ounce) package semisweet
   chocolate morsels
½ cup all-purpose flour
½ cup sugar
¼ teaspoon salt
½ teaspoon baking powder
2 eggs, well beaten
1 cup mashed bananas (about 2
   medium)
1 teaspoon vanilla extract
½ cup chopped pecans
Chocolate Frosting

Melt chocolate in top of a double boiler;
cool slightly. Combine dry ingredients in a
mixing bowl; add chocolate, eggs, bananas,
and vanilla. Beat on medium speed of electric mixer until well mixed. Stir in pecans.
   Spread batter in a well-greased 8-inch
square baking pan. Bake at 350° for 35 to 40
minutes. Cool. Frost with Chocolate Frosting. Cut into 2-inch squares. Yield: 16
squares.

Chocolate Frosting:

3 tablespoons butter or margarine
2 tablespoons cocoa
1½ cups sifted powdered sugar
2 tablespoons milk

Combine butter and cocoa in a saucepan;
place over low heat, stirring constantly until
smooth. Add powdered sugar and milk. Beat
with electric mixer until light and fluffy. Add
more milk, if necessary, to make spreading
consistency. Yield: about 1 cup.

Oatmeal Brownies

½ cup self-rising flour
1 cup sugar
2 eggs, well beaten
½ cup butter or margarine, melted
½ cup cocoa
½ cup quick-cooking oats, uncooked
½ cup chopped pecans

Combine flour, sugar, and eggs in a large
mixing bowl; mix well. Combine butter and
cocoa, and stir into flour mixture. Add oats
and pecans, mixing until well blended.
   Spread batter in a well-greased 8-inch
square pan. Bake at 350° for 30 minutes or
until done. Cool and cut into squares. Yield:
about 16 squares.

Prune Bars

1 cup diced prunes
1 cup chopped walnuts
1 cup firmly packed brown sugar
¾ cup all-purpose flour
1½ teaspoons baking powder
¼ teaspoon salt
3 eggs, slightly beaten
Powdered sugar

Combine prunes, walnuts, brown sugar,
flour, baking powder, and salt; mix
thoroughly. Add eggs, blending well. Spread
dough evenly in a greased 9-inch square
pan. Bake at 325° about 30 minutes or until
done. Cool 10 to 15 minutes. Cut into bars;
roll each in powdered sugar. Yield: about
1½ dozen.

Marmalade Squares

1 cup all-purpose flour
1 teaspoon baking powder
¼ teaspoon salt
¼ cup shortening
¼ cup butter or margarine
1 egg, beaten
1 tablespoon milk
½ cup orange marmalade
Topping (recipe follows)

Combine flour, baking powder, and salt; cut in shortening and butter until mixture resembles coarse meal. Blend in egg and milk, mixing until smooth.

Spread dough in a greased 8-inch square pan. Spread marmalade evenly over dough, and spoon topping over marmalade. Bake at 375° for 30 minutes. Cool completely; cut into squares. Yield: about 1½ dozen.

Topping:

⅓ cup butter or margarine, melted
1 egg, beaten
1 cup sugar
½ cup flaked coconut
1 teaspoon grated orange rind

Combine all ingredients, mixing well. Yield: about 1½ cups.

Anise Cookies

½ cup butter or margarine, softened
1 cup sugar
1 egg, beaten
½ teaspoon vanilla extract
1¾ cups all-purpose flour
½ teaspoon salt
½ teaspoon baking powder
1½ teaspoons anise seeds, crushed

Cream butter and sugar until light and fluffy; stir in egg and vanilla. Add remaining ingredients, mixing well.

Roll dough into 1-inch balls; place on lightly greased baking sheets. Press each ball with tines of a fork. Bake at 350° for 15 to 20 minutes or until lightly browned. Yield: about 3 dozen.

Note: These cookies store well in an airtight container.

Chocolate Balls

1 tablespoon cocoa
½ cup powdered sugar
¼ cup bourbon
1 tablespoon light corn syrup
½ cup finely ground pecans
1¼ cups finely crushed vanilla wafers
2 egg whites
Chocolate sprinkles

Sift cocoa and sugar together; set aside. Combine bourbon and corn syrup in a bowl; stir in cocoa mixture, pecans, and vanilla wafers.

Roll mixture into 1-inch balls. Dip each ball into egg white, and roll in chocolate sprinkles. Store in a covered container or freeze for later use. Yield: about 20.

Chocolate Frosted Cookies

½ cup butter or margarine, softened
½ cup sifted powdered sugar
¼ teaspoon salt
1 teaspoon vanilla extract
1¼ cups all-purpose flour
Creamy Nut Filling
Chocolate Frosting

Cream butter and sugar until light and fluffy; add salt and vanilla, beating well. Gradually stir in flour, mixing until well blended.

Shape dough into 1-inch balls, and place on ungreased cookie sheets. Using index finger or a thimble dipped in flour, press a hole in center of each ball. Bake at 350° for

12 to 15 minutes or until lightly browned.
While cookies are still warm, fill center of each with about 1 teaspoon Creamy Nut Filling. Cool completely, and spread with Chocolate Frosting. Yield: about 3 dozen.

Creamy Nut Filling:

1 (3-ounce) package cream cheese, softened
1 cup sifted powdered sugar
2 tablespoons all-purpose flour
1 teaspoon vanilla extract
½ cup chopped walnuts
¼ cup flaked coconut

Combine cream cheese, powdered sugar, flour, and vanilla; beat until smooth. Stir in walnuts and coconut. Yield: about 1 cup.

Chocolate Frosting:

½ cup semisweet chocolate morsels
2 tablespoons butter or margarine
2 tablespoons water
½ cup sifted powdered sugar

Combine chocolate, butter, and water in a small saucepan; place over low heat, stirring until chocolate and butter are melted. Remove from heat, and stir in powdered sugar; beat until smooth.
If the frosting gets too thick to spread smoothly, blend in a few more drops of water. Yield: about 1 cup.

Coconut Macaroons

1⅓ cups coconut
⅓ cup sugar
2 egg whites
2 tablespoons all-purpose flour
½ teaspoon vanilla extract
⅛ teaspoon salt

Combine all ingredients, mixing well. Drop by level tablespoonfuls onto a greased cookie sheet. Bake at 350° for 20 minutes. Yield: 1½ dozen.

Filled Butter Cookies

1 cup butter or margarine, softened
¼ cup sugar
1 teaspoon almond extract
½ teaspoon salt
2 cups all-purpose flour
Sesame seeds
Raspberry preserves

Cream butter and sugar until light and fluffy. Add almond extract, salt, and flour, mixing well. Shape dough into 1-inch balls, and coat with sesame seeds. Place on a lightly greased baking sheet. Flatten cookies slightly, and indent centers with thumb. Fill with preserves. Bake at 400° for 10 to 12 minutes. Yield: about 2½ dozen.

Shortbread

½ cup butter or margarine, softened
¼ cup sugar
1¼ cups all-purpose flour
⅛ teaspoon salt
Powdered sugar

Cream butter and sugar until light and fluffy; add flour and salt, mixing well. Pat into a 9-inch square pan lined with waxed paper (or roll into 1-inch balls and press down lightly for cookies).
Bake at 325° about 20 minutes or until lightly browned. Let cool in pan. Dust with powdered sugar. Break shortbread into pieces, or cut into squares. Yield: 16 squares.

Oven-Fried Apple Rings

2 Winesap apples, peeled and cored
2 to 3 tablespoons butter or margarine
2 tablespoons sugar
2 tablespoons brown sugar
½ teaspoon ground cinnamon
⅛ teaspoon ground nutmeg
Fresh mint sprigs

Slice apples into rings. Place half in a shallow baking dish. Dot with 1 tablespoon butter. Combine sugar and seasonings; sprinkle half over apples. Repeat layers. Bake at 350° for 45 to 55 minutes or until apples are tender. Garnish with mint. Yield: 2 servings.

Grilled Bananas

2 slightly underripe bananas, unpeeled
Toppings (choices follow)

Lay bananas on flattest side. Carefully slit skin the length of banana, and loosen. Spoon in choice of topping; carefully close skin. Cook on grill 15 minutes. Yield: 2 servings.

Toppings:

Choose from the following: honey combined with ginger and brandy to taste; orange marmalade; or brown sugar combined with curry powder to taste.

Baked Cranberries

1 cup cranberries
½ cup water
½ cup plus 1 tablespoon sugar
¼ teaspoon ground cinnamon
¼ cup walnuts, chopped

Sort and wash cranberries. Combine cranberries, water, and sugar in a shallow 1-quart casserole. Cover and bake at 400° for 15 minutes. Remove from oven, and sprinkle with cinnamon (do not stir). Return to oven, and bake an additional 15 minutes. Sprinkle with walnuts. May be served hot or cold. Yield: 2 servings.

Fruit-Filled Grapefruit

1 large grapefruit, halved
¼ cup whipping cream, whipped
¼ cup commercial sour cream
1 cup orange sections, seeded
½ cup flaked coconut
½ cup miniature marshmallows

Remove sections and membrane from grapefruit shells. Place shells in ice water to keep firm. Combine grapefruit sections and remaining ingredients; chill several hours. Drain grapefruit shells, and fill with fruit mixture. Yield: 2 servings.

Pears in Caramel Cream

2 firm pears, peeled, cored, and quartered
¼ cup sugar
1 tablespoon butter or margarine
⅓ cup whipping cream

Place pears in a buttered shallow baking pan; sprinkle with sugar, and dot with butter. Bake at 475° for 15 minutes or until sugar turns brown; baste several times. Pour cream over pears, stirring gently. Bake 2 additional minutes. Serve warm. Yield: 2 servings.

Baked Custard

2 eggs, slightly beaten
3 tablespoons sugar
⅛ teaspoon salt
1½ teaspoons vanilla extract
Dash of ground nutmeg
1½ cups milk, scalded
Ground nutmeg

Combine all ingredients except milk, stirring until blended. Gradually add scalded milk, stirring constantly. Pour mixture into two 10-ounce custard cups. Sprinkle with nutmeg. Set custard cups in a 9-inch square pan; pour hot water into pan to a depth of 1 inch. Bake at 350° for 45 minutes or until knife inserted in center comes out clean. Remove custard cups from water, and cool. Chill thoroughly. Yield: 2 servings.

Old-Fashioned Rice Pudding

1 cup cooked rice
1 cup milk
2½ tablespoons sugar
Dash of salt
1 tablespoon butter or margarine
¼ teaspoon vanilla extract

Combine rice, milk, sugar, salt, and butter in a medium saucepan. Cook over medium heat until thickened (about 20 minutes), stirring often. Add vanilla. Spoon into serving dishes. Serve hot or cold. Yield: 2 servings.

Variations: For an extra touch, top rice pudding with whipped cream, fruit preserves, chocolate candy, or diced fruit.

Mocha-Mallow Parfaits

12 large marshmallows
½ cup water
1½ teaspoons instant coffee granules
½ cup whipping cream, whipped
¼ cup chocolate wafer crumbs

Combine marshmallows, water, and coffee granules in a small saucepan; cook over medium heat until marshmallows are melted, stirring occasionally. Cool mixture thoroughly. Fold in whipped cream. (Chill until slightly thickened if mixture is thin.) Alternate layers of coffee mixture and wafer crumbs in parfait glasses, beginning and ending with coffee mixture. Place the parfaits in the refrigerator to chill until serving time. Yield: 2 servings.

Hot Water Pastry

2 cups all-purpose flour
½ teaspoon baking powder
1 teaspoon salt
⅓ cup boiling water
⅔ cup shortening

Combine flour, baking powder, and salt. Pour boiling water over shortening, and beat until creamy. Add flour mixture, stirring until well mixed. Shape dough into a ball; chill. Yield: pastry for 2 single-crust 9-inch pies.

Basic Pastry

2 cups all-purpose flour
1 teaspoon salt
⅔ cup plus 2 tablespoons shortening
4 to 6 tablespoons cold water

Combine flour and salt; cut in shortening with pastry blender until mixture resembles coarse meal. Sprinkle cold water evenly over surface; stir with a fork until all dry ingredients are moistened. Shape dough into a ball; chill. Yield: pastry for double-crust 9-inch pie or 6 tart shells.

Graham Cracker Crust

2½ cups graham cracker crumbs
2 tablespoons light brown sugar
¼ cup ground pecans
½ cup butter or margarine, softened

Combine graham cracker crumbs, sugar, and pecans; stir in butter, and mix well. Press mixture firmly and evenly into a 9-inch pieplate. Bake at 350° for 12 to 15 minutes. Yield: one 9-inch graham cracker crust.

Fudge Pie

2 (1-ounce) squares unsweetened
    chocolate
½ cup butter or margarine
2 eggs, well beaten
1 cup sugar
¼ cup all-purpose flour
Vanilla ice cream (optional)

Melt chocolate and butter over medium
heat. Combine eggs, sugar, and flour; stir
into chocolate mixture. Pour into an 8-inch
piepan. Bake at 350° for 20 to 25 minutes.
(Center of pie will be soft.) Serve hot with
vanilla ice cream, if desired. Yield: one 8-
inch pie.

Chocolate Refrigerator Pie

2 (1-ounce) squares unsweetened
    chocolate
¾ cup sugar
Dash of salt
¼ cup plus 1 tablespoon all-purpose
    flour
1 (13-ounce) can evaporated milk,
    divided
2 egg yolks, well beaten
1 cup water
2 cups miniature marshmallows
¼ cup butter or margarine
1 (9-inch) graham cracker crust
1 cup whipping cream
¼ cup sugar
Grated unsweetened chocolate

Melt chocolate squares in top of a double
boiler over boiling water. Add ¾ cup sugar,
salt, flour, and ⅓ cup evaporated milk; mix
well.

Add a small amount of chocolate mixture
to egg yolks, and mix well; add yolk mixture
to remaining hot mixture, mixing well. Stir in
water and remaining evaporated milk. Cook

over boiling water until smooth and thickened, stirring constantly. Remove from heat.
Add marshmallows and butter, stirring until
melted. Allow mixture to cool.

Pour filling into crust. Cover and chill
thoroughly. Combine whipping cream and
¼ cup sugar; beat at high speed of electric
mixer until stiff peaks form. Spread over filling; sprinkle with grated chocolate. Refrigerate until served. Yield: one 9-inch pie.

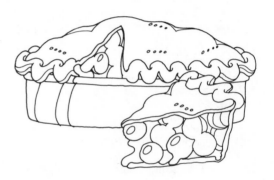

Coconut Meringue Pie

2 eggs, separated
½ cup sugar
¼ cup plus 1 tablespoon all-purpose
    flour
1 cup evaporated milk
1 cup water
1 cup flaked coconut
Dash of salt
1 teaspoon vanilla extract
¼ cup butter or margarine
1 baked 9-inch pastry shell
¼ cup sugar
¼ teaspoon cream of tartar

Beat egg yolks. Combine yolks, ½ cup sugar,
flour, milk, water, coconut, and salt in a
medium saucepan; blend thoroughly. Cook
over medium heat, stirring frequently, until
thickened. Remove from heat; stir in vanilla
and butter. Spoon mixture into pastry shell.

Beat egg whites (at room temperature) until foamy. Gradually add ¼ cup sugar and cream of tartar; continue beating until stiff peaks form. Spread meringue over filling, sealing to edge of pastry. Bake at 400° about 10 minutes or until lightly browned. Cool. Refrigerate until serving time. Yield: one 9-inch pie.

Luscious Lemon Meringue Pie

1½ cups sugar
¼ cup plus 2 tablespoons cornstarch
¼ teaspoon salt
½ cup cold water
½ cup fresh lemon juice
3 egg yolks, well beaten
2 tablespoons butter or margarine
1½ cups boiling water
1 teaspoon grated lemon rind
Few drops yellow food coloring
1 baked 9-inch pastry shell
Meringue

Mix sugar, cornstarch, and salt in a 2- or 3-quart saucepan using a wire whisk. Gradually stir in cold water, then lemon juice, blending until smooth. Add egg yolks, blending thoroughly. Add butter. Add boiling water gradually, stirring constantly with a wooden spoon. Slowly bring mixture to a boil, stirring gently and constantly over medium heat. Reduce heat slightly as mixture begins to thicken. Boil slowly for 1 minute. Remove from heat and stir in grated rind and food coloring. Pour hot filling into baked pastry shell. Let stand, allowing a thin film to form while preparing the Meringue. Yield: one 9-inch pie.

Meringue:

3 egg whites
¼ teaspoon cream of tartar
¼ cup plus 2 tablespoons sugar

Beat egg whites (at room temperature) in a small, deep bowl with electric mixer. Beat until frothy; add cream of tartar. Beat at high speed until soft peaks form. Reduce speed to medium, and gradually add sugar, 1 tablespoon at a time. Beat at high speed until stiff peaks form.

Mound meringue on hot filling around edge of pie. Using a narrow spatula, push meringue gently against inner edge of pastry shell, sealing well. Cover remaining filling by swirling meringue from edge of pie to center, forming decorative peaks. Bake at 350° for 12 to 15 minutes or until golden brown. Cool on wire rack at room temperature away from drafts for 2 hours before serving. Use a sharp knife and dip into hot water after each cut for a "clean cut" serving. Yield: enough for one 9-inch pie.

Whipped Lemon Pie

⅔ cup water
⅓ cup lemon juice
1 (3-ounce) package lemon-flavored gelatin
½ cup sugar
1 teaspoon grated lemon rind
1 cup evaporated milk
2 tablespoons lemon juice
1 (9-inch) graham cracker crust

Combine water and ⅓ cup lemon juice in a small saucepan; bring to a boil. Remove from heat; add gelatin and sugar, stirring until dissolved. Stir in lemon rind. Chill until consistency of unbeaten egg white.

Place evaporated milk in freezer about 15 to 20 minutes or until ice crystals form around edges; beat at high speed of electric mixer about 1 minute or until stiff. Add 2 tablespoons lemon juice; beat about 2 minutes or until very stiff. Fold into gelatin. Spoon mixture into crust. Chill several hours or until set. Yield: one 9-inch pie.

Sweet Potato Pie

2 cups cooked, mashed sweet potatoes
1 egg, slightly beaten
¼ cup sugar
¼ cup milk
2 tablespoons butter or margarine, melted
1 teaspoon ground cinnamon
1 unbaked 9-inch pastry shell

Combine first 6 ingredients, and beat at medium speed of electric mixer until well blended. Spoon into pastry shell. Bake at 425° for 35 minutes or until knife inserted comes out clean; cool. Yield: one 9-inch pie.

Grasshopper Tarts

½ cup chocolate wafer crumbs
2 tablespoons butter or margarine, melted
1 cup marshmallow creme
1 tablespoon green crème de menthe
1 tablespoon white crème de cacao
½ cup whipping cream, whipped

Combine wafer crumbs and butter, stirring well; press firmly into bottom of two 5-inch tart pans.

Combine marshmallow creme and liqueur in a small mixing bowl; beat 1 minute at high speed of electric mixer. Fold in whipped cream; spoon mixture into crusts. Freeze. Yield: two 5-inch tarts.

Brandied Peach Coffee

2 tablespoons instant coffee granules, divided
2½ cups cold water, divided
2 tablespoons peach brandy
2 scoops peach ice cream
Whipped cream
2 maraschino cherries

Place 2½ teaspoons coffee granules in each of two 10-ounce glasses. Set aside remaining coffee granules. To each glass add ½ cup water, stirring until coffee dissolves, and stir in ¾ cup water. Stir into each glass 1 tablespoon brandy; add 1 scoop ice cream. Top each with whipped cream, ½ teaspoon coffee granules, and a cherry. Yield: 2 servings.

Brandied Chocolate Fondue

1½ teaspoons cornstarch
1 tablespoon half-and-half
1½ teaspoons vegetable oil
½ teaspoon instant coffee granules
Dash of ground cinnamon
½ cup milk
½ cup semisweet chocolate morsels
1 tablespoon brandy
Pound cake, cut into 1-inch squares
Marshmallows
Apples, cubed (or strawberries)

Combine cornstarch, half-and-half, and oil in top of a double boiler. Blend in coffee granules, cinnamon, and milk. Cook over medium heat, stirring constantly, until slightly thickened. Add chocolate morsels and brandy. Cook, stirring constantly, until smooth.

Transfer to a fondue pot; keep warm while serving. Dip pound cake squares, marshmallows, and apple cubes into chocolate. Yield: about 1 cup.

Page 183: *Choose your favorite dessert from Summer Fruits and Cream (page 49), Pots de Crème (page 87), or Orange Cheesecake (page 173).*

Page 184: *A colorful and delicious fresh vegetable sauce makes a difference in these Baked Fish Fillets (page 185).*

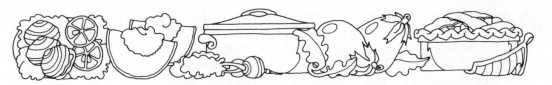

FISH AND SHELLFISH

Baked Fish in Tomato Sauce

½ cup chopped onion
¼ cup chopped celery
¼ cup chopped parsley
1 pound fish fillets
½ teaspoon salt
⅛ teaspoon pepper
2 tablespoons vegetable oil
¼ to ½ teaspoon paprika or red pepper
1 (8-ounce) can tomato sauce

Combine onion, celery, and parsley. Place in a greased 12- × 8- × 2-inch baking dish.

Sprinkle each fillet with salt and pepper; arrange over vegetables. Pour oil over fish, and sprinkle with paprika. Bake at 375° for 10 minutes.

Pour tomato sauce over fish, and bake 30 minutes longer or until fish flakes easily when tested with a fork. Yield: 2 servings.

Baked Fish Fillets

2 (8- to 10-ounce) fish fillets
3 fresh mushrooms, sliced
1 tablespoon butter or margarine
2 medium-size ripe tomatoes, peeled and coarsely chopped
1 small onion, sliced
½ medium carrot, sliced
1 tablespoon chopped chives
1 tablespoon dried basil leaves
1 small clove garlic, crushed
½ teaspoon salt
¼ teaspoon pepper

Dry fillets thoroughly; set aside.

Sauté mushrooms in butter 3 minutes; add remaining ingredients, and simmer 10 minutes. Pour half of sauce in a lightly buttered baking dish; add fillets and top with remaining sauce.

Bake at 350° about 20 minutes or until fish flakes easily when tested with a fork. Yield: 2 servings.

Broiled Fish Puff

1 pound fish fillets
1 tablespoon butter or margarine, melted
1 tablespoon lemon juice
½ teaspoon salt
Dash of pepper
¼ cup mayonnaise or salad dressing
2 tablespoons sweet pickle relish
1½ tablespoons chopped parsley
1½ tablespoons minced pimiento
2 teaspoons minced onion
1 egg white, stiffly beaten

Dry fillets thoroughly; arrange on a shallow heatproof platter. Combine butter and lemon juice; drizzle over fish, and sprinkle with salt and pepper. Broil 3 inches from heat 10 to 12 minutes.

Combine remaining ingredients except egg white; fold mixture into beaten egg white. Spread egg white mixture evenly over fish. Broil 1 minute or until golden brown. Yield: 2 servings.

Steamed Fish Fillets

¾ pound fish fillets
Soy sauce to taste
⅓ cup sliced green onion
¼ cup very hot peanut oil
Lemon juice (optional)

Place fish on a rack above boiling water; cover and steam 2 to 3 minutes on each side or until fish turns white. Place fillets in a heatproof serving dish; sprinkle with soy sauce and onion. Pour hot oil over fish. When sizzling stops, serve immediately. Sprinkle with lemon juice, if desired. Yield: 2 servings.

Note: Have everything ready for this dish before starting, as it only takes about 5 minutes to prepare.

Fried Fish

1 pound fish fillets
½ teaspoon salt
Pepper
1 egg, beaten
2 tablespoons water
¼ teaspoon prepared mustard
⅛ teaspoon onion powder
1¼ cups cracker crumbs
¼ cup butter or margarine

Dry fish thoroughly, and cut into serving-size portions. Sprinkle both sides with salt and pepper. Combine egg, water, mustard, and onion powder.

Dip both sides of fish into egg mixture, and coat with cracker crumbs; repeat process.

Fry fish in melted butter over low heat until golden brown on both sides. Drain on paper towels. Yield: about 2 servings.

Use fish as an economical dish. It has very little waste. A pound of fish, dressed or filleted, will yield two full size servings.

Crunchy Fried Fillets

Salt
1 pound frozen perch fillets, thawed
All-purpose flour
1 egg, beaten
3 tablespoons water
25 to 30 saltine crackers, crushed
Vegetable oil

Lightly salt fillets; dredge each in flour. Beat egg and water; dip floured fillets in egg mixture. Coat well with cracker crumbs, pressing crumbs into fish. Fry fillets in hot oil over medium heat until browned. Drain on absorbent paper. Yield: about 2 servings.

Oven-Fried Fish Fillets

1 pound sole or flounder fillets
¼ cup mayonnaise
Breadcrumbs
Paprika
½ teaspoon salt
¼ teaspoon pepper
Lemon wedges

Thinly coat fish fillets with mayonnaise; dredge each in breadcrumbs. Arrange in a greased 13- × 9- × 2-inch baking pan; sprinkle fillets with seasonings.

Bake at 450° for about 12 minutes or until fish flakes easily when tested with a fork. Garnish fillets with lemon wedges. Yield: 2 servings.

Fried Catfish

3 small catfish, cleaned and dressed
½ teaspoon salt
⅛ teaspoon pepper
½ (2-ounce) bottle hot sauce
1 cup self-rising cornmeal
Vegetable oil

Sprinkle catfish with salt and pepper. Marinate fish in hot sauce for 1 to 2 hours in the refrigerator.

Place cornmeal in a paper bag; drop in catfish one at a time, and shake until coated completely. Fry in deep hot oil over high heat until fish float to the top and are golden brown; drain fish well. Serve hot. Yield: 2 servings.

Fried Flounder

1 cup all-purpose flour
1½ teaspoons instant minced onion
1 teaspoon salt
½ teaspoon pepper
1 (16-ounce) package frozen flounder
  fillets, thawed
1 tablespoon onion juice
Vegetable oil

Combine flour, minced onion, salt, and pepper; mix well. Sprinkle fish with onion juice, and coat well with flour mixture. Fry in about ¼ inch hot oil until golden brown, turning once. Yield: 2 servings.

Sherry-Baked Flounder

1 (4-ounce) can sliced mushrooms
2 (8- to 10-ounce) flounder fillets,
  skinned
Seasoned salt
1 slice Swiss cheese, folded in half
1 slice tomato
1 small onion, sliced
1 tablespoon butter or margarine
2½ teaspoons all-purpose flour
½ teaspoon seasoned salt
½ cup half-and-half
3 tablespoons dry sherry
Hot cooked rice

Drain mushrooms, reserving liquid. Add enough water to liquid to make ⅓ cup; set aside.

Sprinkle fillets on all sides with seasoned salt; starting at wide end, roll up each fillet. Place, seam side down, in a greased 9-inch square baking dish. Place cheese and tomato slice between the rolls; set aside.

Sauté onion and mushrooms in butter until golden. Stir in flour, ½ teaspoon seasoned salt, half-and-half, mushroom liquid, and sherry. Bring to a boil; cook until thickened, and pour over fish. Bake at 400° for 20 minutes or until fish flakes easily when tested with a fork. Serve with hot cooked rice. Yield: 2 servings.

Codfish Casseroles

1 (16-ounce) package frozen cod fillets,
  slightly thawed
2 to 3 tablespoons lemon juice
¼ cup butter or margarine, melted and
  divided
½ teaspoon salt
¼ teaspoon pepper
3 tablespoons dry breadcrumbs
Minced parsley
Lemon wedges (optional)
Pimiento strips (optional)

Cut fish into 1-inch cubes, and place in 2 well-greased individual casseroles. Combine lemon juice and 2 tablespoons melted butter; drizzle half over each casserole, and sprinkle with salt and pepper. Bake at 450° for 20 minutes or until fish flakes easily.

Combine breadcrumbs and remaining 2 tablespoons melted butter, tossing lightly. Sprinkle breadcrumbs and parsley over fish. Garnish with lemon and pimiento, if desired. Yield: 2 servings.

If soups, stews, or other foods are too salty, add a teaspoon of vinegar and a teaspoon of sugar and reheat.

Baked Mackerel

2 to 3 mackerel fillets
Seasoned salt
Pepper
Butter or margarine
½ cup butter or margarine
Juice of 3 lemons
1 to 2 tablespoons Worcestershire sauce

Sprinkle fillets with seasoned salt and pepper; dot with butter. Arrange in a greased 12-× 8- × 2-inch baking dish. Bake at 350° for 10 minutes. Place under broiler to lightly brown fillets.

Combine ½ cup butter, lemon juice, and Worcestershire sauce in a small saucepan. Place over low heat until butter melts. Pour sauce over fillets; continue baking at 350° for 20 to 30 minutes or until fish flakes easily when tested with a fork. Yield: 2 servings.

Salmon and Cheese Casserole

1 (7¾-ounce) can red salmon, drained and flaked
¼ cup chopped celery
1 tablespoon chopped green onion or snipped chives
3 tablespoons commercial sour cream
¼ teaspoon dry mustard
¼ teaspoon salt
1 cup (4 ounces) shredded Swiss cheese, divided

Combine first 6 ingredients; stir in ¾ cup cheese. Spoon into two greased 1-cup baking dishes; sprinkle with remaining cheese.

Place casseroles on a baking sheet; bake at 350° for 20 minutes. Yield: 2 servings.

For just a squirt of lemon, poke a hole in one end of the lemon and squeeze.

Tuna Florentine

1 (10-ounce) package frozen chopped spinach
3 tablespoons butter or margarine
3 tablespoons all-purpose flour
1½ cups milk
1 chicken-flavored bouillon cube, crushed
2 tablespoons minced onion
½ teaspoon garlic powder
¼ cup shredded Swiss cheese
1 (3-ounce) can chopped mushrooms, drained
1 (7-ounce) can tuna, drained
Salt and pepper to taste

Cook spinach according to package directions; drain, and set aside.

Melt butter over low heat; blend in flour. Add milk, bouillon cube, onion, garlic powder, and cheese; cook until thickened, stirring constantly. Add mushrooms and tuna, mixing well. Season to taste; serve over spinach. Yield: 2 servings.

Tuna Casserole

1 small onion, chopped
½ small green pepper, chopped
1½ tablespoons butter or margarine
¼ cup all-purpose flour
1½ cups milk
½ teaspoon salt
Dash of pepper
1 (7-ounce) can solid-pack light tuna in oil, drained and flaked
½ cup biscuit mix
2 tablespoons cold water
¼ cup shredded Cheddar cheese

Sauté onion and green pepper in butter until vegetables are tender. Blend in flour, and cook over low heat until bubbly. Gradually add milk; cook until smooth and thickened, stirring constantly. Stir in salt, pepper, and tuna. Spoon mixture into a lightly greased 1-quart casserole.

Combine biscuit mix and water. Mix with a fork until a soft dough forms; beat vigorously 20 strokes.

Smooth dough into a ball on a lightly floured board; knead 5 times. Roll to ¼-inch thickness, and sprinkle with cheese. Roll dough up jellyroll fashion, and cut into 4 slices. Place on tuna mixture. Bake at 325° for 30 to 40 minutes or until lightly browned. Yield: 2 servings.

Spaghetti with Clam Sauce

⅓ cup olive oil
3 to 4 cloves garlic, crushed
¼ cup chopped parsley
1 (8-ounce) can minced clams
Salt and pepper to taste
Hot cooked spaghetti or linguine

Heat olive oil in a heavy saucepan; add garlic, and sauté 1 minute. Add parsley, and sauté 2 minutes.

Drain clams, reserving juice. Add clam juice to saucepan, and cook until juice is reduced by half (10 to 15 minutes). Add clams and heat through. Season with salt and pepper. Serve over cooked spaghetti. Yield: 2 servings.

Broiled Crab and Shrimp

1 (6-ounce) package frozen crab and shrimp, thawed and drained
2 tablespoons mayonnaise
2 tablespoons plain yogurt
1 tablespoon minced fresh parsley
1 teaspoon instant minced onion
¼ teaspoon salt
⅛ teaspoon curry powder
⅛ teaspoon white pepper

Combine all ingredients, mixing well. Spoon mixture into two (6-ounce) ovenproof dishes. Broil 4 to 5 minutes. Yield: 2 servings.

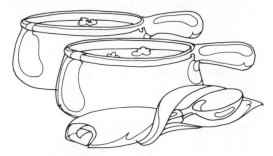

Crab Claws

1½ quarts water
3 tablespoons salt
Crab boil (optional)
1½ pounds fresh crab claws
½ cup minced green onion
¼ cup minced parsley
1 stalk celery, minced
2 cloves garlic, crushed
½ cup olive oil
¼ cup tarragon vinegar
1 tablespoon lemon juice
French bread

Combine water and salt in a Dutch oven; add crab boil according to package directions, if desired. Bring water to a boil; add crab claws. Cover and return to boiling point. Reduce heat, and simmer 5 to 7 minutes or until crab claws are bright red.

Drain; let cool long enough to handle. Remove shell from large portion of crab claw. Place crab claws in a large shallow baking dish.

Combine remaining ingredients except French bread in a jar; shake well. Pour marinade over crab claws. Cover tightly, and chill 4 to 5 hours.

Remove crab claws from marinade, reserving marinade. Serve claws with French bread; use marinade as a dipping sauce for claws and bread. Yield: 2 servings.

Crab Cakes

1 (6-ounce) package frozen crabmeat, thawed, drained, and flaked or 1 (6½-ounce) can crabmeat, drained and flaked
½ cup seasoned breadcrumbs
2 tablespoons butter or margarine, melted
1 egg, slightly beaten
½ carrot, scraped and grated
¾ teaspoon chopped parsley
1 teaspoon mayonnaise
¾ teaspoon Worcestershire sauce
½ teaspoon salt
¼ teaspoon dry mustard
⅛ teaspoon pepper
1 egg, slightly beaten
1 tablespoon water
½ cup dry breadcrumbs
2 tablespoons butter or margarine

Combine first 11 ingredients; stir well. Shape into ½-inch-thick patties (mixture will be slightly loose). Cover and chill mixture for 1 hour.

Combine 1 egg and water; beat well. Dip patties in egg mixture; dredge in breadcrumbs. Sauté crab cakes in butter, turning once, until golden brown. Drain on paper towels. Yield: 2 servings.

Baked Crab and Avocado

1 tablespoon minced green onion
1½ tablespoons butter or margarine
1½ tablespoons all-purpose flour
¼ cup milk
1 (6-ounce) package frozen crabmeat, thawed, drained, and flaked
2 teaspoons lemon juice
½ teaspoon salt
1 avocado

Sauté onion in butter until tender. Blend in

flour; cook over low heat until bubbly, stirring constantly. Add milk; cook, stirring constantly, until thickened. Stir in crabmeat, lemon juice, and salt; set aside.

Cut avocado in half; carefully remove pulp to within ¼ inch of edges, reserving shells. Chop pulp. Stir into crabmeat mixture. Spoon crabmeat mixture into shells. Bake at 325° for 20 minutes. Yield: 2 servings.

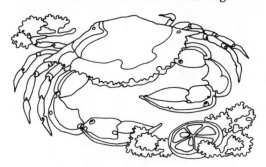

Creamed Crab in Patty Shells

1 (3-ounce) can sliced mushrooms
1 tablespoon butter or margarine
1 tablespoon plus 1 teaspoon all-purpose flour
2 drops hot sauce
⅔ cup evaporated milk
¼ cup shredded process American cheese
1 tablespoon chili sauce
1 (6-ounce) package frozen lump crabmeat, thawed and drained
2 to 4 baked patty shells

Drain mushrooms, reserving liquid. Melt butter in a saucepan over medium heat; blend in flour. Add water to mushroom liquid to make ¼ cup; gradually add liquid, hot sauce, and milk to flour mixture. Cook until thickened, stirring constantly.

Stir in cheese until melted. Add chili sauce, mushrooms, and crabmeat; heat until hot but not boiling. Serve in patty shells. Yield: 2 servings.

Crab Casserole

¼ cup butter or margarine, divided
¾ cup breadcrumbs, divided
⅓ cup half-and-half
1 egg, beaten
1½ teaspoons chopped fresh parsley
¾ teaspoon dry mustard
¼ teaspoon salt
Dash of pepper
½ pound fresh or thawed frozen
    crabmeat

Melt 3 tablespoons butter in a medium saucepan. Add ½ cup breadcrumbs and half-and-half; cook until slightly thickened, stirring constantly. Add egg, parsley, mustard, salt, and pepper; remove from heat. Stir in crabmeat.

Pour mixture into a greased 1-quart casserole. Melt remaining 1 tablespoon butter, and stir in remaining breadcrumbs; sprinkle over casserole. Bake at 350° for 30 minutes. Yield: about 2 servings.

Sherried Crab with Noodles

1 (3-ounce) can mushroom caps
1 tablespoon butter or margarine
½ cup finely chopped onion
¼ cup finely sliced celery
1 tablespoon all-purpose flour
½ cup commercial sour cream
¼ teaspoon salt
Dash of pepper
1 (6-ounce) package frozen crabmeat,
    thawed and drained
¼ cup sherry
Butter or margarine
½ (8-ounce) package spinach noodles,
    cooked

Drain mushrooms, reserving liquid; set aside. Melt butter in a small saucepan. Add onion and celery; sauté over low heat 4 minutes. Add mushrooms and flour, and stir until flour is well blended.

Combine sour cream and reserved mushroom liquid, stirring well. Add sour cream mixture, salt, and pepper to vegetable mixture, stirring well. Add crabmeat and sherry; cook over low heat 5 minutes.

Butter spinach noodles generously, and arrange on a serving platter. Spoon crabmeat mixture over noodles. Yield: 2 servings.

Baked Oysters

2 dozen freshly shucked oysters in half
    shells
2 cloves garlic, minced
¼ cup butter or margarine, softened
2 tablespoons dry white wine
2 to 4 tablespoons fine dry breadcrumbs
2 teaspoons Worcestershire sauce
Grated Parmesan cheese

Arrange oysters on a heatproof tray. Combine garlic, butter, wine, breadcrumbs, and Worcestershire sauce to make a paste. Cover oysters with paste. Sprinkle a heavy layer of Parmesan cheese over the paste-topped oysters. Bake at 350° about 10 minutes or until cheese is brown. Yield: 2 servings.

Bacon-Wrapped Fried Oysters

2 eggs, beaten
¼ cup milk
2 dozen fresh oysters, drained
About 1 cup cracker meal
12 bacon strips, cut in half
Vegetable oil

Combine eggs and milk in a shallow dish. Dip oysters in egg mixture, then in cracker meal; repeat process. Wrap each oyster with bacon; secure with a wooden pick. Fry in shallow hot oil until golden. Drain on paper towels. Yield: 2 dozen.

Barbecued Oysters

1 dozen oysters
3 tablespoons oyster liquid
2 tablespoons tomato paste
1 tablespoon chili sauce
1 tablespoon lemon juice
½ teaspoon Worcestershire sauce
¼ teaspoon prepared horseradish
⅛ teaspoon onion salt
Dash of salt
3 tablespoons bacon-flavored cracker
  crumbs

Place oysters in a single layer in a shallow baking dish. Combine oyster liquid, tomato paste, chili sauce, lemon juice, Worcestershire sauce, horseradish, and salt in a saucepan; cook over medium heat 20 minutes.

Pour sauce over oysters; prick oysters with a fork to allow sauce to penetrate. Sprinkle with cracker crumbs. Bake at 350° for 25 minutes. Yield: 2 servings.

Crumb-Topped Oysters

1 dozen unshucked oysters
½ cup herb-seasoned stuffing mix,
  crushed
¼ cup minced parsley
⅛ teaspoon salt
Dash of pepper
Dash of ground mace
½ teaspoon Worcestershire sauce
2 drops hot sauce
2 tablespoons butter or margarine,
  melted
1 tablespoon lemon juice
2 slices bacon, cooked and crumbled
1 tablespoon chopped pimiento

Wash and rinse oysters thoroughly in cold water. Shuck oysters, reserving deep half of shells; place oysters in colander to drain. Set aside.

Combine stuffing mix, parsley, seasonings, Worcestershire sauce, and hot sauce in a medium saucepan; place over medium heat, and gradually add melted butter. Stir until mixture is moistened.

Place oysters in shells; arrange in a shallow roasting pan lined with crumpled foil. Spoon lemon juice over each oyster; cover with 1 tablespoon stuffing mixture. Sprinkle with bacon and pimiento. Bake at 500° for 3 to 5 minutes or until edges of oysters begin to curl. Serve hot. Yield: 2 servings.

Sauteed Scallops

¼ cup all-purpose flour
½ teaspoon salt
Dash of pepper
⅔ pound scallops
¼ cup milk
2 tablespoons butter or margarine
⅛ teaspoon lemon juice

Combine flour, salt, and pepper in a shallow dish. Dip scallops in milk; coat with flour mixture. Melt butter with lemon juice; sauté scallops in butter mixture until lightly browned (about 5 to 7 minutes). Yield: about 2 servings.

Baked Scallops

3 tablespoons soy sauce
2 tablespoons wine vinegar
2 teaspoons sugar
½ teaspoon ground ginger
½ clove garlic, pressed
½ teaspoon grated lime rind
⅔ pound scallops

Combine all ingredients except scallops, mixing well. Place scallops in an 8-inch square baking dish; pour marinade over scallops; turn to coat scallops with marinade.

Refrigerate at least 1 hour, spooning marinade over scallops frequently. Bake at 400° for 10 minutes. Yield: 2 servings.

Grilled Scallops

1 pound fresh scallops
3 tablespoons butter or margarine, melted
2 teaspoons lime juice
1 teaspoon salt
⅛ teaspoon ground thyme or oregano
⅛ teaspoon pepper
1 to 2 drops hot sauce
¼ pound sliced bacon, cut in half crosswise and lengthwise

Place scallops in a bowl. Combine remaining ingredients except bacon; pour over scallops. Cover and marinate in refrigerator 30 minutes to 1 hour. Drain well, reserving marinade.

Wrap 1 strip bacon around each scallop, and thread on skewers. Place skewers on grill 4 inches from medium heat. Cook until bacon is done, basting with marinade and turning occasionally. Yield: 2 servings.

Scallops Florentine

¾ pound scallops
2 tablespoons butter or margarine
¾ cup milk
¼ cup dry white wine
2 tablespoons chopped green onion
2 teaspoons cornstarch
1 (10-ounce) package frozen chopped spinach, thawed and well drained
Shredded mozzarella cheese

Combine scallops, butter, milk, wine, and onion in a saucepan; cook over low heat 10 minutes. Combine cornstarch and a small amount of hot liquid; mix until smooth, and stir into hot mixture. Cook until slightly thickened, stirring constantly (do not boil).

Spoon spinach into a 1-quart greased casserole. Pour scallop mixture over spinach, and sprinkle with cheese. Bake at 350° about 10 minutes or until bubbly. Yield: about 2 servings.

Cold Marinated Scallops

½ pound scallops, cut into bite-size pieces
1 tablespoon butter or margarine
¼ cup vegetable oil
1 egg yolk, beaten
1 tablespoon instant minced onion
1 tablespoon chopped fresh parsley
1½ teaspoons chopped chives
1 tablespoon lemon juice
1 tablespoon commercial sour cream
½ teaspoon dried dillweed
½ teaspoon lemon pepper
½ teaspoon Dijon mustard
¼ teaspoon dried tarragon leaves
¼ teaspoon salt
¼ teaspoon anchovy paste
2 tablespoons diced pimiento
2 stalks celery, chopped
Parsley sprigs
Cherry tomatoes

Sauté scallops in butter 2 minutes; cool, drain, and spoon into a shallow dish. Combine remaining ingredients except parsley sprigs and tomatoes; stir well, and pour over scallops. Cover and chill overnight.

Spoon scallops onto a serving plate; garnish with parsley sprigs and tomatoes. Yield: 2 generous servings.

Keep herbs and spices in alphabetical order for convenience. If a spice does not have a strong, clear aroma as soon as you open the container, it is time to replace it.

Broiled Butterfly Shrimp

1 pound large fresh shrimp, peeled and deveined
Salt to taste
Lemon pepper to taste
Paprika
½ cup butter or margarine, melted
½ cup lemon juice
Toast points

Butterfly shrimp by cutting along outside curve almost through; flatten. Place cut side down in a shallow pan; sprinkle with salt, lemon pepper, and a generous amount of paprika. Pour melted butter over shrimp. Bake at 350° for 8 minutes.

Pour lemon juice over shrimp. Broil 5 minutes. Spoon shrimp over toast points; serve with the lemon-butter liquid. Yield: 2 servings.

New Orleans Barbecued Shrimp

1 pound large fresh shrimp
¼ cup butter or margarine
1½ tablespoons olive oil
1 tablespoon chili sauce
2 teaspoons Worcestershire sauce
2 teaspoons lemon juice
½ lemon, thinly sliced
1 clove garlic, minced
1 teaspoon minced fresh parsley
½ teaspoon red pepper
¼ teaspoon ground oregano
⅛ teaspoon hot pepper sauce
French bread

Wash shrimp well. Split shell down the back; peel and devein; Pat dry and place in a heavy plastic bag. Combine remaining ingredients except French bread in a small pan. Simmer 10 minutes. Cool; pour over shrimp

and mix thoroughly. Refrigerate and allow to marinate 2 to 8 hours, turning bag several times to coat shrimp with marinade.

Preheat oven to 300°. Arrange shrimp and marinade in a shallow pan. Bake until just pink (about 15 or 20 minutes). Do not overbake. Serve in soup bowls with chunks of French bread to soak up the sauce. Yield: 2 servings.

Boiled Shrimp in Beer

1 quart water
2 cups stale beer
¼ cup pickling spice
1 small onion, sliced
½ lemon, sliced
2 tablespoons salt
1 pound large fresh shrimp, peeled and deveined

Combine first 6 ingredients in a Dutch oven; bring to a boil. Add shrimp, and return to a boil. Cover and cook 1 minute. Remove from heat and allow shrimp to steam 10 minutes. Drain shrimp. Serve hot or cold with cocktail sauce. Yield: 2 servings.

Grilled Shrimp

½ cup orange juice
¼ cup vinegar
¼ cup vegetable oil
¼ cup soy sauce
½ teaspoon salt
¾ pound fresh shrimp, peeled and deveined
Lemon wedges

Combine first 5 ingredients; add shrimp, and marinate several hours. Alternate shrimp and lemon wedges on skewers. Grill over medium coals 3 to 4 minutes or until done, basting frequently with marinade.

Heat remaining marinade, and serve with the shrimp. Yield: 2 servings.

Batter Fried Shrimp

1 pound fresh shrimp
½ cup all-purpose flour
¼ teaspoon sugar
¼ teaspoon salt
1 egg, slightly beaten
½ cup cold water
1 tablespoon vegetable oil
Vegetable oil

Peel shrimp, leaving the last section of shell and tail intact. Butterfly shrimp by cutting along outside curve almost through; remove vein. Flatten shrimp, and set aside.

Combine flour, sugar, salt, egg, water, and 1 tablespoon oil; beat until smooth.

Dip shrimp into batter, and fry in deep hot oil until golden. Yield: 2 servings.

Cold Pickled Shrimp

3 cups water
1 pound shrimp
Bay leaves
3 small onions, thinly sliced
½ cup olive oil
2 tablespoons tarragon vinegar
1 tablespoon pickling spice
1 teaspoon salt
¼ teaspoon dry mustard
Dash of red pepper
Cherry tomatoes
Parsley

Bring water to a boil; add shrimp and return to a boil. Lower heat and simmer 3 to 5 minutes. Drain well. Rinse shrimp with cold water; peel and devein, leaving the tails intact.

Place a layer of shrimp in a flat-bottomed container. Place 5 bay leaves on top of shrimp; cover shrimp with a layer of onion slices. Repeat layering until all shrimp are used.

Combine next 6 ingredients, mixing well. Pour marinade over shrimp. Cover; chill 24 hours, stirring mixture occasionally. Remove shrimp from marinade, and arrange in a serving dish. Garnish with cherry tomatoes and parsley. Yield: 2 servings.

Curried Shrimp

1½ cups water
½ pound fresh shrimp
3 tablespoons chopped onion
1 small clove garlic, minced
2 tablespoons chopped green pepper
2 tablespoons butter or margarine
1½ tablespoons all-purpose flour
1 teaspoon curry powder
1 cup half-and-half
2 teaspoons lemon juice
¼ teaspoon salt
Dash of pepper
Dash of ground ginger
Dash of chili powder
Hot cooked rice

Bring water to a boil; add shrimp and return to a boil. Lower heat and simmer 3 to 5 minutes. Drain well; rinse with cold water. Chill. Peel and devein shrimp.

Sauté onion, garlic, and green pepper in butter until vegetables are tender. Add flour and curry powder; cook over low heat until bubbly, stirring constantly. Gradually stir in half-and-half; cook until smooth and thickened, stirring constantly.

Add lemon juice, remaining seasonings, and shrimp to sauce; heat thoroughly. Serve over rice. Yield: 2 servings.

Shrimp and Cheese Casserole

1½ cups water
½ pound fresh shrimp
2 tablespoons butter or margarine
1 tablespoon plus 1½ teaspoons
    all-purpose flour
¾ cup milk
¼ teaspoon salt
Dash of pepper
Dash of paprika
2 tablespoons dry sherry
Grated Parmesan chesse

Bring water to a boil; add shrimp and return to a boil. Lower heat and simmer 3 to 5 minutes. Drain well; rinse with cold water. Peel and devein shrimp.

Melt butter in a heavy saucepan over low heat; add flour, stirring until smooth. Cook 1 minute, stirring constantly. Gradually add milk; cook over medium heat until thickened and bubbly. Stir in salt, pepper, paprika, sherry, and shrimp.

Spoon into two 10-ounce ramekins; sprinkle each with Parmesan cheese. Broil 3 to 4 inches from heat until cheese is lightly browned. Yield: 2 servings.

Shrimp Creole

½ onion, chopped
½ green pepper, chopped
1 stalk celery, chopped
1 clove garlic, crushed
1½ teaspoons vegetable oil
1 (15-ounce) can tomato sauce
1 teaspoon ground oregano
1 bay leaf
1 (8-ounce) package frozen shrimp,
    thawed
Hot cooked rice

Sauté onion, green pepper, celery, and garlic in oil until tender. Add tomato sauce, oregano, and bay leaf; simmer 20 minutes. Stir in shrimp, and simmer 5 minutes. Remove bay leaf before serving over hot cooked rice. Yield: 2 servings.

Sauteed Garlic Shrimp

2 cloves garlic, minced
¼ cup butter or margarine
3 tablespoons lemon juice
2 tablespoons dry vermouth
1 tablespoon soy sauce
2 teaspoons Worcestershire sauce
2 teaspoons tarragon vinegar
Dash of salt
2 drops hot sauce
1 pound shrimp, peeled and deveined
Hot cooked rice

Sauté garlic in butter in a skillet; combine the next 7 ingredients, and gradually add mixture to skillet. Add shrimp; cook 5 minutes or until shrimp are done, stirring frequently; Serve over rice. Yield: 2 to 3 servings.

Shrimp Scampi

¼ cup butter or margarine
1 tablespoon olive oil
12 jumbo shrimp, peeled and deveined
2 cloves garlic, crushed
1 tablespoon chopped parsley
1 tablespoon dry white wine
1½ teaspoons lemon juice
Salt and pepper to taste

Heat butter and olive oil in a medium skillet; add shrimp, and sauté until done (about 5 minutes).

Pour off pan drippings into small saucepan. Add remaining ingredients; cook over high heat 1 minute. Pour sauce over shrimp. Yield: 2 servings.

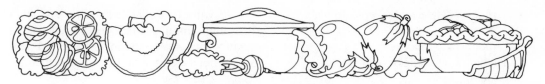

MEATS

Chili with Beef Cubes

1 tablespoon finely chopped beef suet
1 (¾-pound) beef round steak, cut into 1-inch squares
1 medium onion, chopped
2 small tomatoes, peeled and quartered
¼ cup water
1 small clove garlic, crushed
¾ teaspoon dark brown sugar
¾ teaspoon chili powder
¾ teaspoon red wine vinegar
Salt and pepper to taste

Melt suet in a 9-inch skillet; add beef and onion, and cook until meat is browned. Stir in remaining ingredients; cover and simmer 1 to 1½ hours or until meat is tender. Yield: 2 servings.

Everyday Chili

1 cup finely chopped onion
1 clove garlic, minced
1 pound lean ground beef
1 tablespoon vegetable oil
¼ cup boiling water
2 to 3 tablespoons chili powder
1 (16-ounce) can tomatoes, undrained
1 teaspoon salt
1 teaspoon ground oregano
½ teaspoon ground basil
¾ cup water
1 (15-ounce) can kidney beans, undrained

Sauté onion, garlic, and ground beef in hot oil until browned; drain.

Combine ¼ cup boiling water and chili powder. Stir well to dissolve chili. Add tomatoes, salt, oregano, basil, and chili powder mixture to meat mixture. Cover and simmer, about 1 hour, stirring occasionally. Add ¾ cup water and beans to meat mixture. Simmer 25 to 30 minutes longer. Yield: 3 to 4 servings.

Note: Store remaining chili in tightly covered container in refrigerator or package in freezer container and freeze.

Barbecued Hamburgers

⅓ cup catsup
¾ teaspoon Worcestershire sauce
⅛ teaspoon celery salt
Dash of hot sauce
½ pound ground beef
1 tablespoon finely chopped onion
Salt and pepper to taste
2 hamburger buns, split, toasted, and buttered

Combine catsup, Worcestershire sauce, celery salt, and hot sauce in a saucepan; bring to a boil, and set aside.

Combine beef, onion, salt, and pepper. Shape into 2 patties ½ inch thick. Place on grill 3 to 5 inches from coals; cook 3 to 5 minutes on each side or to desired degree of doneness. Baste occasionally with sauce.

Serve on buns with remaining sauce. Yield: 2 servings.

Grilled Cheeseburgers

½ pound ground beef
3 tablespoons quick-cooking oats,
  uncooked
1½ tablespoons finely chopped onion
½ teaspoon salt
Dash of pepper
3 tablespoons tomato juice
2 hamburger buns
2 Cheddar cheese slices
2 onion slices
2 tomato slices

Combine first 6 ingredients. Shape into 2 patties ½ inch thick.

Place patties on grill 3 to 5 inches from coals; cook 3 to 5 minutes on each side or to desired degree of doneness.

Place patties on bottom of buns. Top each with cheese, onion, and tomato; close with bun tops. Yield: 2 servings.

Hamburgers in Wine Sauce

¼ cup minced onion
1 tablespoon butter or margarine
½ pound ground beef
½ teaspoon salt
Dash of pepper
Dash of ground thyme
2 teaspoons butter or margarine, divided
2 teaspoons vegetable oil
¼ cup red wine or beef-flavored
  bouillon

Sauté onion in 1 tablespoon butter until tender. Combine onion, beef, salt, pepper, and thyme; mix well. Shape into 2 patties. Heat 1 teaspoon butter and oil in a skillet; add patties and cook over medium-high heat 6 to 10 minutes, depending on desired degree of doneness. Turn once. Remove to a hot platter.

Add wine to skillet, and cook over high heat until amount is reduced by half and is slightly thickened. Stir in remaining 1 teaspoon butter, and spoon sauce over patties. Yield: 2 servings.

Sour Cream Beefburgers

½ pound ground beef
½ cup coarse breadcrumbs
2 green onions, finely chopped
3 tablespoons commercial sour cream
1½ teaspoons Worcestershire sauce
¼ teaspoon salt
¼ teaspoon pepper

Combine all ingredients, mixing thoroughly. Shape mixture into 2 patties. Place waxed paper between patties; place in a plastic bag, and refrigerate several hours.

Broil patties 3 to 6 minutes on each side, depending on desired degree of doneness. Yield: 2 servings.

Grilled Hamburgers

¾ pound lean ground beef
¾ cup corn flakes, crushed (optional)
½ cup commercial sour cream
2 tablespoons Worcestershire sauce
1½ teaspoons instant minced onion
¾ teaspoon salt
2 hamburger buns split
2 thin slices onion
2 thin slices tomato

Combine first 6 ingredients; shape into 2 patties. Cook 3 to 4 inches from hot coals 3 to 6 minutes; turn and cook 3 to 6 minutes, depending on desired degree of doneness. Place patties on bottom of buns. Top each with onion and tomato slices; close with bun tops. Yield: 2 servings.

Beef and Ham Burgers

¼ pound ground beef
¼ pound ground cooked ham
¼ cup commercial sour cream
2 tablespoon finely chopped onion
⅛ teaspoon salt
Dash of pepper
Commercial barbecue sauce
1 slice process American cheese, halved
2 hamburger buns, toasted
Cherry tomatoes
Sliced sweet pickles
Lettuce
Sliced onion

Combine first 6 ingredients. Shape into 2 large patties. (Mixture will be sticky.) Place on grill over hot coals; cook 4 to 8 minutes on each side or until desired degree of doneness. Baste patties frequently with barbecue sauce during cooking. Top patties with cheese during last 2 to 3 minutes of cooking.

Serve on toasted buns. Garnish with tomatoes, pickles, lettuce, and onion. Yield: 2 servings.

Hamburger Steak

¾ to 1 pound ground round
2 slices bread, finely torn
1 egg, beaten
2 tablespoons red wine
½ cup half-and-half
1 tablespoon chopped parsley
¾ teaspoon salt
½ teaspoon pepper
2 tablespoons butter or margarine
1 (4-ounce) can sliced mushrooms, drained
1 cup beef gravy

Combine beef, bread, egg, wine, half-and-half, parsley, salt, and pepper; mix lightly,

and shape into 4 oval patties. Melt butter in a skillet, and brown patties on both sides.

Add mushrooms to patties, and cook about 3 minutes. Add gravy and bring to a boil; cover and simmer over low heat about 10 minutes or until meat is thoroughly cooked. Yield: 2 generous servings.

Salisbury Steak

½ pound ground round
1 tablespoon onion juice
½ teaspoon salt
Dash of pepper
Horseradish Sauce

Combine ground round, onion juice, salt, and pepper; mix thoroughly. Shape meat into 2 patties. Broil patties 3 to 6 minutes on each side, depending on desired degree of doneness. Serve immediately with Horseradish Sauce. Yield: 2 servings.

Horseradish Sauce:

1½ tablespoons breadcrumbs
Dash of dry mustard
3 tablespoons whipping cream
1½ tablespoons grated fresh horseradish
Salt and pepper to taste
1½ teaspoons vinegar

Combine all ingredients; cook over low heat until sauce is thoroughly heated. Yield: about ⅓ cup.

Beef-Stuffed Manicotti

4 manicotti shells
3 quarts boiling water
Salt
½ pound ground chuck
1 small onion, finely chopped
½ green pepper, finely chopped
1 (15-ounce) can tomato sauce
1 to 1½ teaspoons dried oregano leaves
1 teaspoon ground thyme
1 bay leaf
1 cup (4 ounces) shredded mozzarella cheese, divided

Cook manicotti shells in boiling salted water for 10 minutes; drain. Rinse in cold water; drain and set aside.

Sauté ground chuck, onion, and green pepper until brown; drain. Add tomato sauce, oregano, thyme, and bay leaf; simmer over low heat 10 minutes. Add ½ cup cheese, stirring until melted.

Arrange manicotti shells in two individual baking dishes; stuff with half of meat mixture. Pour remaining meat mixture over shells; sprinkle with remaining cheese. Bake at 300° for 30 minutes. Yield: 2 servings.

Meatballs in Bacon

½ pound ground beef
¼ cup cold water
2 teaspoons instant minced onion
½ teaspoon salt
¼ teaspoon seasoned pepper
4 slices bacon, cut in half crosswise

Combine first 5 ingredients, mixing well; shape into 8 meatballs. Roll bacon pieces around meatballs, and secure with wooden picks. Sauté over medium heat until bacon is crisp and brown; drain off fat. If meatballs are not done, cover and simmer an additional 5 to 7 minutes. Yield: 2 servings.

Oriental Meatballs

¾ pound ground chuck
3 tablespoons minced onion
1 egg
¼ teaspoon salt
¼ cup soy sauce, divided
2 tablespoons vegetable oil
1 (8-ounce) can pineapple chunks
1 green pepper, cut in strips
1 cup sliced cooked carrots
¼ cup sliced water chestnuts
1½ tablespoons sugar
1½ tablespoons vinegar
1 tablespoon cornstarch
1 (6-ounce) can pineapple juice
Hot cooked rice

Combine ground chuck, onion, egg, salt, and 2 tablespoons soy sauce; mix well and shape into 2-inch balls. (Balls hold shape better if chilled before cooking.) Sauté meatballs in oil until brown; remove to a platter, and keep warm. Reserve drippings.

Drain pineapple, and reserve liquid; set aside. Sauté pepper in reserved drippings 2 minutes. Add pineapple chunks, carrots, and water chestnuts; sauté 3 minutes. Add meatballs to skillet.

Combine remaining 2 tablespoons soy sauce, sugar, vinegar, cornstarch, pineapple juice, and reserved pineapple liquid in a small saucepan. Bring to a boil, stirring until thick and clear. Pour sauce over mixture in skillet, and simmer 5 minutes. Serve over hot rice. Yield: 2 servings.

Page 201: *Pastas provide an endless variety of dishes such as Beef-Stuffed Manicotti (page 200) and Cracked Wheat Salad (page 97).*

Page 202: *Cut a 7-bone pot roast into separate portions for Island Steak Strip Kabobs (page 205), Beef and Cucumber Soup (page 206), and Steak Fingers Oriental (page 205).*

German Meatballs

¾ pound ground beef
1 egg, beaten
1 tablespoon breadcrumbs
1 tablespoon instant minced onion
1 tablespoon parsley flakes
¾ teaspoon salt
Dash of pepper
1½ teaspoons lemon juice
1½ tablespoons beef-flavored bouillon
   granules
1½ cups boiling water
1½ tablespoons all-purpose flour
2 tablespoons cold water
1½ teaspoons Worcestershire sauce
2 tablespoons pickle relish
Hot cooked noodles

Combine first 8 ingredients; shape into 2-inch balls.

Combine bouillon granules and boiling water. Add meatballs, and heat to boiling. Lower heat; turn meatballs. Cover and simmer 30 minutes. Remove meatballs, and keep warm. Skim fat from broth; keep broth simmering.

Combine flour and cold water; gradually stir into broth. Add Worcestershire sauce and pickle relish. Cook over medium heat, stirring constantly, until sauce thickens and bubbles. Pour sauce over meatballs. Serve over noodles. Yield: 2 servings.

Freezer Meat Loaf

2 pounds lean ground beef
1 cup crushed corn flakes
¾ cup tomato soup, undiluted
1 egg, slightly beaten
1 small onion, chopped
1 teaspoon salt
2 slices bacon
1 cup boiling water, divided

Combine first 6 ingredients, mixing well. Spoon half of mixture into an 8½- × 4½- × 3-inch loafpan. Spoon remaining mixture into an aluminum foil-lined 8½- × 4½- × 3-inch loafpan. Place a bacon strip on top of each loaf. Pour ½ cup boiling water over each. Bake at 350° for 45 minutes.

For 2 servings, serve unlined loaf immediately. To freeze remaining loaf for later use, cool and wrap tightly in aluminum foil before placing in freezer. After meat loaf is frozen, remove from pan, and return wrapped loaf to freezer. To serve, return to pan, thaw in aluminum foil, and reheat at 350°. Yield: about 4 servings.

Spaghetti for Two

½ pound ground beef
1 (4-ounce) can tomato paste
1 cup water
¼ cup diced green pepper
¼ cup minced onion
1 bay leaf
½ teaspoon garlic salt
¼ teaspoon salt
¼ teaspoon pepper
¼ teaspoon chili powder
¼ teaspoon hot sauce
1 (2-ounce) can sliced mushrooms,
   drained
Hot cooked spaghetti

Cook ground beef until browned, and drain well; stir in tomato paste and water. Bring to a boil, and stir in next 8 ingredients. Reduce heat; cover and simmer 40 minutes, adding water as needed.

Stir in mushrooms, and simmer 5 additional minutes; remove bay leaf. Serve over spaghetti. Yield: 2 servings.

To reheat cooked pasta or rice, place it in a strainer over a pan of boiling water. Cover and steam 10 to 15 minutes.

Layered Taco Casserole

½ pound ground beef
½ cup chopped onion
1 clove garlic, minced
½ cup tomato sauce
2 tablespoons water
2 teaspoons chili powder
⅛ teaspoon whole oregano, crushed
1 cup kidney beans, undrained
1 cup corn chips, crushed
⅔ cup shredded lettuce

Brown ground beef, onion, and garlic in a medium skillet; drain.

Combine meat mixture, tomato sauce, water, and seasonings in a medium bowl; stir well. Place half of meat mixture in a lightly greased 1-quart casserole; top with half of kidney beans. Sprinkle with half of crushed corn chips. Repeat layers.

Cover and bake at 350° for 25 to 30 minutes. Uncover and bake an additional 5 minutes. To serve, top casserole with shredded lettuce. Yield: 2 generous servings.

Beef Burgundy

½ large onion, thinly sliced
1½ teaspoons butter or margarine
½ pound boneless lean beef, cubed
1½ teaspoons all-purpose flour
Salt and pepper to taste
Dash of ground marjoram
Dash of ground thyme
¼ cup beef bouillon
½ cup Burgundy or dry red wine
1 (4-ounce) can whole mushrooms, drained
Hot cooked noodles

Sauté onion in butter until tender; remove from skillet, and set aside. Add beef to skillet, and sauté until brown. Stir in flour, seasonings, bouillon, and wine.

Cover and cook over low heat 1½ hours or until tender. Stir in mushrooms and sautéed onion. Serve over noodles. Yield: 2 servings.

Beef Cubes in Beer

1 pound boneless chuck, cut into 1-inch cubes
⅓ cup all-purpose flour
¼ cup butter or margarine, divided
2 tablespoons chopped parsley
½ teaspoon dried thyme
1 tablespoon wine vinegar
1 cup beer
½ teaspoon salt
¼ teaspoon pepper
½ bay leaf, crumbled
3 onions, sliced
½ teaspoon sugar

Dredge beef in flour; brown on all sides in 2 tablespoons butter. Add parsley, thyme, vinegar, beer, salt, pepper, and bay leaf; bring to a boil. Reduce heat; cover and simmer 1 hour or until meat is tender.

Sauté onion in remaining butter; add sugar, and cook until onion is slightly glazed. Add onion to beef, and simmer 15 minutes. Yield: 2 generous servings.

Three Meals From a Beef 7-Bone Pot Roast

(1½ to 2 inches thick, about 4 pounds)

Cut around blade bone and remove sections A and B. Section A is the top blade and the most tender part of this cut. Remove membrane separating section A into two pieces; cut each into slices ½ inch thick. Panfry to rare or medium or prepare Steak Fingers Oriental.

Divide remaining meat by cutting along natural seam between sections C and D. Remove bone from D. Cut meat from D and

B into cubes. Use for Beef and Cucumber Soup (recipe on page 206).

Braise section C as pot roast. Or chill and cut into thin strips to stir-fry or to prepare Island Steak Strip Kabobs.

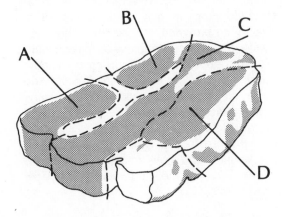

Island Steak Strip Kabobs

1 (¾-pound) boneless beef chuck blade roast
1 (8¼-ounce) can pineapple chunks
⅓ cup soy sauce
⅓ cup vegetable oil
¼ teaspoon ground ginger
⅛ teaspoon dry mustard
1 clove garlic, minced
1 medium-size green pepper, cut into 8 to 12 square pieces (blanch, if desired)
Cherry tomatoes (optional)

Partially freeze meat; cut meat across grain into ⅛-inch-thick slices. Cut each slice in half lengthwise.

Drain pineapple, reserving syrup. Combine syrup, soy sauce, oil, ginger, dry mustard, and garlic in small saucepan; cook over low heat 10 minutes, stirring occasionally. Cool. Place beef strips and marinade in dish or plastic bag, turning to coat all sides. Cover dish or tie bag securely and marinate in refrigerator 6 to 8 hours or overnight.

Remove beef strips from marinade. Thread strips of beef (weaving back and forth) on skewers alternating with pineapple chunks and green pepper pieces. Arrange kabobs on rack in broiler pan. Broil 3 to 4 inches from heat for 3 to 5 minutes on each side, brushing with marinade. Garnish servings with tomatoes, if desired. Yield: 2 servings.

Steak Fingers Oriental

1 (½- to ¾-pound) boneless beef chuck top blade roast
3 to 4 tablespoons butter or margarine, divided
¼ pound fresh mushrooms, sliced
¼ cup sliced green onion
1 cup shredded Chinese cabbage, cut ¾ inch thick
¼ teaspoon salt
1 tablespoon plus 1 teaspoon all-purpose flour
⅔ cup water
1 tablespoon soy sauce
1 clove garlic, minced
⅛ teaspoon pepper
Green onion (optional)
Hot cooked rice

Remove membrane (connective tissue) separating top blade into 2 pieces; cut each piece lengthwise in half. Melt 2 tablespoons butter in large skillet; add mushrooms and sauté 2 minutes over medium heat, stirring gently. Add green onion and cabbage, and continue cooking and stirring 1 to 2 minutes. Remove from skillet; add remaining 1 to 2 tablespoons butter. Brown steak pieces, allowing 2 minutes for each side; season with salt. Stir in flour; gradually add water, soy sauce, garlic, and pepper and cook slowly, stirring, until sauce thickens. Quickly stir in vegetable mixture and heat through. Garnish with green onion, if desired. Serve with rice. Yield: 2 servings.

Beef and Cucumber Soup

1 (¾-to 1-pound) boneless beef chuck blade roast, cut in ¾-inch pieces (include bone, if desired)
2 cups water
1½ teaspoons salt
1 small clove garlic, minced
¼ teaspoon dried dillweed
2 green onions with tops, sliced
1 carrot, cut into julienne strips
1 stalk celery
1 medium cucumber, peeled, halved, and thinly sliced
1 tablespoon all-purpose flour
2 tablespoons water

Combine beef pieces, bone, water, salt, garlic, and dillweed in a large saucepan. Cover tightly and cook slowly 1 to 1½ hours. Add white portion of onions, carrot, and celery; continue cooking, covered, 30 minutes or until meat is tender and vegetables are done. Stir in cucumber and reserved green onion tops and continue cooking, covered, 5 minutes. Combine flour and water; stir into soup. Remove bone. Cook until slightly thickened. Yield: 2 generous servings.

Traditional Pot Roast

1 (2½-pound) boneless chuck roast
2 tablespoons vegetable oil
½ cup water
3 medium potatoes, peeled and quartered
3 medium carrots, cut into 2-inch pieces
3 medium onions, quartered
1 tablespoon all-purpose flour
1 (8-ounce) carton commercial sour cream

Brown roast on all sides in hot oil in a large Dutch oven; add water. Reduce heat; cover and simmer 2½ hours. Add potatoes, carrots, and onion. Cover and simmer 30 minutes or until vegetables are tender.

Remove roast and vegetables to a serving dish. Drain off drippings, leaving 2 tablespoons in pan; reserve remainder. Stir flour into drippings in pan; cook over medium heat until browned, stirring constantly. Add water to reserved drippings to make 1 cup; stir into flour and cook, stirring constantly, until smooth and slightly thickened. Add sour cream and cook, stirring constantly, until thoroughly heated. Serve gravy with roast. Yield: 5 to 6 servings.

Note: To freeze, divide remaining beef, vegetables, and gravy into serving-size portions. Wrap in moisture vapor-proof paper and freeze.

Cube Steaks with Wine Sauce

2 (½-pound) cube steaks
Salt and pepper to taste
¼ teaspoon vegetable oil
1½ tablespoons butter or margarine
2 carrots, cut into strips
2 small onions, halved or quartered
1 teaspoon chopped parsley
¼ cup dry rosé wine
¼ cup evaporated milk
¼ teaspoon beef-flavored bouillon granules

Season steaks with salt and pepper; brown in oil and butter. Remove from skillet and set aside.

Add carrots, onion, and parsley to skillet; sauté 5 minutes, stirring frequently. Add wine and steaks; cover and cook over low heat until steaks are tender. Remove with slotted spoon, reserving cooking liquid.

Add evaporated milk and bouillon to cooking liquid; cook, stirring constantly, until smooth. Return steaks and vegetables to skillet; heat thoroughly. Yield: 2 servings.

Marinated Flank Steak

1 (1-pound) flank steak
2 teaspoons instant meat tenderizer
1 teaspoon sugar
2 tablespoons dry sherry
2 tablespoons soy sauce
1 tablespoon honey
1 teaspoon salt

Pierce steak with a fork, and place in a shallow dish.

Combine remaining ingredients, mixing well; pour over flank steak. Let stand at room temperature 3 to 4 hours.

Remove steak from marinade and place on a lightly greased rack in a broiler pan. Broil 6 inches from heat 4 to 5 minutes on each side. To serve, slice across grain in thin slices. Yield: 2 servings.

Beef Fillets for Two

2 (1¼- to 1⅓-inch-thick) fillets of beef
3 tablespoons butter or margarine, divided
½ pound fresh mushrooms, sliced
1½ teaspoons minced shallots or green onion
¼ cup Burgundy or dry red wine
½ teaspoon butter or margarine, softened
½ teaspoon all-purpose flour
1 tablespoon Burgundy or dry red wine

Sauté fillets in 1 tablespoon butter 4 minutes on each side; remove from skillet, and keep warm. Drain and discard pan drippings.

Melt 1 tablespoon butter in skillet over low heat; sauté mushrooms and shallots 2 to 3 minutes. Stir in ¼ cup Burgundy; cook over high heat until wine is reduced to half.

Combine ½ teaspoon butter and flour; stir to form a smooth paste. Add to mushroom mixture; cook, stirring constantly, 30 seconds. Add remaining tablespoon butter and

1 tablespoon Burgundy; stir until butter melts. Spoon sauce over fillets. Serve at once. Yield: 2 servings.

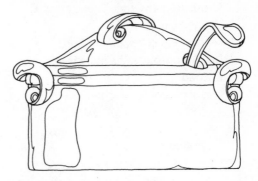

Beef Strips in Sauce

1 (1-pound) sirloin steak or filet mignon
½ cup all-purpose flour
½ teaspoon salt
¼ teaspoon pepper
2 tablespoons vegetable oil
1 tablespoon butter or margarine
1 teaspoon beef-flavored bouillon granules or 1 beef bouillon cube
1 cup hot water
1 tablespoon commercial sour cream
2 tablespoons grated Parmesan cheese
Hot cooked noodles

Slice beef diagonally into ¼-inch strips.

Combine flour, salt, and pepper. Dredge beef in flour mixture; shake to remove excess flour.

Heat oil and butter in a medium skillet. Sauté beef strips, a few at a time, to brown both sides. Remove browned strips; set aside and repeat to brown all beef strips.

Dissolve bouillon granules in water; add bouillon and sour cream to skillet. Mix well over low heat. Return beef to skillet and stir carefully. Do not allow to boil.

Pour beef and sauce into a shallow greased casserole; top with Parmesan cheese. Broil until lightly brown. Serve with hot cooked noodles. Yield: 2 servings.

Steak Diane Flambe

2 cups sliced fresh mushrooms or 2
(4-ounce) cans sliced mushrooms,
drained
¼ cup finely chopped shallots
⅔ to ¾ cup butter or margarine,
divided
1 teaspoon chopped chives
2 teaspoons chopped parsley
½ teaspoon Worcestershire sauce
½ teaspoon salt
2 teaspoons freshly ground pepper
2 (8-ounce) filets mignons, halved
crosswise
⅓ cup cognac
3 tablespoons dry sherry

Sauté mushrooms and shallots in ½ cup butter in a small saucepan 5 minutes. Add
chives, parsley, Worcestershire sauce, and
seasonings, and simmer 15 minutes. Set
aside.

Sauté filets in the remaining butter until
desired degree of doneness. Heat cognac
over medium heat; do not boil. Ignite and
pour over filets. When flame is extinguished,
add sherry. Transfer filets to a heated platter;
spoon mushroom mixture over filets. Serve
immediately. Yield: 2 to 4 servings.

Special Steak for Two

1 pound (¾-inch-thick) New York strip,
tenderloin, rib eye, or club steak
½ clove garlic
Freshly ground pepper to taste
1 tablespoon butter or margarine
¼ cup dry vermouth or dry sherry
¼ teaspoon Worcestershire sauce
2 tablespoons chopped chives or green
onion tops
Salt to taste

Rub steak with garlic, and season with pepper. Melt butter in a large, heavy skillet; add
vermouth, Worcestershire sauce, and
chives. Simmer mixture 5 minutes.

Add steak to skillet; cook over high heat 3
to 5 minutes on each side for rare, 5 to 7
minutes for medium, or 7 to 10 minutes for
well done. Sprinkle with salt, and serve immediately. Yield: 2 servings.

Country-Fried Round Steak

1 (¾-pound) boneless round steak
1 egg, beaten
Grated rind and juice of 1 lemon
¼ teaspoon salt
¼ teaspoon pepper
¼ cup fine dry breadcrumbs
¼ cup fine cracker crumbs
Vegetable oil

Trim excess fat from steak; pound to ¼-inch
thickness. Cut steak into serving-size pieces.

Combine egg, lemon rind and juice, salt,
and pepper; beat well. Combine breadcrumbs and cracker crumbs. Dip steak into
egg mixture; dredge in crumb mixture. Cook
steak cutlets in hot oil until done, turning
once. Yield: 2 servings.

Baked Swiss Steak

1 (½- to ¾-pound) boneless round
steak, about ¾ inch thick
½ teaspoon salt
2 tablespoons all-purpose flour
2 tablespoons vegetable oil
1 (8-ounce) can stewed tomatoes
¼ cup chopped carrots
¼ cup chopped celery
1 tablespoon chopped onion
¼ teaspoon Worcestershire sauce
2 tablespoons shredded sharp American
cheese

Cut meat into 2 portions; pound ¼ inch thick. Combine salt and flour, and coat meat well in flour mixture. Brown meat in oil; remove meat from skillet, and place in a small shallow baking dish.

Blend remaining flour with drippings in skillet. Add remaining ingredients except cheese; cook, stirring constantly, until mixture boils. Pour over meat; cover and bake at 350° about 2 hours or until meat and vegetables are tender.

Sprinkle cheese over meat, and return to oven a few minutes or until cheese melts. Yield: 2 servings.

Shortribs for Two

1 to 1½ pounds beef shortribs
All-purpose flour
3 tablespoons shortening
1½ cups water
¼ cup red wine
½ teaspoon bottled brown bouquet
   sauce
2 tablespoons all-purpose flour
2 teaspoons salt
½ teaspoon pepper
Pinch of dried rosemary leaves
Parsley sprigs
1 teaspoon onion flakes
2 medium potatoes, peeled and sliced
4 carrots, sliced

Cut ribs into serving pieces; dredge in flour, and brown in hot shortening in either a heavy skillet or a Dutch oven.

Combine water, red wine, bouquet sauce, 2 tablespoons flour, and seasonings in a mixing bowl. Pour mixture over meat; simmer, covered, 1 hour. Add vegetables; cook over medium heat until vegetables and meat are tender. Yield: 2 servings.

When cutting thin slices of raw meat, place meat in freezer for 30 minutes to make slicing easier.

Barbecued Beef Ribs for Two

1 (8-ounce) can tomato sauce
1 cup catsup
⅓ cup firmly packed brown sugar
2 tablespoons lemon juice
1 teaspoon instant minced onion
½ teaspoon garlic powder
4 to 6 large meaty beef ribs

Combine all ingredients except ribs, stirring mixture well. Add ribs; cover and marinate 8 hours or overnight in refrigerator.

Grill over medium heat 40 to 50 minutes or to desired degree of doneness, basting with marinade and turning occasionally. Yield: 2 servings.

Note: Rib-eye steaks may be substituted for beef ribs. Grill steaks to desired degree of doneness.

Liver and Onions

½ cup all-purpose flour
¾ teaspoon salt
⅛ teaspoon pepper
¼ teaspoon paprika
¾ pound beef liver, cut into 2-inch
   pieces
2 cloves garlic, crushed
½ jalapeño pepper, thinly sliced
2 to 3 tablespoons vegetable oil
1 medium onion, sliced
1 to 2 cups water

Combine flour, salt, pepper, and paprika in a plastic bag; add liver and shake until well coated with flour; set aside.

Sauté garlic and jalapeño pepper in oil until tender. Add liver, and brown slowly on both sides. Place onion slices on top of liver. Add water; cover and simmer over low heat 30 to 40 minutes, stirring occasionally. Yield: 2 servings.

Liver Stroganoff

¾ pound calves or beef liver
All-purpose flour
¼ cup butter or margarine, divided
1 tablespoon chopped fresh parsley
¼ cup chopped onion
3 tablespoons chopped green onion tops
½ cup sliced fresh mushrooms
1 clove garlic, minced
1½ tablespoons all-purpose flour
⅔ cup consommé
½ teaspoon salt
¼ teaspoon freshly ground pepper
3 drops hot sauce
½ cup commercial sour cream
Hot cooked noodles or rice

Dredge liver in flour. Cook in 2 tablespoons melted butter in a large skillet just until liver loses its pink color and is lightly browned. Remove and set aside to cool. Cut into narrow strips.

Sauté parsley, onion, onion tops, mushrooms, and garlic in remaining 2 tablespoons butter. Blend in 1½ tablespoons flour; cook 1 minute, stirring constantly. Gradually stir in consommé; add salt, pepper, and hot sauce. Cook over medium heat, stirring constantly, until thickened and bubbly.

Add liver to sauce, and simmer 10 minutes. Remove from heat, and add sour cream. Heat thoroughly, but do not boil. Serve over noodles. Yield: 2 servings.

Grilled Lamb Chops

4 to 6 (1-inch-thick) lamb chops
¼ cup soy sauce
¼ cup water
1 tablespoon sugar
¼ teaspoon toasted sesame seeds
¼ teaspoon fresh ground ginger
1 small clove garlic, minced
Pepper to taste

Place meat in a shallow dish. Combine remaining ingredients; pour over meat. Cover and marinate in refrigerator 8 hours. Remove meat from the marinade.

Grill chops 5 to 6 inches from low to medium heat 30 to 35 minutes; turn several times. Yield: 2 servings.

Chinese Lamb Chops

¼ cup soy sauce
1½ tablespoons olive oil
1 tablespoon lemon juice
1½ teaspoons vinegar
1 small onion, grated
1½ teaspoons sugar
⅛ teaspoon pepper
1 clove garlic, crushed
1 bay leaf
Pinch of ground oregano
2 shoulder lamb chops, about ½
   inch thick
Cooked rice or noodles (optional)

Combine all ingredients except lamb chops and rice. Pour over lamb chops; refrigerate and marinate at least 2 hours, turning the meat occasionally to coat with marinade.

Place chops and soy sauce mixture in skillet; cover and simmer about 30 to 40 minutes or until tender. Discard bay leaf. Serve with rice or noodles, if desired. Yield: 2 servings.

Baked Lamb Chops

2 (½-inch-thick) loin lamb chops
1 tablespoon vegetable oil
3 tablespoons orange juice
2 tablespoons soy sauce
½ teaspoon ground ginger
⅛ teaspoon garlic salt
⅛ teaspoon pepper
⅛ teaspoon sugar
1 small orange, peeled and sectioned

Trim excess fat from chops. Lightly brown chops in hot oil, and drain on paper towels. Place chops in a shallow baking dish.

Combine orange juice, soy sauce, ginger, garlic salt, pepper, and sugar; pour marinade over chops. Cover and refrigerate 2 hours, turning once. Remove from refrigerator, but do not uncover.

Bake at 350° for 45 to 55 minutes or until chops are tender. Place orange sections on chops. Replace cover; bake 10 minutes. Spoon sauce over chops before serving. Yield: 2 servings.

Grilled Ham

1 (1-inch-thick) slice cooked ham (about ¾ pound)
½ cup ginger ale
½ cup orange juice
¼ cup firmly packed brown sugar
2 tablespoons vegetable oil
2 teaspoons wine vinegar
1 teaspoon dry mustard
¼ teaspoon ground ginger
⅛ teaspoon ground cloves

Score fat edge of ham. Combine remaining ingredients; pour over ham in a shallow baking dish. Refrigerate overnight or let stand at room temperature 1 hour, spooning marinade over ham several times.

Place ham on grill over slow coals; cook about 15 minutes on each side, brushing often with marinade. Heat remaining marinade; serve with ham. Yield: 2 servings.

Baked Ham Slice

1 (1-pound) slice smoked ham
1½ teaspoons prepared mustard
½ (8¼-ounce) can pineapple slices
1 tablespoon butter or margarine, melted
1 tablespoon all-purpose flour
¼ cup sherry

Place ham in a shallow baking dish, and spread with mustard. Drain pineapple, reserving juice; add enough water to juice to measure ½ cup, if needed. Arrange halved pineapple slices over the ham.

Combine butter and flour in a saucepan; gradually stir in reserved pineapple juice and sherry. Cook, stirring constantly, until mixture is thickened and smooth. Pour sauce over ham, and bake, uncovered, at 350° for 1 hour, basting several times with sauce. Yield: 2 servings.

Ham and Zucchini Stir-Fry

⅔ cup chicken broth, undiluted
¼ cup soy sauce
1 tablespoon sugar
1 teaspoon grated fresh ginger or ¼ teaspoon ground ginger
¼ teaspoon salt
2 cloves garlic, minced or crushed
2 teaspoons cornstarch
Vegetable oil
½ pound fully cooked ham, cut into 3- × ¼-inch strips
1 large carrot, thinly sliced
1 large zucchini, thinly sliced
1 large onion, thinly sliced
Hot cooked rice (optional)

Combine broth, soy sauce, sugar, ginger, salt, and garlic; stir well. Gradually add to cornstarch; mix well. Set aside.

Pour oil around top of hot wok, coating sides until bottom is covered with oil. Add ham; stir-fry until lightly browned. Add vegetables; stir-fry 2 minutes or until crisp-tender. Add broth mixture; cook, stirring, until thickened and bubbly. Serve with rice, if desired. Yield: 2 servings.

After removing a roast from the oven, let it rest 15 minutes for easier carving.

Green Noodles and Ham

½ cup chopped cooked ham
½ tomato, peeled and chopped
½ onion, chopped
1 clove garlic, minced
2 tablespoons butter or margarine
1 cup whipping cream
½ cup grated Parmesan cheese
¼ cup shredded Cheddar cheese
½ teaspoon ground nutmeg
2 cups cooked spinach noodles

Sauté ham, tomato, onion, and garlic in butter until onion is tender. Combine whipping cream, cheese, and nutmeg in a saucepan; heat thoroughly. Combine ham mixture and sauce. Serve over hot noodles. Yield: 2 servings.

Ham Shortcake

½ cup sliced mushrooms
2 tablespoons butter or margarine
2 tablespoons all-purpose flour
¾ cup milk
⅛ teaspoon salt
Pepper to taste
⅛ teaspoon steak sauce
¾ cup diced cooked ham
Patty shells or toast cups

Sauté mushrooms in butter; blend in flour, and cook until bubbly. Gradually add milk; cook until smooth and thickened, stirring constantly. Add seasonings, steak sauce, and ham; heat mixture thoroughly. Serve in patty shells or toast cups. Yield: 2 servings.

Easy Pork Chops

2 (1-inch-thick) lean pork chops
Commercial Italian salad dressing
Salt and pepper
⅓ cup Italian-seasoned breadcrumbs

Brush pork chops generously with salad dressing. Sprinkle with salt and pepper; coat with breadcrumbs. Place pork chops on a rack in a shallow pan. Bake at 350° for 50 to 60 minutes or until done. Yield: 2 servings.

Pork Chops in Sour Cream Gravy

2 (¾-inch-thick) loin pork chops
Vegetable oil
1 small onion, thinly sliced
¼ teaspoon caraway seeds
¼ teaspoon salt
¼ teaspoon paprika
⅛ teaspoon dried dillweed
Dash of garlic powder
⅓ cup water
⅓ cup commercial sour cream

Brown pork chops in a small amount of hot oil; drain. Add onion, seasonings, and water; cover and simmer over low heat about 1 hour or until chops are tender.

Transfer chops to a warm platter. Add sour cream to meat drippings; blend well. Heat thoroughly, but do not boil; spoon over pork chops. Yield: 2 servings.

Vegetable-Stuffed Pork Chops

½ cup chopped celery
1 tablespoon chopped onion
¼ teaspoon poultry seasoning
2 tablespoons butter or margarine
1 cup soft breadcrumbs
2 (1-inch-thick) pork loin chops, cut with pockets
Salt and pepper to taste
1 tablespoon shortening
¾ cup water, divided
½ green pepper, cut in ½-inch strips
3 carrots, cut in ½-inch slices

Combine celery, onion, and poultry seasoning; sauté in butter 5 minutes or until vegetables are tender. Stir in breadcrumbs.

Season pockets of pork chops with salt and pepper; stuff with breadcrumb mixture, and secure with wooden picks. Brown chops on both sides in shortening. Pour ¼ cup water over chops; cover and simmer 30 minutes. Add green pepper, carrots, and ½ cup water; cover and simmer 15 minutes or until vegetables are crisp-tender. Yield: 2 servings.

Skillet Pork Chops

2 to 3 (½- to ¾-inch-thick) loin
  pork chops
1½ tablespoons butter or margarine
¾ cup chopped onion
½ teaspoon salt
⅛ teaspoon pepper
1 teaspoon cornstarch
2 teaspoons prepared mustard
1 cup water
1 beef-flavored bouillon cube
1 teaspoon Worcestershire sauce

Sauté pork chops in butter until brown; set aside, reserving drippings. Sauté onion in drippings until tender. Add salt, pepper, cornstarch, and mustard; stir well. Add water, bouillon, and Worcestershire sauce; stir until bouillon is dissolved. Place pork chops in skillet, and simmer 20 to 30 minutes or until done. Yield: 2 servings.

Grilled Pork Chops

¼ cup soy sauce
2 tablespoons brown sugar
2 tablespoons dry sherry
½ teaspoon ground cinnamon
¼ teaspoon garlic salt
Dash of ground ginger
2 (1-inch-thick) center cut pork chops

Combine first 6 ingredients; stir well. Arrange pork chops in a single layer in a dish. Pour marinade over chops; cover and refrigerate overnight.

Grill chops 6 to 8 inches from heat over gray-white coals 1 hour or until done, basting with marinade and turning occasionally. Yield: 2 servings.

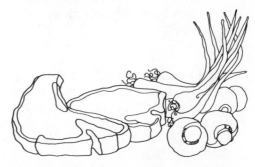

Pork Chops in Mushroom Gravy

2 (1-inch-thick) loin pork chops
2 tablespoons all-purpose flour
1 teaspoon paprika
Salt and pepper
1 tablespoon vegetable oil
1 small onion, minced
½ green pepper, minced
6 to 8 mushrooms, chopped
1 cup milk
Juice of ½ lemon

Remove excess fat from edge of chops. Combine flour, paprika, salt, and pepper; dredge chops in mixture. Set aside remaining flour mixture. Brown chops in oil, and remove to a shallow casserole.

Add onion, green pepper, and mushrooms to skillet; sauté until soft. Add reserved flour mixture; cook, stirring, 3 minutes. Blend in milk, and cook until thickened, stirring constantly; stir in lemon juice. Pour sauce over chops; cover and bake at 350° for 1 hour. Remove cover, and bake 10 more minutes. Yield: 2 servings.

Rice-Stuffed Pork Chops

½ cup uncooked wild rice
3 cups water, divided
1 teaspoon salt
2 tablespoons chopped fresh parsley
⅓ cup slivered almonds
1 (1⅜-ounce) package onion soup mix
2 (1½-inch-thick) loin pork chops
Vegetable oil
Pepper to taste

Combine rice, 2 cups cold water, and salt; bring to a boil. Simmer 40 minutes or until rice is tender. Add parsley and almonds, stirring to mix. Set aside.

Bring 1 cup water to a boil; add onion soup mix. Set aside.

Cut deep pockets in chops. Brown in hot oil; cool. Stuff with rice mixture, and place in a 2-quart casserole. Pour onion soup mixture over chops and sprinkle with pepper. Cover and bake at 350° for 1 hour or until chops are tender. Yield: 2 servings.

Pork Tenderloin with Pears

1 (8-ounce) can pear halves
2 tablespoons soy sauce
6 pork tenderloin slices (about 1 pound)
1 to 2 tablespoons butter or margarine
½ teaspoon crystallized ginger
½ teaspoon ground cinnamon sugar
Pinch of ground nutmeg
Salt and pepper to taste
Hot cooked rice

Drain pears, reserving juice. Combine pear juice and soy sauce in a shallow dish. Add pork; cover, and marinate 1 hour at room temperature or overnight in refrigerator. Drain pork, reserving marinade. Sauté pork in butter until golden brown; set aside and keep warm.

Combine marinade, ginger, cinnamon sugar, nutmeg, salt, and pepper in a saucepan; simmer 5 minutes. Add pears and simmer 3 minutes, basting with marinade. Serve with pork and rice. Yield: 2 servings.

Stir-Fry Pork

1 pound boneless lean pork, cut into ¼-inch strips
1½ tablespoons sherry
1½ tablespoons soy sauce
2 tablespoons vegetable oil
¼ pound fresh mushrooms, sliced
1 teaspoon cornstarch
¼ cup chicken stock or water

Combine pork, sherry, and soy sauce, tossing lightly. Let stand 15 to 20 minutes; drain.

Sauté pork in oil over high heat 2 minutes, stirring constantly; drain on paper towels, and set aside.

Stir mushrooms into pan drippings in skillet. Cook over medium heat 2 to 3 minutes or until tender, stirring occasionally. Add meat to mushrooms, mixing well. Combine cornstarch and chicken stock, stirring to make a smooth paste. Add to pan and cook over medium heat, stirring constantly, until thickened. Yield: 2 servings.

Sausage and Sauerkraut

1 (16-ounce) can sauerkraut, undrained
1 pound Polish sausage, cut into 1-inch pieces

Cook sauerkraut over low heat 5 minutes; add sausage. Cover and cook over low heat an additional 15 minutes. Yield: 2 servings.

Home-Baked Pepperoni Pizza

¾ teaspoon dry yeast
⅓ cup warm milk (105° to 115°)
¾ teaspoon sugar
¼ teaspoon salt
1 tablespoon vegetable oil
1⅓ cups all-purpose flour
Pizza sauce
Sliced pepperoni
Chopped green pepper
Sliced mushrooms
Shredded mozzarella cheese
Grated Parmesan cheese

Dissolve yeast in milk in a medium bowl. Stir in sugar, salt, and oil. Gradually add flour, stirring after each addition. Dough will be stiff.

Turn dough onto a lightly floured surface; knead until smooth and elastic. Shape into a ball and place in a greased bowl, turning to grease both sides. Cover and let rise in a warm place (85°), free from drafts, about 1 hour or until doubled in bulk.

Roll dough into a 12- or 15-inch circle on a floured surface and place on a well-greased pizza pan. Spread pizza sauce over dough. Sprinkle pepperoni, green pepper, mushrooms, mozzarella, and Parmesan cheese over sauce. Bake at 450° for 12 to 15 minutes or until bubbly. Let stand 5 minutes before cutting. Yield: one 12- to 15-inch pizza.

Veal Scallopini

¾ pound (⅛-inch-thick) veal cutlets
Salt and pepper
About 1 tablespoon all-purpose flour
1 tablespoon butter or margarine
¼ cup dry Marsala or Madeira wine
½ cup sliced fresh mushrooms
1 tablespoon water

Cut veal into large pieces. Season both sides lightly with salt and pepper; sprinkle lightly with flour.

Sauté veal in butter until well browned on both sides. Stir in wine and mushrooms; cook 1 minute over medium heat, stirring frequently.

Place veal on a serving platter. Add water to drippings, stirring and scraping bottom of skillet to loosen browned bits. Cook until bubbly; pour over veal. Yield: 2 servings.

Veal with Mushrooms and Peppers

2 tablespoons vegetable oil
2 tablespoons lemon juice
½ teaspoon salt
½ teaspoon paprika
½ teaspoon prepared mustard
⅛ teaspoon ground nutmeg
1 clove garlic, minced
¾ pound veal sirloin steak or shoulder, cut into serving-size pieces
2 tablespoons all-purpose flour
1 to 2 tablespoons butter or margarine
⅔ cup chicken broth
½ medium-size green pepper, seeded and cut into rings
1 cup sliced fresh mushrooms
1 medium onion, sliced and separated into rings

Combine oil, lemon juice, salt, paprika, mustard, nutmeg, and garlic. Pour marinade over veal; marinate 15 minutes. Remove veal from marinade, reserving marinade.

Dredge veal in flour; brown on both sides in butter. Place veal in a 1½-quart casserole. Combine marinade, broth, green pepper, and mushrooms; pour over veal. Cover and bake at 350° for 30 minutes. Remove cover; top with onion rings. Bake, uncovered, 15 minutes. Yield: 2 servings.

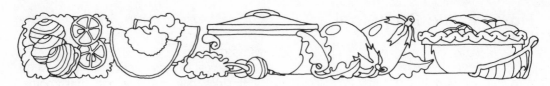

POULTRY

Baked Chicken and Broccoli

2 whole chicken breasts, split
2 tablespoons butter or margarine, melted
1 (10-ounce) package frozen broccoli
1 (10¾-ounce) can cream of mushroom soup, undiluted
½ cup milk
½ cup (2 ounces) shredded Cheddar cheese
¼ cup breadcrumbs
Paprika

Place chicken in a 9-inch square pan, and drizzle with butter. Bake at 375° for 40 minutes. Cook broccoli according to package directions; drain. Arrange around chicken.

Combine soup, milk, and cheese; pour over chicken and broccoli. Sprinkle with breadcrumbs and paprika. Bake an additional 20 minutes. Yield: 2 servings.

Chicken Dijon

2 whole chicken breasts, split, boned, and skinned
2 tablespoons butter or margarine
1 tablespoon all-purpose flour
½ cup chicken broth
¼ cup half-and-half
1 tablespoon Dijon mustard

Sauté chicken in butter over low heat about 20 minutes or until tender. Remove chicken to a warm platter.

Blend flour into pan drippings; cook over low heat, stirring constantly, until bubbly. Gradually stir in broth and half-and-half; cook until smooth and thickened, stirring constantly. Stir in mustard. Add chicken; cover and simmer about 10 minutes. Yield: 2 servings.

Chicken Dinner in a Skillet

2 whole chicken breasts, split
2 tablespoons butter or margarine
1 (11-ounce) can Cheddar cheese soup, undiluted
¼ cup water
2 medium potatoes, peeled and quartered
2 stalks celery, cut into 2-inch slices
½ cup sliced carrots
1 bay leaf
¼ teaspoon poultry seasoning

Brown chicken on both sides in butter; add remaining ingredients to skillet. Bring to a boil; cover and simmer 30 minutes, stirring occasionally. Remove bay leaf.

For 2 servings, serve 2 chicken pieces and half the sauce immediately.

To freeze remainder, line a 1-quart casserole with aluminum foil; spoon remaining mixture into prepared dish.

Wrap foil securely around mixture, and place in freezer. After mixture is frozen, remove from dish and return the wrapped portion to freezer.

To serve, unwrap mixture; return to a 1-quart casserole dish, and thaw in refrigerator. Bake at 350° for 30 to 35 minutes or until bubbly. Yield: 4 servings.

Chicken Florentine

1 (10-ounce) package frozen chopped spinach
1 egg, beaten
¼ cup grated Parmesan cheese, divided
¾ cup Italian-style breadcrumbs
2 whole chicken breasts, split, boned, and skinned
Salt and pepper to taste
3 tablespoons butter or margarine, melted

Cook spinach according to package directions; drain well, and allow to cool. Combine spinach, egg, and 1 tablespoon Parmesan cheese; set aside. Combine breadcrumbs and remaining Parmesan cheese in a shallow pan; set aside.

Sprinkle chicken breasts with salt and pepper; roll each in breadcrumb mixture. Place in a greased 9-inch square baking pan.

Divide spinach mixture evenly and spread on each chicken breast to form a ½-inch-thick layer. Sprinkle with remaining breadcrumb mixture, and drizzle with butter. Bake chicken at 350° for 35 to 40 minutes. Yield: 2 servings.

Chicken Kabobs

1 whole chicken breast, boned and skinned
3 tablespoons lemon juice
½ teaspoon garlic powder
½ teaspoon ground ginger
3 tablespoons vegetable oil
⅛ teaspoon salt
12 to 14 medium-size fresh mushrooms
8 to 10 pineapple chunks

Cut chicken into 1½-inch pieces. Place in a small bowl. Combine remaining ingredients except mushrooms and pineapple chunks. Mix well. Pour lemon juice mixture over chicken. Turn or toss to coat. Cover and refrigerate 2 hours, stirring several times.

Rinse mushrooms and pat dry. Drain chicken, reserving marinade. Thread skewers alternately with chicken pieces, mushrooms, and pineapple chunks. Brush with marinade.

Arrange kabobs on broiler rack. Broil 5 to 6 inches from heat, turning several times until chicken is tender (about 6 to 8 minutes). Yield: 2 servings.

Chicken and Ham Casserole

2 tablespoons butter or margarine, melted
2 tablespoons all-purpose flour
1 cup milk
½ cup chopped cooked chicken or turkey
½ cup chopped cooked ham
½ cup cooked rice or macaroni
¼ cup chopped celery
¼ teaspoon salt
¼ teaspoon pepper
½ cup (2 ounces) shredded process American cheese
Dash of paprika

Combine butter and flour in a saucepan; cook over low heat, stirring until bubbly. Gradually add milk; cook, stirring constantly, until thickened and smooth. Remove from heat. Add chicken, ham, rice, celery, salt, and pepper. Spoon mixture into a lightly greased 1-quart casserole. Bake at 400° for 15 minutes or until bubbly. Remove from oven; sprinkle with cheese and paprika, and bake an additional 5 minutes or until cheese melts. Yield: 2 servings.

Chicken with Olives

2 whole chicken breasts, split, boned, and skinned
3 to 4 tablespoons olive oil
3 to 4 tablespoons butter or margarine
½ cup white wine, divided
6 to 8 sliced pimiento-stuffed olives
Parsley to taste

Wash and dry chicken breasts; brown on both sides in olive oil and butter. Cover and cook 8 to 10 minutes. Turn chicken, and add ¼ cup wine and olives; cook 10 minutes. Turn chicken again, and cook until tender.

Remove chicken to a serving platter; add remainder of wine and parsley to drippings. Bring mixture to a boil; serve hot over chicken. Yield: 2 servings.

Orange Marinated Chicken

2 whole chicken breasts, split and skinned
¼ cup orange juice
½ teaspoon salt
¼ teaspoon ground marjoram
¼ teaspoon dried basil leaves
½ teaspoon garlic salt
¼ teaspoon pepper

Wash chicken and dry well with absorbent towels. Combine remaining ingredients. Pour mixture over chicken, and refrigerate 1 hour. Bake, uncovered, at 350° for 45 to 55 minutes, basting occasionally. Yield: 2 servings.

Rosemary Chicken

Salt and pepper to taste
2 whole chicken breasts, split and skinned
¼ teaspoon dried rosemary leaves, crushed
¼ cup butter or margarine, melted

Salt and pepper chicken; place in a shallow baking pan. Sprinkle with rosemary, and drizzle with butter. Cover and bake at 325° for 40 to 45 minutes or until chicken is tender. Yield: 2 servings.

Sauteed Chicken

1 whole chicken breast, split, boned, and skinned
Salt and pepper to taste
½ cup breadcrumbs
¼ cup grated Parmesan cheese
1 egg, beaten
3 tablespoons butter or margarine

Place each half of chicken breast on a sheet of waxed paper; flatten to ¼-inch thickness, using a meat mallet or rolling pin. Season with salt and pepper.

Combine breadcrumbs and cheese. Dip chicken in egg, and coat well with breadcrumb mixture. Sauté in butter 4 to 5 minutes on each side or until well browned and tender. Yield: 2 servings.

Saucy Chicken

1 (4-ounce) can whole mushrooms, drained
½ cup commercial Italian salad dressing
2 tablespoons all-purpose flour
Salt and pepper
2 whole chicken breasts, split
2 tablespoons vegetable oil
1 (10¾-ounce) can cream of mushroom soup, undiluted
½ cup water
1 cup dry white wine
Hot cooked noodles

Marinate mushrooms in Italian dressing overnight; drain. Combine flour, salt, and pepper; dredge chicken in flour mixture. Brown in hot oil in an electric skillet. Add remaining flour mixture to skillet, and stir until smooth. Add soup, water, and mushrooms; cover and cook over low heat 45 minutes to 1 hour. After 30 minutes, stir in wine. Serve over cooked noodles. Yield: 2 servings.

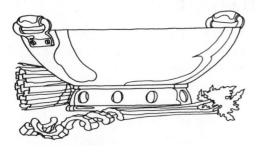

Stir-Fry Chicken

2 tablespoons soy sauce
1 tablespoon cornstarch
1 whole chicken breast, skinned, boned, and cut into ⅛-inch strips
¼ cup vegetable oil, divided
⅓ cup roasted cashew nuts
1 small onion
¼ pound green beans, cut diagonally in ½-inch pieces
2 medium carrots, peeled and cut diagonally in ⅛-inch slices
1 stalk celery, sliced
1 clove garlic, minced
½ cup chicken broth
1 teaspoon cornstarch

Combine soy sauce and 1 tablespoon cornstarch; mix well. Add chicken, and stir until coated; set aside.

Heat 1 tablespoon oil in a wok until hot; add nuts, stirring constantly, until browned (about 30 seconds). Remove nuts, and set aside. Add another tablespoon oil to pan; add chicken, and stir-fry 1 to 2 minutes. Remove chicken, and set aside.

Cut onion into ¼-inch slices; cut slices in half crosswise. Add remaining oil to wok, and heat to smoking. Add vegetables and garlic; cover and cook 1 minute, shaking wok to prevent vegetables from sticking. Remove cover; cook, stirring constantly, an additional 2 to 4 minutes.

Combine broth and 1 teaspoon cornstarch. Add chicken and broth mixture to vegetables; stir until thickened. Stir in cashews. Yield: 2 servings.

Buttermilk Fried Chicken

½ cup all-purpose flour
¾ teaspoon salt
¼ teaspoon paprika
¼ teaspoon ground thyme
¼ teaspoon ground marjoram
Pinch of pepper
2 whole chicken breasts, split
½ cup buttermilk
Vegetable oil

Combine first 6 ingredients; stir well.

Dip each piece of chicken in buttermilk; dredge in flour mixture, coating well. Heat 1 inch of oil in a skillet; add chicken, and cook over medium heat 20 minutes or until golden brown, turning occasionally. Drain on paper towels. Yield: 2 servings.

Oven Fried Chicken

4 chicken breast halves, thighs, or legs
¼ cup butter or margarine, melted
Salt and pepper
1 to 1½ cups finely crushed cheese crackers

Dip chicken in butter; sprinkle with salt and pepper. Roll pieces in cracker crumbs until thoroughly coated. Place in a greased 12- × 8- × 2-inch baking dish. Bake, uncovered, at 350° for 1 hour. Yield: 2 servings.

To prevent grease from spattering while frying, invert a colander over the skillet to catch grease and allow steam to escape.

Cheese-Topped Chicken

1 (2- to 3-pound) broiler-fryer, halved
Salt and pepper
2 cups (8 ounces) shredded Cheddar
  cheese
1 jalapeño pepper, seeded and minced
1½ tablespoons green pepper, chopped
3 tablespoons chopped celery
1 small onion, chopped
½ cup chopped olives, drained
Celery leaves (optional)

Sprinkle chicken with salt and pepper; place in a well-greased 12- × 8- × 2-inch baking dish. Cover with foil and bake at 350° for 1 to 1½ hours or until tender. Drain excess juices.

Combine remaining ingredients except celery leaves; spoon on top of chicken. Bake at 325° about 15 minutes or until cheese melts. Garnish with celery leaves, if desired. Yield: 2 servings.

Curried Chicken

1 (2- to 3-pound) broiler-fryer, halved
½ teaspoon salt
⅓ cup butter or margarine, melted
1 teaspoon Worcestershire sauce
1 teaspoon curry powder
½ teaspoon oregano leaves
¼ teaspoon dry mustard
¼ teaspoon garlic powder
⅛ teaspoon paprika
1 to 2 drops hot sauce
3 tablespoons sherry or chicken
  bouillon
Spiced peaches (optional)
Parsley (optional)

Sprinkle chicken with salt, and place skin side down in a greased 12- × 8- × 2-inch baking dish. Combine next 9 ingredients, mixing well; brush over chicken. Bake at 350° for 1 to 1½ hours or until tender, turning and basting with pan drippings several times. Garnish with spiced peaches and parsley, if desired. Yield: 2 servings.

Herbed Chicken

1 (2- to 3-pound) broiler-fryer, halved
¼ cup butter or margarine, melted
½ teaspoon salt
½ teaspoon ground sage
½ teaspoon parsley flakes
¼ teaspoon onion powder
Dash of pepper

Place chicken in a shallow baking pan. Combine butter and seasonings, mixing well; brush on chicken. Bake, uncovered, at 325° for 1½ hours. Yield: 2 servings.

Sherried Chicken

1 (2- to 3-pound) broiler-fryer, halved
Seasoned salt
2 tablespoons tarragon vinegar
2 tablespoons vegetable oil
1 clove garlic, minced
2 tablespoons chopped fresh parsley
2 tablespoons butter or margarine,
  melted
½ cup plus 2 tablespoons sherry,
  divided
1 cup sliced fresh mushrooms

Sprinkle chicken with seasoned salt.

Combine vinegar, oil, garlic, and parsley. Sauté 1 portion of chicken in half the vinegar mixture until lightly browned, turning once. Repeat procedure.

Place both chicken halves in a greased 13- × 9- × 2-inch baking pan; add butter and ½ cup sherry. Bake at 350° for 1 hour or until done. Add 2 tablespoons sherry and mushrooms; bake 5 to 10 minutes or until thoroughly heated. Yield: 2 servings.

Soy-Grilled Chicken

½ cup soy sauce
¼ cup sherry
¼ cup honey
1 clove garlic, crushed
¼ teaspoon ground ginger
3 tablespoons butter or margarine, melted
1 (2- to 3-pound) broiler-fryer, halved

Combine first 6 ingredients; cook 5 minutes, stirring constantly. Arrange chicken in a shallow pan; cover with sauce, and marinate 15 minutes.

Place chicken, skin side up, on grill. Cook 1 hour or until tender; turn often and baste about every 10 minutes. Watch carefully to prevent burning. Yield: 2 servings.

Chicken Pie for Two

1 (5-ounce) can boned chicken, drained
6 small white onions, peeled
1 cup biscuit mix
2 tablespoons butter or margarine, melted
2 tablespoons all-purpose flour
¼ teaspoon salt
Dash of pepper
¼ teaspoon Worcestershire sauce
1 chicken-flavored bouillon cube
½ cup milk
2 teaspoons sherry
½ cup minced celery
Milk
Parsley (optional)

Cut chicken into bite-size pieces; set aside. Cook onions, covered, in boiling salted water for 10 minutes or until tender; drain.

Prepare biscuit mix according to package directions; roll out dough and cut into 2-inch circles.

Combine butter and flour in top of double boiler; cook until bubbly. Add salt, pepper, Worcestershire sauce, bouillon cube, and ½ cup milk; cook, stirring constantly, until smooth and thickened. Remove from heat, and blend in sherry.

Arrange chicken, onions, and celery in 2 individual casseroles or a 1-quart casserole; add sauce, and top with biscuits. Brush biscuits with milk. Bake at 425° for 30 minutes or until biscuits are browned. Garnish with parsley, if desired. Yield: 2 servings.

Chicken a la King

2 tablespoons chopped green pepper
1 (2-ounce) can sliced mushrooms, drained
2 tablespoons butter or margarine
2 tablespoons all-purpose flour
½ teaspoon salt
Dash of pepper
½ cup chicken broth
½ cup half-and-half
½ cup diced cooked chicken
2 tablespoons chopped pimiento
2 frozen patty shells, baked

Sauté green pepper and mushrooms in butter in a medium skillet until green pepper is tender. Combine flour, salt, and pepper; add to vegetables, stirring until smooth. Cook 1 minute, stirring constantly. Gradually add chicken broth and half-and-half; cook over medium heat, stirring constantly, until thickened and bubbly.

Stir in chicken and pimiento; cook until thoroughly heated. Divide filling between patty shells. Yield: 2 servings.

When a sauce curdles, remove pan from heat and plunge into a pan of cold water to stop cooking process. Beat sauce vigorously or pour into a blender and beat.

Chicken Livers over Rice

4 slices bacon
2 tablespoons all-purpose flour
Dash of pepper
½ pound chicken livers
1 tablespoon chopped onion
1 (10¾-ounce) can cream of mushroom
 soup, undiluted
¼ cup water
1 cup hot cooked rice

Fry bacon until crisp; drain, crumble, and set aside. Reserve 2 tablespoons drippings. Combine flour and pepper; dredge livers in flour. Brown livers and onion in reserved bacon drippings; cover, and cook over low heat 8 to 10 minutes.

Combine soup and water; add to livers. Heat thoroughly, and serve over hot rice. Top with bacon. Yield: 2 servings.

Sherried Chicken Livers

¾ pound chicken livers
2 tablespoons butter or margarine
¼ teaspoon crushed sage
⅛ teaspoon salt
Dash of pepper
2 tablespoons sherry
Toast points

Sauté livers in butter over low heat; add seasonings. Cook 5 minutes, stirring constantly. Remove livers from pan; set aside and keep warm. Add sherry to liquid in pan. Cook 3 minutes, stirring constantly. Pour mixture over chicken livers; serve on toast points. Yield: 2 servings.

Use kitchen shears to cut shells from shrimp, to snip parsley, to trim pastry shells, and to cut many foods. This saves time and gives a neat-looking cut.

Tarragon Chicken Livers

¾ pound chicken livers
Salt and pepper to taste
All-purpose flour
Vegetable oil
¼ cup chopped onion
1 tablespoon tarragon vinegar
¼ cup chicken broth
2 teaspoons all-purpose flour
¼ cup commercial sour cream

Sprinkle livers with salt and pepper; dredge in flour. Brown in ¼ inch of hot oil; remove from skillet, and drain well. Reserve 2 tablespoons pan drippings. Keep livers warm in oven while preparing sauce.

Sauté onion in reserved drippings; add vinegar, and cook until evaporated. Add broth, stirring to loosen pan particles; simmer 2 to 3 minutes.

Combine 2 teaspoons flour and sour cream; add to broth. Heat thoroughly, stirring constantly; do not boil. Pour over livers. Yield: 2 servings.

Cornish Hen for Two

1 (1½-pound) Cornish hen, split
 lengthwise
Salt and pepper
1 slice bacon, cut in half
1½ teaspoons lemon juice
½ teaspoon chicken-flavored bouillon
 granules
½ cup hot water

Sprinkle hen halves with salt and pepper; place cut side down in a large shallow roasting pan. Place half a slice of bacon on top of each half, and sprinkle with lemon juice.

Dissolve bouillon granules in hot water, and pour in pan. Bake at 375° for 1 hour and 15 minutes or until juice runs clear when thigh is pierced with a fork; baste often with pan drippings. Yield: 2 servings.

Apricot-Glazed Cornish Hens

1 cup herb-seasoned stuffing mix
¼ cup hot water
2 tablespoons butter or margarine, melted
2 (1-pound) Cornish hens
½ cup apricot preserves
½ cup water
1 (¾-ounce) envelope brown gravy mix
Dash of ground cloves

Combine stuffing, ¼ cup water, and butter; mix well. Stuff hens with dressing, and truss securely. Place hens breast side up in a 9-inch square baking pan.

Combine preserves, ½ cup water, gravy mix, and cloves in a small saucepan; cook over medium heat, stirring constantly, just until sauce reaches a boil. Spoon half of sauce over hens; use remainder for basting.

Bake at 350° for 1 hour or until juice runs clear when thigh is pierced with a fork; baste hens occasionally with sauce during baking. Yield: 2 servings.

Cornish Hen in Wine Sauce

1 (1½-pound) Cornish hen, split lengthwise
Garlic salt
Salt and pepper
1 small onion, chopped
1 (2-ounce) can sliced mushrooms, drained
1½ tablespoons butter or margarine
¼ cup dry white wine
3 tablespoons commercial sour cream

Sprinkle hen halves with seasonings; place cut side down in a lightly greased 12- × 8- × 2-inch baking dish. Cover with foil, and bake at 350° for 30 minutes. Remove foil, and bake an additional 30 minutes.

Sauté onion and mushrooms in butter over medium heat 5 minutes; stir in wine. Pour wine mixture over hen halves. Bake an additional 25 minutes or until juice runs clear when thigh is pierced with a fork.

Place hen halves on a serving platter, reserving pan drippings. Stir sour cream into pan drippings, and pour over Cornish hen. Yield: 2 servings.

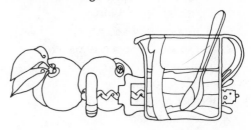

Wine-Basted Turkey Breast

1 (5- to 6-pound) turkey breast, thawed
Butter or margarine
3 tablespoons butter or margarine
2 tablespoons finely chopped parsley
½ cup dry white wine

Wipe turkey dry with paper towel. Rub thoroughly with butter. Arrange on rack in roaster. Bake at 325° for 25 minutes per pound or until meat thermometer reaches 170°.

Melt 3 tablespoons butter in a small saucepan. Add parsley; cook over medium heat 2 to 3 minutes. Add wine and heat thoroughly.

Brush turkey with wine-butter mixture several times during last 1 hour of cooking time. Let turkey stand 10 to 15 minutes before slicing. Skim fat off pan drippings; spoon drippings over turkey to serve. Yield: about 10 servings.

Note: Remaining turkey can be sliced and chopped and used in Turkey Salad Casserole, Quick Turkey Étouffée, or any other dish calling for cooked turkey. To freeze unused turkey, slice and place in freezer in a tightly covered container.

Quick Turkey Etouffee

¼ cup butter or margarine
2 teaspoons shortening
½ cup chopped onion
⅓ cup chopped celery
3 tablespoons chopped green onion
2 tablespoons chopped green pepper
1 tablespoon chopped parsley
1 cup diced cooked turkey
3 tablespoons dry sherry
2 tablespoons chopped pimiento
½ teaspoon bottled brown bouquet
    sauce (optional)
½ teaspoon hot sauce
¼ teaspoon sugar
1 teaspoon salt
¼ teaspoon black pepper
⅛ teaspoon red pepper
1 clove garlic, crushed
Hot cooked rice

Melt butter and shortening in a medium skillet; sauté onion, celery, green onion, green pepper, and parsley until tender. Add remaining ingredients except rice, stirring well. Cover and simmer 10 minutes. Serve over rice. Yield: 2 servings.

Turkey Salad Casserole

2 (1-ounce) packages potato chips
¼ cup shredded sharp Cheddar cheese
½ teaspoon butter or margarine
¼ cup chopped walnuts
1 cup diced cooked turkey
1 cup thinly sliced celery
1 teaspoon grated onion
⅛ teaspoon salt
¼ cup mayonnaise or salad dressing
1 tablespoon lemon juice

Crush potato chips to make 1 cup; combine potato chips and cheese. Place half of potato chip mixture in a lightly greased 8-inch square baking dish. Set remaining potato chip mixture aside.

Melt butter in a small skillet over low heat; add walnuts and sauté until lightly toasted (about 15 minutes), stirring occasionally. Drain nuts on absorbent paper.

Combine nuts, turkey, celery, onion, salt, mayonnaise, and lemon juice; spoon over potato chip mixture in baking dish. Sprinkle with remaining potato chip mixture. Bake at 450° for 10 to 15 minutes or until hot and bubbly. Yield: 2 servings.

Quail in Wine Sauce

½ cup all-purpose flour
Salt and pepper to taste
4 to 5 quail, cleaned
¼ cup butter or margarine
½ cup sliced mushrooms
¼ cup chopped onion
½ cup white wine
1 tablespoon chopped parsley
½ cup whipping cream
Cooked wild rice
Parsley sprigs (optional)

Combine flour, salt, and pepper. Dredge quail in seasoned flour, and brown in butter in a large skillet. Remove quail from skillet; set aside. Add mushrooms and onion to skillet, and cook until tender.

Return quail to skillet; add wine and chopped parsley. Reduce heat; cover and simmer 30 minutes. Remove quail from skillet; add whipping cream to pan drippings, stirring until smooth. Heat thoroughly.

Arrange quail and rice on serving platter; garnish with parsley, if desired. Serve with sauce. Yield: 2 servings.

Keep bacon drippings in a covered container in the refrigerator; use for browning meats or seasoning vegetables.

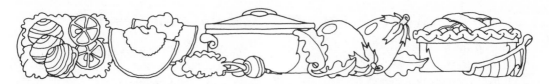

SALADS AND DRESSINGS

Apple-Stuffed Avocado

¼ cup cubed apple
¼ cup finely chopped celery
2 tablespoons commercial French
   dressing
1 large avocado, peeled and halved
2 tablespoons mayonnaise
Paprika
Lettuce (optional)

Combine apple and celery; add French dressing, and mix well. Spoon into avocado halves. Top each half with 1 tablespoon mayonnaise; sprinkle with paprika. Serve on lettuce, if desired. Yield: 2 servings.

Avocado Fruit Salad

1 grapefruit
1 avocado
½ cup mayonnaise
¼ cup commercial sour cream
3 tablespoons powdered sugar
1 mint leaf
¼ cup halved strawberries
Toasted slivered almonds

Section grapefruit and remove seeds, reserving juice with fruit. Cut avocado in half lengthwise; twist gently to separate, and remove seed. Scoop out avocado using a melon ball scoop, leaving shells intact; set aside shells. Toss avocado balls with grapefruit to keep from darkening.

Combine mayonnaise, sour cream, sugar,

mint, and strawberries in container of electric blender; blend until smooth.

Drain fruit, and spoon into avocado shells; sprinkle with almonds. Serve with dressing. Yield: 2 servings.

Sherried Cherry Salad

½ cup chopped fresh Bing cherries
¼ cup chopped celery
¼ cup chopped walnuts
½ cup fresh pineapple chunks, chilled,
   or ½ (8-ounce) can pineapple chunks,
   drained and chilled
Lettuce leaves
Sherry Salad Dressing
Mint sprigs (optional)

Combine cherries, celery, and walnuts; stir well and chill. Stir in pineapple just before serving (cherry juice will discolor pineapple). Serve fruit on lettuce leaves. Top with Sherry Salad Dressing; garnish with mint leaves, if desired. Yield: 2 servings.

Sherry Salad Dressing:

1½ tablespoons vegetable oil
1 tablespoon commercial sour cream
1½ teaspoons lemon juice
1½ teaspoons cream sherry
Pinch of sugar
Pinch of salt
Dash of white pepper

Combine all ingredients; beat well. Yield: about ¼ cup.

Creamy Cranberry Salad

½ cup fresh cranberries
½ cup miniature marshmallows
1 to 2 tablespoons sugar
½ cup diced unpeeled tart apple
¼ cup seedless grapes
¼ cup chopped pecans or walnuts
Pinch of salt
½ cup frozen whipped topping, thawed

Sort and wash cranberries; grind finely. Combine cranberries, marshmallows, and sugar; cover and chill overnight. Add apple, grapes, pecans, and salt; mix well. Fold in whipped topping. Chill. Yield: 2 servings.

Fruited Cottage Cheese Salad

⅔ cup cream-style cottage cheese
⅛ teaspoon finely chopped mint
2 teaspoons sugar
About 1 cup diced fresh pineapple
Lettuce leaves
1 medium orange, peeled and sectioned
Fresh mint sprigs

Combine cottage cheese, chopped mint, and sugar; chill thoroughly. Just before serving, add pineapple; spoon onto lettuce leaves. Top with orange sections, and garnish with fresh mint. Yield: 2 servings.

Gingered Fruit Compote

1 apple, cored and sliced
1 orange, peeled and sectioned
1 banana, sliced
¼ cup orange juice
2 teaspoons grated fresh ginger

Combine all ingredients; cover and chill 2 hours. Yield: 2 servings.

Green Grape Salad

¾ cup seedless green grapes
¾ cup diced apple
½ cup sliced celery
½ cup walnuts or pecans coarsely chopped
¼ cup mayonnaise
1½ teaspoons milk
1 teaspoon lemon juice
Salt and pepper to taste
Lettuce leaves

Combine grapes, apple, celery, and walnuts in a medium bowl. Gently toss to combine. Combine mayonnaise, milk, and lemon juice in a small bowl. Stir into grape mixture. Add salt and pepper to taste. Serve on lettuce leaves. Yield: 2 servings.

Sherried Orange Salad

1 tablespoon lemon juice
1½ tablespoons vegetable oil
Pinch of salt
Red pepper to taste
Sugar to taste
⅛ teaspoon sherry
2 oranges, peeled and sliced
2 tablespoons coarsely chopped pecans
6 maraschino cherries, halved
Lettuce leaves

Combine lemon juice, oil, salt, pepper, sugar, and sherry; beat well. Combine orange slices, pecans, and cherries; spoon onto lettuce. Top with dressing. Yield: 2 servings.

Fresh Peach Salad

¼ cup crushed pineapple, drained
¼ cup shredded coconut
¼ cup cottage cheese
¼ cup commercial sour cream
2 fresh peaches, peeled, seeded, and
  halved

Combine pineapple, coconut, cottage cheese, and sour cream in a medium bowl, stirring well. Chill.

Fill peach halves with mixture and serve immediately. Yield: 2 servings.

Swedish Slaw

½ cup sugar
½ cup vinegar
½ teaspoon dry mustard
½ teaspoon ground turmeric
½ medium head cabbage, chopped
½ medium-size green pepper, chopped
½ medium onion, chopped

Combine sugar, vinegar, mustard, and turmeric in a saucepan; boil mixture 1 minute.

Combine cabbage, green pepper, and onion in a large mixing bowl. Pour hot mixture over slaw, stirring well. Chill. Yield: 2 servings.

Carrot-Date Slaw

¼ cup commercial sour cream
2 tablespoons milk
2 teaspoons lemon juice
½ teaspoon sugar
Dash of salt
1½ cups shredded carrots
¼ cup chopped dates

Combine all ingredients; stir well. Chill thoroughly. Yield: 2 servings.

Crunchy Cauliflower Salad

1 cup sliced cauliflower flowerets
½ cup shredded carrot
½ cup chopped celery
1 tablespoon minced green pepper
¼ cup mayonnaise
2 tablespoons milk
1 teaspoon vinegar
1 teaspoon frozen or dried chopped
  chives
¼ teaspoon salt
Dash of pepper
Lettuce leaves

Combine first 4 ingredients; chill. Combine remaining ingredients except lettuce leaves; mix well, using a wire whisk. Chill.

Pour dressing over vegetables; toss well. Serve on lettuce leaves. Yield: 2 servings.

Greek Salad

⅓ bunch romaine
4 radishes, sliced
2 green onions, tops included, cut into
  ½-inch pieces
½ small red onion, sliced
2 tablespoons olive oil
1½ tablespoons red wine vinegar
Pinch of dried oregano leaves
10 to 12 Greek olives
6 to 8 (½-inch) cubes feta cheese
Anchovies (optional)

Tear lettuce into bite-size pieces. Toss lettuce, radishes, and green and red onions in a medium bowl. Cover and refrigerate.

Combine oil, vinegar, and oregano in a small jar. Cover and shake well. Refrigerate.

When ready to serve, shake dressing thoroughly; add to salad. Toss to combine. Top with olives, feta cheese, and anchovies, if desired. Yield: 2 servings.

Special Egg Salad

4 hard-cooked eggs, chopped
4 slices bacon, cooked and crumbled
1 teaspoon chopped onion
¼ teaspoon olive oil
1½ teaspoons prepared mustard
2 to 3 tablespoons mayonnaise
1 teaspoon vinegar
Salt and pepper to taste

Combine all ingredients; mix well. Chill salad until serving time. Yield: 2 servings.

Macaroni Salad for Two

1 cup cooked elbow macaroni, cooled
1 hard-cooked egg, chopped
2 tablespoons chopped celery
2 tablespoons chopped onion
3 tablespoons mayonnaise or salad dressing
1 teaspoon sugar
1 teaspoon vinegar
¼ teaspoon salt
¼ teaspoon prepared mustard
Pepper to taste

Combine all ingredients, stirring lightly; cover and chill several hours before serving. Yield: 2 servings.

Potato Salad for Two

2 to 3 medium potatoes
¼ cup chopped onion
1 stalk celery, finely chopped
⅓ cup chopped green pepper
2 tablespoons chopped pimiento
2 teaspoons hot water
2 teaspoons vinegar
⅓ cup mayonnaise
½ teaspoon salt

Place potatoes in boiling salted water to cover; cook 20 to 25 minutes or until tender. Drain and cool; peel and cut into ¾-inch cubes. Combine potatoes, onion, celery, green pepper, and pimiento.

Combine water, vinegar, mayonnaise, and salt; mix well. Spoon over potato mixture; toss lightly. Chill. Yield: 2 servings.

Potato Salad with Cottage Cheese

2 cups cooked cubed potatoes
¼ cup sliced celery
2 tablespoons chopped green pepper
2 tablespoons chopped pimiento
1 tablespoon minced onion
1 tablespoon chopped sweet pickle
½ cup mayonnaise
½ teaspoon salt
Dash of pepper
½ teaspoon dry mustard
1½ teaspoons lemon juice
½ cup small-curd cottage cheese
Lettuce or other greens

Combine potatoes, celery, green pepper, pimiento, onion, and pickle; toss lightly. Chill. Combine mayonnaise, seasonings, and lemon juice; add to potato mixture. Add cottage cheese; stir gently. Serve over lettuce. Yield: 2 servings.

Hot Potato Salad

2 teaspoons butter or margarine
2 teaspoons all-purpose flour
⅔ cup milk
½ teaspoon salt
⅛ teaspoon dried dillweed
Dash of pepper
¼ cup mayonnaise or salad dressing
1 tablespoon finely chopped onion
1½ cups diced cooked potatoes
Paprika

Melt butter in a heavy saucepan over low heat; blend in flour, and cook 1 minute. Gradually add milk; cook over medium heat, stirring constantly, until thickened and bubbly. Stir in salt, dillweed, and pepper; add mayonnaise, stirring well. Stir in onion and potatoes. Sprinkle with paprika. Serve warm. Yield: 2 servings.

Easy Rice Salad

¾ cup water
¾ cup instant rice
¼ cup chopped celery
2 tablespoons chopped dill pickle
1 tablespoon chopped onion
1 tablespoon chopped parsley
¼ teaspoon dry mustard
½ cup mayonnaise
Salt and pepper
Hard-cooked egg slices or stuffed olive
   slices

Bring water to a boil, and stir in rice. Cover; remove from heat, and let stand 5 minutes. Add celery, dill pickle, onion, parsley, mustard, and mayonnaise; chill at least 1 hour. Add salt and pepper to taste; garnish with egg or olive slices. Yield: 2 servings.

Rice and Vegetable Salad

4 slices bacon, cooked and crumbled
1½ cups cooked rice
½ cup cooked English peas
½ cup thinly sliced celery
¼ cup mayonnaise
2 tablespoons diced pimiento
2 tablespoons minced fresh chives
⅛ teaspoon salt
⅛ teaspoon pepper
Pimiento-stuffed olives

Combine all ingredients except olives; toss. Garnish with olives; chill. Yield: 2 servings.

Spinach Salad with Mushrooms

½ pound fresh spinach
¼ pound fresh mushrooms
¼ cup vegetable oil
2 tablespoons wine vinegar
2 teaspoons grated onion
1 teaspoon Dijon mustard
½ teaspoon salt
½ teaspoon sugar
Freshly ground pepper
2 slices bacon, cooked and crumbled

Remove stems from spinach; wash leaves thoroughly, and pat dry. Tear into bite-size pieces. Quickly rinse mushrooms in cold water; drain well, and slice thin.

Combine oil, vinegar, onion, mustard, salt, sugar, and pepper in a jar; shake well to blend. Combine spinach, mushrooms, and dressing in a salad bowl; toss until well coated. Top with bacon. Yield: 2 servings.

Cottage Cheese-Stuffed Tomatoes

2 tomatoes
Salt
¼ cup small-curd cottage cheese
½ teaspoon Worcestershire sauce
¼ teaspoon chopped chives
2 slices bacon, cooked and crumbled
¼ teaspoon prepared horseradish
Salt to taste
Lettuce leaves

Slice off top and scoop out pulp from each tomato; reserve pulp for use in other recipes. Sprinkle inside of shells with salt, and invert on absorbent towel.

Combine remaining ingredients except lettuce leaves; fill tomatoes with mixture. Serve on lettuce leaves. Yield: 2 servings.

Fresh Tomato Aspic

1 envelope unflavored gelatin
1 cup cold water, divided
1 chicken-flavored bouillon cube
½ cup tomato juice
1 tablespoon lemon juice
1 teaspoon dried dillweed
½ teaspoon salt
¼ teaspoon hot sauce
2 tablespoons chopped green onion
1 cup peeled and chopped fresh
    tomatoes
½ cup peeled and chopped cucumber
Lettuce leaves (optional)

Soften gelatin in ½ cup cold water; add bouillon cube. Place over low heat, stirring constantly, until gelatin and bouillon cube dissolve. Remove from heat, and add remaining ½ cup water, tomato juice, lemon juice, dillweed, salt, hot sauce, and green onion. Chill gelatin mixture until consistency of unbeaten egg white.

Fold tomatoes and cucumber into thickened gelatin, and spoon mixture into 2 to 3 individual molds. Chill until firm; unmold. Serve aspic on lettuce leaves, if desired. Yield: 2 servings.

Beef and Bean Salad

¼ cup mayonnaise or salad dressing
2 teaspoons chili sauce
2 teaspoons sweet pickle relish
⅛ teaspoon salt
1 cup cubed cooked beef
½ cup drained red kidney beans
½ cup chopped celery
3 tablespoons chopped onion
1 hard-cooked egg, chopped

Combine first 4 ingredients, and mix well; add remaining ingredients, and toss well. Refrigerate 24 hours before serving. Yield: 2 servings.

Chicken Salad Supreme

1 whole chicken breast
1 cup seedless white grapes, halved
½ cup chopped pecans
¼ to ⅓ cup mayonnaise
2 tablespoons commercial sour cream
2 teaspoons lime juice
½ teaspoon salt
1 pineapple, cut in half lengthwise and
    cored

Place chicken in boiling salted water to cover and cook until tender (about 25 minutes); drain and cool. Skin and bone chicken; coarsely chop meat.

Combine chicken, grapes, pecans, mayonnaise, sour cream, and lime juice. Toss gently, and add salt. Cover and refrigerate about 2 hours or until thoroughly chilled.

Scoop pulp from pineapple, leaving ½-inch thick shells. Cut pulp into bite-size pieces. Set aside fruit pieces and shells.

To serve, mound chicken salad in pineapple shells. Garnish or serve with pineapple pieces. Yield: 2 servings.

Ham and Avocado Salad

½ cup cubed cooked ham
2 hard-cooked eggs, chopped
1 sweet pickle, chopped
1 green onion, chopped
¾ cup chopped celery
¼ cup mayonnaise
1½ teaspoons sweet pickle juice
1 avocado, peeled and sliced
¼ cup cashew nuts
8 cherry tomatoes

Combine first 7 ingredients, mixing well. Spoon ham mixture on avocado slices, and garnish with nuts and tomatoes. Yield: 2 servings.

Pork Salad

⅓ cup mayonnaise
½ teaspoon Dijon mustard
2 tablespoons whipping cream
1½ teaspoons apple brandy or apple
　juice
2 cups julienne cold roast pork
1 small apple, thinly sliced
1 tablespoon raisins
Lettuce leaves
1 tablespoon chopped parsley

Combine mayonnaise, mustard, whipping cream, and apple brandy; mix well, and set aside.

Combine pork, apple, and raisins; toss with mayonnaise mixture. Serve on lettuce, and garnish with parsley. Yield: 2 servings.

Crab Louis Salad

¼ cup mayonnaise
¼ cup chili sauce
1 tablespoon chopped green pepper
1 tablespoon chopped sweet pickle
2 teaspoons chopped onion
2 teaspoons lemon juice
¾ cup lump crabmeat or ½ (12-ounce)
　package frozen lump crabmeat,
　thawed and drained
Lettuce leaves
1 tomato, quartered
1 green pepper, sliced
1 hard-cooked egg, sliced into rings
Pimiento strips

Combine mayonnaise, chili sauce, chopped green pepper, sweet pickle, onion, and lemon juice; blend well. Add crabmeat, tossing lightly. Chill thoroughly.

At serving time, spoon salad on lettuce. Garnish with tomato quarters, green pepper slices, egg slices, and pimiento strips. Yield: 2 servings.

Tuna Goddess Salad

1 (7-ounce) can white tuna in water
Crisp salad greens
1 cup sliced mushrooms
½ pound fresh asparagus spears,
　steamed
2 hard-cooked eggs, quartered
4 to 6 ripe olives
4 to 6 cherry tomatoes
Goddess Dressing

Drain tuna well. Spread crisp salad greens on two salad plates. Arrange tuna in center and surround with mushrooms, asparagus, eggs, ripe olives, and tomatoes. Serve with Goddess Dressing. Yield: 2 servings.

Goddess Dressing:

½ cup mayonnaise
1 tablespoon finely chopped green
　onion
1 tablespoon finely chopped parsley
¾ to 1 teaspoon dried tarragon leaves
1 teaspoon lemon juice
Dash of pepper

Combine all ingredients in container of electric blender; process on low speed about 30 seconds or until smooth. Yield: about ½ cup.

Shrimp and Melon Salad

2 teaspoons lemon juice
1 cup diced, cooked shrimp
½ cup diced cantaloupe or honeydew
½ cup cold cooked rice
¼ teaspoon salt
⅛ teaspoon white pepper
¼ cup mayonnaise
Parsley

Sprinkle lemon juice over shrimp; add cantaloupe, rice, salt, and pepper. Toss lightly, and stir in mayonnaise. Chill. Garnish with parsley. Yield: about 2 servings.

Louisiana Shrimp Salad

½ pound medium shrimp, cooked,
   peeled, and deveined
1 hard-cooked egg, chopped
½ cup chopped celery
¼ cup chopped onion
1 tablespoon chopped dill pickle
¼ cup mayonnaise
2 teaspoons catsup
¼ teaspoon Worcestershire sauce
Salt and pepper to taste
Lettuce leaves (optional)

Combine all ingredients except lettuce; mix
well. Serve on lettuce, if desired. Yield: 2
servings.

Angel Salad Dressing

½ cup mayonnaise
¼ cup whipping cream, whipped
2 tablespoons raspberry preserves

Combine ingredients, stirring gently. Serve
over fruit salads. Yield: about 1 cup.

Tangy Blue Cheese Dressing

½ cup wine vinegar with garlic
¼ cup red wine
2 tablespoons vegetable oil
2 tablespoons sugar
2 tablespoons catsup
1 clove garlic, pressed
1 teaspoon paprika
1 teaspoon steak or meat sauce
1 teaspoon Worcestershire sauce
1 teaspoon prepared mustard
1 (2-ounce) package blue cheese,
   crumbled

Combine all ingredients, mixing well. Serve
over tossed salad. Yield: 1 cup.

Blue Cheese French Dressing

½ cup mayonnaise
¼ cup catsup
¼ cup commercial French dressing
¼ teaspoon Worcestershire sauce
1 (2-ounce) package blue cheese,
   crumbled
¼ teaspoon salt

Combine all ingredients, mixing well. Store,
covered, in refrigerator. Stir well before serving over tossed salad. Yield: about 1¼ cups.

Buttermilk Salad Dressing

½ cup buttermilk
½ cup mayonnaise
½ teaspoon garlic powder
¼ teaspoon onion powder
2 teaspoons parsley flakes
¼ teaspoon salt
⅛ teaspoon white pepper

Combine all ingredients, mixing well. Chill
at least 4 hours. Serve with coleslaw or
tossed salad. Yield: 1 cup.

Cooked Coleslaw Dressing

2 eggs
1 cup sugar
1 teaspoon dry mustard
1 tablespoon all-purpose flour
½ to 1 cup vinegar
Salt to taste
Red and black pepper to taste

Beat eggs until light and fluffy. Add sugar,
beating well. Stir in mustard and flour. Add
vinegar, salt, and pepper. Cook over low
heat, stirring constantly, until smooth and
thickened. Cool before tossing with coleslaw. Yield: 1½ cups.

Cucumber Salad Dressing

½ (3-ounce) package cream cheese, softened
½ cup mayonnaise or salad dressing
½ cup diced cucumber
½ teaspoon salt
Dash of paprika

Mash cream cheese; add mayonnaise, and beat until smooth. Add cucumber, salt, and paprika; stir until well blended. Cover; chill 3 to 4 hours. Serve over fresh vegetables. Yield: about 1 cup.

French Dressing

½ cup vegetable oil
⅓ cup distilled vinegar
¼ cup tarragon vinegar or red wine vinegar
¼ cup catsup
¼ cup chili sauce
2 tablespoons sugar
1½ teaspoons prepared mustard
1½ teaspoons Worcestershire sauce
1½ teaspoons prepared horseradish
1 small onion, finely chopped
Salt to taste

Combine all ingredients; stir well. Chill. Store, covered, in refrigerator. Stir well before serving over citrus or salad greens. Yield: about 2 cups.

Whipped Cream Fruit Dressing

½ cup pineapple juice
1 egg yolk, beaten
Juice of ½ lemon
¼ cup sugar
2 teaspoons prepared mustard
Dash of salt
½ cup whipping cream, whipped

Combine all ingredients except whipped cream in a small saucepan. Cook over low heat, stirring occasionally, until smooth and thickened (about 30 minutes). Cool; fold in whipped cream just before serving. Serve over fruit. Yield: about 1½ cups.

Honey Dressing

⅓ cup sugar
½ teaspoon dry mustard
½ teaspoon celery seeds
¼ teaspoon salt
¼ teaspoon paprika
Dash of pepper
½ cup vegetable oil
2 tablespoons honey
¼ cup lemon juice
1 teaspoon vinegar
½ teaspoon grated onion

Combine all ingredients in a small bowl; mix thoroughly. Refrigerate 8 hours before serving. Serve over fresh fruit. Yield: 1 cup.

Italian Dressing

¾ cup olive oil
¼ cup wine vinegar
2 teaspoons minced fresh chives
1 teaspoon salt
1 teaspoon minced parsley
⅛ teaspoon black pepper
⅛ teaspoon red pepper
⅛ teaspoon dillseeds
1 clove garlic

Combine all ingredients in a jar. Cover tightly, and shake vigorously. Chill several hours. Remove garlic clove before serving. Serve dressing over salad greens. Yield: about 1 cup.

Louis Dressing

½ cup mayonnaise
⅓ cup chili sauce
1½ tablespoons minced celery
1½ tablespoons minced dill pickle
1½ teaspoons lemon juice
1 teaspoon Worcestershire sauce
¼ teaspoon prepared horseradish

Combine all ingredients, stirring well; chill. Store, covered, in refrigerator. Serve over seafood, ham, or salad greens. Yield: 1 cup.

Homemade Mayonnaise

2 egg yolks or 1 whole egg
2 tablespoons vinegar or lemon juice, divided
1 teaspoon dry mustard
½ teaspoon salt
Dash of red pepper
1 cup vegetable oil

Combine egg yolks or egg, 1 tablespoon vinegar, mustard, salt, and pepper in small mixing bowl. Beat with an electric mixer at medium speed until well blended. Continue beating, adding ¼ cup oil, drop by drop. Add remaining oil 1 tablespoon at a time, beating constantly. Slowly beat in remaining vinegar. Place in jar with tight-fitting lid. Store in refrigerator. Yield: 1¼ cups.

Blender Method:

Measure ¼ cup oil and all other ingredients into blender container. Blend at high speed for 5 seconds. While blending at high speed, add remaining oil very slowly until thick and smooth. If necessary, turn off blender occasionally and push mixture from sides of container with a rubber spatula. Place in jar with a tight-fitting lid. Store in refrigerator.

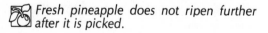 *Fresh pineapple does not ripen further after it is picked.*

Poppy Seed Dressing

¼ cup sugar
½ teaspoon dry mustard
½ teaspoon salt
½ teaspoon pepper
⅛ teaspoon paprika
1½ teaspoons grated onion
½ cup vegetable oil
3 tablespoons vinegar
1½ teaspoons poppy seeds
Red food coloring (optional)

Combine sugar, seasonings, and onion in a mixing bowl. Add oil in a slow steady stream, beating at medium speed of electric mixer. Add vinegar and poppy seeds; beat well. Add a small amount of food coloring to make a soft rose color, if desired.

Store, covered, in refrigerator. Stir well before using. Serve over fruit salads. Yield: about ¾ cup.

Thousand Island Dressing

½ cup catsup
¼ cup relish sandwich spread
¼ cup mayonnaise
1 teaspoon vegetable oil

Combine all ingredients, stirring well; chill. Store, covered, in refrigerator. Serve over tossed greens. Yield: 1 cup.

Yogurt Salad Dressing

1 (8-ounce) carton plain yogurt
¾ cup catsup
1 tablespoon vinegar
Pinch of ground oregano

Combine all ingredients in a small mixing bowl, and mix well. Chill. Serve over tossed salad. Yield: 1½ cups.

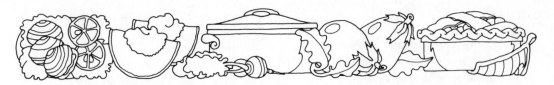

SOUPS AND SAUCES

Blender Avocado Soup

½ ripe avocado, peeled and cut into
   small pieces
¾ cup chicken broth
1½ teaspoons lemon juice
½ cup half-and-half
¼ teaspoon salt
Dash of pepper
Dash of red pepper
Lemon slices (optional)

Combine avocado, broth, and lemon juice in container of electric blender; process until smooth. Add half-and-half, salt, and pepper; stir well. Chill. Garnish with lemon slices, if desired. Yield: 2 servings.

Curried Avocado Soup

½ avocado, peeled and coarsely
   chopped
1 cup chicken broth
½ cup commercial sour cream
2 tablespoons rum (optional)
1½ teaspoons lemon juice
½ teaspoon curry powder
¼ teaspoon seasoned salt
Lemon slices (optional)

Combine first 7 ingredients in container of electric blender; process until smooth. Chill

well. Serve with lemon slices, if desired. Yield: 2 servings.

Hot Broccoli Soup

1 (10-ounce) package frozen chopped
   broccoli
3 tablespoons butter or margarine
½ cup chopped onion
¼ teaspoon salt
2 tablespoons all-purpose flour
1½ cups milk
¼ teaspoon celery salt
⅛ teaspoon garlic powder
½ teaspoon Worcestershire sauce
Commercial sour cream (optional)
Croutons (optional)

Cook broccoli according to package directions. Drain thoroughly to remove excess moisture.

Melt butter in a heavy saucepan. Stir in onion; cook until tender. Add salt and flour; cook 1 minute over medium heat. Gradually stir in milk, seasonings, and Worcestershire sauce; cook over medium heat, stirring constantly, until thickened.

Add drained broccoli to sauce mixture. Stir well. Pour into container of electric blender. Puree all ingredients; return mixture to saucepan. Heat thoroughly. Pour into serving bowls. Garnish with dollop of sour cream and croutons, if desired. Yield: about 2 servings.

Borscht

1 cup finely chopped fresh beets
½ cup finely chopped carrots
½ cup finely chopped onion
2 teaspoons butter or margarine
1 cup beef broth
½ cup finely shredded cabbage
1 tablespoon lemon juice
¼ teaspoon salt
Dash of pepper

Cover beets, carrots, and onion with boiling water; boil 20 minutes. Add butter, broth, and cabbage; cover and simmer 45 minutes. Stir in lemon juice and seasonings. Serve warm. Yield: 2 servings.

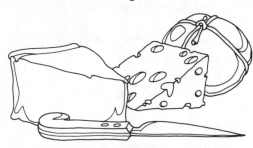

Cheese Soup

1¼ cups milk, divided
½ teaspoon cornstarch
1 tablespoon butter or margarine
Dash of paprika
⅛ teaspoon salt
⅛ teaspoon celery salt
Dash of red pepper
2 tablespoons chopped pimiento
1 cup (4 ounces) shredded process
   American cheese

Combine ¼ cup milk and cornstarch, blending well. Add remaining milk and butter; heat until butter melts. Stir in seasonings; add pimiento and cheese. Cook over low heat, stirring constantly, until cheese melts. Yield: about 2 servings.

Creamy Clam Chowder

1 slice bacon
2 tablespoons diced onion
1 small potato, peeled and diced
½ cup water
½ teaspoon salt
Dash of pepper
1 (8-ounce) can minced clams,
   undrained
1 cup milk
1 tablespoon butter or margarine

Cook bacon until crisp; drain on paper towel, and reserve drippings. Sauté onion in reserved drippings until tender; set aside.
   Combine potato, water, salt, and pepper in a saucepan; cook over medium heat just until potato is tender. Stir in clams, milk, butter, and onion; simmer 3 minutes or until heated through. Sprinkle bacon over each serving of chowder. Yield: 2 servings.

Corn and Okra Soup

1 cup fresh corn
2 cups chicken broth
¼ cup okra, cut into ½-inch pieces
1 small clove garlic, minced
¼ cup chopped celery
½ cup diced cooked chicken
1 teaspoon butter or margarine
¼ teaspoon salt
¼ teaspoon pepper
1 cup hot milk

Combine corn and chicken broth in a Dutch oven. Place over medium heat, and cook 8 to 10 minutes or until corn is tender. Add okra, garlic, celery, and chicken; simmer, uncovered, 20 to 25 minutes. Stir in butter, salt, and pepper. Gradually add milk, stirring constantly; heat thoroughly. Yield: about 2 servings.

Cold Cucumber Soup

1 (8-ounce) carton commercial sour
   cream
2 medium cucumbers, peeled and
   coarsely chopped
1 green onion, coarsely chopped
¼ teaspoon celery salt
¼ teaspoon salt
Dash of pepper
¾ teaspoon dried dillweed
2 teaspoons lemon juice
2 teaspoons Worcestershire sauce

Combine all ingredients in container of an
electric blender; process until smooth. Chill
thoroughly. Yield: 2 servings.

Mushroom Bisque

1 tablespoon butter or margarine
1½ tablespoons all-purpose flour
¼ teaspoon salt
Dash of white pepper
⅔ cup half-and-half, scalded
3 tablespoons chicken broth, heated
¾ cup milk, scalded and divided
¼ cup sliced fresh mushrooms
¼ cup chopped fresh mushrooms
¼ teaspoon minced onion
1 teaspoon butter or margarine

Melt butter in saucepan; stir in flour, salt,
and pepper and blend well. Simmer 2 minutes. Combine half-and-half, broth, and ⅔
cup milk; gradually add to flour mixture,
stirring constantly, until smooth. Cook over
medium heat until thickened. Remove from
heat, and set aside.

   Sauté mushrooms and onion in 1 teaspoon
butter 6 to 8 minutes, stirring frequently. Add
remaining milk; heat to simmering. Stir into
milk mixture; heat thoroughly. Serve immediately. Yield: about 2 servings.

Fish Chowder

1 cup diced potatoes
1 cup boiling water
3 slices bacon, chopped
1 medium onion, chopped
¾ pound fish fillets, cubed
1 cup milk
½ teaspoon salt
⅛ teaspoon pepper
2 tablespoons chopped fresh parsley

Place potatoes in boiling water in a Dutch
oven; cover and cook 10 to 15 minutes. Fry
bacon until transparent; add onion, and
cook until onion is soft and bacon is lightly
browned. Add bacon, onion, bacon drippings, and fish fillets to potatoes. Simmer 10
minutes or until potatoes and fish are done.
Stir in milk, salt, and pepper; simmer 5 minutes. Sprinkle with parsley. Yield: 2 servings.

Oyster Stew

1 cup oysters
1 tablespoon all-purpose flour
¾ teaspoon salt
1 tablespoon water
1 teaspoon Worcestershire sauce
1 tablespoon butter or margarine
1½ cups milk, scalded
½ cup whipping cream, scalded

Drain oysters, reserving liquid; set oysters
aside.

   Combine oyster liquid, flour, salt, water,
and Worcestershire sauce in a saucepan; stir
over low heat until smooth. Add oysters and
butter; simmer 5 minutes or until edges of
oysters curl.

   Combine milk and cream in small saucepan; heat to just below boiling. Stir into
oyster mixture. Cover and remove from heat;
let stand 15 minutes. Reheat over very low
heat, if desired. Yield: 2 servings.

Oyster Soup

1 tablespoon chopped onion
1 tablespoon butter or margarine
1½ tablespoons all-purpose flour
1½ cups milk
½ teaspoon salt
½ pint oysters, undrained
¼ teaspoon chopped parsley

Sauté onion in butter until tender; add flour, stirring until smooth. Cook 1 minute, stirring constantly. Gradually add milk; cook over medium heat, stirring constantly, until thickened and bubbly. Stir in salt.

Cook oysters over medium-low heat until edges start to curl up (about 5 minutes); stir into sauce. Sprinkle parsley over soup, and serve hot. Yield: 2 servings.

Freezer French Onion Soup

2 large onions, coarsely chopped
2 tablespoons bacon drippings
¼ teaspoon salt
Dash of pepper
1 clove garlic, crushed
1 tablespoon all-purpose flour
1½ teaspoons dried parsley flakes or 1½ tablespoons chopped fresh parsley
Dash of ground thyme
½ teaspoon bottled brown bouquet sauce
2 cups chicken stock
½ cup dry white wine
1 tablespoon Cognac or brandy
2 thin slices French bread, toasted
Grated Parmesan cheese

Sauté onion in bacon drippings until tender. Add salt, pepper, garlic, and flour; cook, stirring constantly, until golden brown. Add parsley, thyme, bouquet sauce, chicken stock, and wine; cover and simmer 30 minutes. Stir in Cognac.

Spoon soup into 2 bowls. Top each with 1 slice toast; sprinkle with cheese.

Freeze remaining soup for later use. To serve, thaw and heat in saucepan. Top as directed above. Yield: 3 to 4 servings.

Vegetable Soup

¾ pound meaty soup bones
3 cups water
1½ teaspoons garlic salt
1 teaspoon salt
½ teaspoon pepper
½ teaspoon dried oregano leaves
1 bay leaf
1½ teaspoons minced parsley
½ cup diced carrots
½ cup frozen whole kernel corn
1 (16-ounce) can tomatoes, undrained
½ cup frozen English peas
1 onion, quartered
¼ to ½ cup uncooked barley

Combine first 8 ingredients in a large Dutch oven; bring to a boil, and cook over low heat about 30 minutes. Add remaining ingredients, and simmer 1½ hours. Remove soup bones; cut meat from bones, and return meat to soup. Yield: 2 generous servings.

Chilled Shrimp Bisque

½ medium leek or 4 large green onions
1½ teaspoons butter or margarine
1 medium cucumber, peeled and sliced
1 bay leaf
2½ teaspoons all-purpose flour
2 cups chicken broth
½ teaspoon salt
1 small cucumber, peeled and grated
½ cup whipping cream
2 to 3 teaspoons lemon juice
1½ teaspoons finely chopped parsley
⅓ cup finely chopped cooked shrimp
Commercial sour cream

Slice white portion of leek; reserve green top for another use.

Melt butter in a heavy saucepan; add leek, sliced cucumber, and bay leaf. Cover and cook over low heat about 20 minutes or until vegetables are tender; remove bay leaf.

Stir flour into cucumber mixture; cook 1 minute, stirring constantly. Gradually add broth; cook over medium heat, stirring constantly, until thickened. Stir in salt.

Pour soup mixture into container of electric blender; process 30 seconds. Chill soup at least 4 hours. Just before serving, stir in grated cucumber, whipping cream, lemon juice, parsley, and shrimp. Top each serving with sour cream. Yield: 2 servings.

Caramel Sauce

1½ cups firmly packed brown sugar
⅔ cup light corn syrup
¼ cup butter or margarine
⅛ teaspoon salt
1 (5.33-ounce) can evaporated milk

Combine sugar, corn syrup, and butter in a medium saucepan; cook over medium heat to soft ball stage (234° to 240°), stirring constantly. Remove mixture from heat; stir in salt and milk. Serve warm over ice cream. Yield: about 2¼ cups.

Note: Cool remaining sauce and refrigerate in airtight container up to two weeks. To reheat, place in small saucepan and stir over medium heat until warm.

Cherry Sauce

1 (16-ounce) can pitted dark sweet cherries
2 tablespoons cornstarch
¼ cup sugar
¼ cup Burgundy or dry red wine

Drain cherries, reserving juice.

Combine cornstarch and sugar in a small saucepan; mix well. Gradually stir in cherry juice. Cook over medium heat, stirring constantly, until mixture boils and thickens.

Remove from heat, and stir in Burgundy and cherries. Serve warm over ice cream. Yield: about 1½ cups.

Chocolate-Peanut Butter Sauce

1 (6-ounce) package semisweet chocolate morsels
¼ cup crunchy peanut butter
¼ cup light corn syrup
¼ cup plus 1 tablespoon whipping cream

Melt chocolate morsels in top of a double boiler. Add peanut butter, stirring until well blended. Remove from heat, and stir in corn syrup and whipping cream. Serve warm over ice cream. Yield: about 1¼ cups.

Note: Store in refrigerator. Reheat over low heat before using. If sauce becomes too thick, stir in a small amount of whipping cream.

Special Chocolate Sauce

1 (6-ounce) package semisweet chocolate morsels
¼ cup butter or margarine
1 cup sifted powdered sugar
Dash of salt
½ cup light corn syrup
¼ cup hot water
¼ cup crème de cacao
1 teaspoon vanilla extract

Combine chocolate morsels, butter, sugar, salt, corn syrup, and water in a heavy saucepan. Place over low heat; stir until chocolate melts. Remove from heat, and add liqueur and vanilla.

Serve immediately, or pour hot mixture into hot, sterilized half-pint jars. Cool and store in refrigerator. Serve over ice cream or cake. Yield: about 2 cups.

Cranberry Relish

1 (16-ounce) can whole-berry cranberry
  sauce
½ cup orange marmalade
Grated rind and juice of 1 small lemon
¼ cup chopped walnuts

Combine all ingredients. Chill until ready to
serve. Serve with ham, turkey, or other
meats. Yield: about 2¼ cups.

Lemon Butter

Grated rind and juice of 1 lemon
1 egg
1 cup sugar
2 tablespoons butter or margarine,
  melted
¼ cup water

Combine all ingredients in a saucepan; cook
over low heat until mixture thickens, stirring
constantly. Serve over cake squares or bread.
Yield: about 1 cup.

Raspberry Sauce

1 (10-ounce) package frozen sweetened
  raspberries, thawed and crushed
1 tablespoon cornstarch
½ cup currant jelly

Combine raspberries and cornstarch in a
saucepan, mixing well. Add jelly; cook, stirring constantly, until bubbly. Cook 1 minute.
Strain. Cool and serve over ice cream. Yield:
about 1¼ cups.

Barbecue Seasoning Mix

⅓ cup salt
⅓ cup sugar
2½ tablespoons pepper
1 tablespoon paprika
1½ teaspoons instant lemon peel
¼ teaspoon ground thyme

Combine all ingredients, mixing well. Sprinkle heavily on chicken or other meat before
grilling. (Seasoning may darken slightly on
chicken during grilling.) Yield: about 1 cup.

Barbecue Sauce

2 tablespoons vinegar
¼ cup water
1 tablespoon brown sugar
1½ teaspoons prepared mustard
¾ teaspoon salt
¼ teaspoon pepper
⅛ teaspoon red pepper
1 tablespoon lemon juice
1 small onion, cut into ¼-inch slices
2 tablespoons butter or margarine
¼ cup catsup
1 tablespoon Worcestershire sauce
¾ teaspoon liquid smoke

Combine first 10 ingredients in a medium
saucepan; mix well. Bring to a boil; then
cook, uncovered, over medium heat 20 minutes, stirring occasionally. Stir in remaining
ingredients. Use to baste chicken or other
meat. Yield: about 1¼ cups.

Cucumber Sauce

1 medium cucumber, peeled and
  chopped
1 teaspoon sugar
½ teaspoon salt
1 (8-ounce) carton commercial sour
  cream
1 teaspoon dried dillweed
½ teaspoon pepper

Combine cucumber, sugar, and salt; let
stand 15 minutes. Drain; add remaining ingredients, and stir well. Chill 1 hour. Serve
with poultry, fish, or hamburgers. Yield:
about 2 cups.

Easy Hollandaise Sauce

1 egg yolk, lightly beaten
⅛ teaspoon salt
⅛ teaspoon white pepper
1½ teaspoons water
1 tablespoon lemon juice
1 tablespoon butter or margarine
1 tablespoon butter or margarine,
  melted

Combine egg yolk, salt, pepper, water, and lemon juice in the top of a double boiler; stir well with a wire whisk. Add 1 tablespoon butter; place over simmering water and cook, stirring constantly with a whisk, just until mixture is thickened. Remove from heat; gradually add remaining 1 tablespoon melted butter, stirring constantly with a whisk until desired consistency is reached. Yield: about ¼ cup.

Red Salsa

1 (16-ounce) can whole tomatoes
½ (4-ounce) can chopped green chiles,
  drained
½ large onion, finely chopped
1 tablespoon vegetable oil
½ teaspoon salt
⅛ teaspoon dried oregano leaves
  (optional)
1 small clove garlic, minced
⅛ teaspoon sugar

Drain tomatoes, reserving liquid; finely chop tomatoes. Combine tomatoes, reserved liquid, and remaining ingredients; mix well. Cover salsa and place in refrigerator to chill for at least 2 hours. Serve with tacos or tortillas. Yield: about 2½ cups.

Reheat single servings in a microwave or toaster oven; these use less energy than a standard range.

Seafood Sauce

¾ to 1 cup catsup
¼ teaspoon garlic powder
¼ teaspoon onion powder
½ teaspoon prepared horseradish
1 tablespoon lemon juice
Dash of Worcestershire sauce
Dash of hot sauce
Dash of salt
Dash of pepper

Combine all ingredients; stir well and chill. Serve with boiled shrimp or other seafood. Yield: ¾ to 1 cup.

Shrimp Cocktail Sauce

½ cup chili sauce
½ cup catsup
1 tablespoon prepared horseradish
1 tablespoon vinegar
1½ teaspoons Worcestershire sauce
1 teaspoon lemon juice
Dash of hot sauce

Combine all ingredients, mixing well. Chill sauce at least 30 minutes before serving. Serve with shrimp or other seafood and garnish with lemon wedges, if desired. Yield: about 1 cup.

Tartar Sauce

½ cup mayonnaise or salad dressing
1 tablespoon chopped capers
1 tablespoon chopped sweet pickle
1 tablespoon chopped parsley
¼ teaspoon salt
⅛ teaspoon onion juice
3 drops hot sauce

Combine all ingredients, mixing well; chill thoroughly before serving. Serve with fried fish or other seafood. Yield: about ¾ cup.

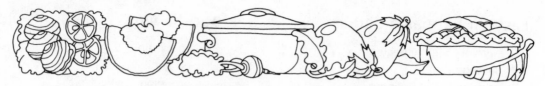

VEGETABLES
AND SIDE DISHES

Asparagus Casserole

2 tablespoons butter or margarine
1 tablespoon all-purpose flour
1 cup milk
¼ cup shredded Cheddar cheese
⅛ teaspoon salt
1½ cups cooked asparagus
⅓ cup buttered breadcrumbs

Melt butter in a small saucepan; add flour and cook over low heat 1 minute, stirring constantly. Gradually add milk; cook over medium heat, stirring constantly, until mixture is thickened and bubbly. Add cheese and salt, stirring until cheese melts.

Place asparagus in a lightly greased 1-quart casserole. Add cheese sauce; sprinkle with breadcrumbs. Bake at 325° for 25 to 30 minutes. Yield: 2 servings.

Asparagus in Garlic Butter

¾ pound asparagus
⅛ to ¼ teaspoon salt
Dash of garlic powder
1½ to 2 tablespoons butter or
    margarine, melted

Snap off tough ends of asparagus. Remove scales with knife or vegetable peeler; cut each spear into thin strips. Place asparagus, salt, garlic powder, and butter in a medium skillet; cover and cook over medium heat, stirring occasionally, for 3 to 5 minutes or until crisp-tender. Yield: 2 servings.

Asparagus with Sour Cream Topping

1 (10½-ounce) can asparagus tips, well
    drained
½ cup commercial sour cream
2 tablespoons mayonnaise
2 tablespoons grated Parmesan cheese

Arrange asparagus in a 10- × 6- × 2-inch baking dish; set aside. Combine remaining ingredients; mix well and spread over asparagus. Broil until lightly browned and bubbly (do not overcook). Serve immediately. Yield: 2 servings.

Note: Sauce can be served over broccoli, cauliflower, or any vegetable.

Asparagus Goldenrod

2 tablespoons butter or margarine
2 tablespoons all-purpose flour
¾ cup milk
¼ teaspoon salt
Dash of pepper
⅓ cup small-curd cottage cheese
1 pound fresh asparagus, cooked
1 slice toast, cut in half
1 hard-cooked egg, finely chopped

242

Melt butter in a heavy saucepan over low heat; blend in flour, and cook 1 minute, stirring constantly. Gradually add milk; cook over medium heat, stirring constantly, until thickened and bubbly. Stir in salt and pepper. Fold in cottage cheese; cook over low heat 1 minute.

Place asparagus on toast on a serving platter and top with sauce; sprinkle with chopped egg. Yield: 2 servings.

Lima Beans with Ground Beef

1 cup fresh lima beans
¼ pound ground beef
1 medium onion, sliced
1 clove garlic, pressed
1 (16-ounce) can whole tomatoes, drained
½ teaspoon crushed red pepper
½ teaspoon salt
½ teaspoon chili powder
¼ cup shredded Cheddar cheese

Cook beans in boiling water until tender (20 to 30 minutes); drain, reserving 1 cup liquid.

Cook ground beef, onion, and garlic in a small Dutch oven until meat is browned. Add lima beans, reserved liquid, tomatoes, and seasonings. Cover and simmer 50 minutes; stir cheese into bean mixture. Cover and cook an additional 10 minutes. Yield: 2 servings.

Creole Lima Beans

2 cups fresh lima beans
2 slices bacon
2 tablespoons finely chopped onion
1 tablespoon chopped green pepper
1 cup canned whole tomatoes, undrained
½ teaspoon salt
Dash of pepper

Cook beans in boiling salted water in a saucepan until tender (20 to 30 minutes); drain. Return beans to saucepan, and set aside.

Cook bacon until crisp. Remove from skillet, reserving 2 tablespoons drippings; crumble bacon, and set aside. Sauté onion and green pepper in reserved drippings until tender.

Stir onion mixture, bacon, and remaining ingredients into beans; cover and simmer 15 minutes. Yield: 2 servings.

Green Bean Medley

1 cup fresh green beans, cut in 2-inch pieces
2 to 4 slices bacon
¼ cup chopped onion
2 large tomatoes, peeled and chopped
1 large whole pimiento, chopped
⅛ teaspoon salt
Dash of freshly ground pepper
¼ cup shredded process American cheese

Cook beans, uncovered, in boiling salted water 2 to 3 minutes; cover and cook 20 to 30 more minutes or until tender. Drain and set aside.

Fry bacon until crisp; remove from pan, and drain on paper towels, reserving drippings. Crumble bacon. Sauté onion in drippings until tender.

Combine all ingredients except cheese, tossing gently. Spoon into a lightly greased 1-quart casserole; sprinkle cheese on top. Bake at 350° for 15 minutes. Yield: about 2 servings.

Barbecued Pork and Beans

1 (8-ounce) can pork and beans,
　undrained
3 tablespoons chopped onion
2 tablespoons diced green pepper
1 slice bacon, diced
1 clove garlic, minced
2 tablespoons catsup
1 tablespoon brown sugar or
　maple-flavored syrup
1½ teaspoons Worcestershire sauce
⅛ teaspoon dry mustard
¼ teaspoon salt
Dash of pepper
1 tablespoon butter or margarine

Combine all ingredients except butter, mixing well. Spoon into a lightly greased small casserole, and dot with butter. Bake at 425° for 25 to 30 mintues. Yield: 2 servings.

Glazed Beets

½ pound fresh beets
2 teaspoons cornstarch
3 tablespoons water
2 tablespoons strawberry jelly
1 tablespoon lemon juice
⅛ teaspoon salt
⅛ teaspoon pumpkin pie spice
1 tablespoon butter or margarine

Cook beets, covered, in a small amount of boiling salted water until tender (about 35 minutes). Drain, peel, and slice beets; set aside.

　Combine cornstarch, 3 tablespoons water, jelly, lemon juice, salt, and pumpkin pie spice. Cook, stirring constantly, over medium heat until mixture is thickened and bubbly. Stir in beets and butter, stirring gently until butter melts and beets are thoroughly heated. Yield: 2 servings.

Creamy Cabbage

½ medium head cabbage, chopped
2 tablespoons milk
1 tablespoon all-purpose flour
½ teaspoon salt
Dash of pepper
3 tablespoons milk
3 tablespoons slivered almonds

Combine cabbage and 2 tablespoons milk in a medium skillet; cover and cook over medium heat 5 to 8 minutes or until crisp-tender. Combine flour, salt, and pepper; sprinkle over cabbage, and mix well. Cook 2 to 3 minutes over low heat, stirring constantly. Stir in 3 tablespoons milk; cook, stirring constantly, until cabbage is lightly coated with white sauce. Spoon mixture into serving dish, and sprinkle almonds over top. Yield: 2 servings.

Orange-Flavored Carrots

½ pound carrots, thinly sliced
¼ cup orange juice
¼ teaspoon salt
½ teaspoon grated orange rind
1 tablespoon brown sugar
1 tablespoon sliced almonds
2 teaspoons butter or margarine
¼ teaspoon parsley flakes

Combine carrots, orange juice, and salt in a pressure cooker. Adjust cooker according to manufacturer's directions; cook at 15 pounds pressure for 3 minutes. Before opening, reduce pressure according to manufacturer's directions; open pressure cooker. Add orange rind, sugar, almonds, and butter, stirring over low heat until butter melts; sprinkle with parsley flakes. Yield: 2 servings.

　Note: If preferred, carrots, orange juice, and salt may be cooked in a covered saucepan over medium heat 12 to 15 minutes.

Stir-Fried Celery and Carrot Strips

2 tablespoons butter or margarine
3 cups thinly sliced celery
1 carrot, cut into julienne strips
1 small onion, chopped
1½ teaspoons soy sauce
¼ teaspoon salt
¼ cup toasted sliced almonds

Melt butter in electric skillet or wok. Add celery, carrot, and onion; sauté until almost tender (about 7 minutes). Stir in soy sauce, salt, and almonds. Cook and stir until celery is crisp-tender (about 2 minutes). Yield: 2 servings.

Corn Casserole

1 egg
2 tablespoons milk
¼ cup cracker crumbs
1 (8½-ounce) can cream-style corn
2 tablespoons butter or margarine, melted
1 small carrot, grated
3 tablespoons chopped green pepper
2 tablespoons chopped celery
2 tablespoons chopped onion
2 drops hot sauce
¼ teaspoon sugar
¼ teaspoon salt
¼ cup shredded Cheddar cheese

Combine egg and milk; beat until well blended. Add cracker crumbs; set aside until all liquid is absorbed.

Add remaining ingredients except cheese to cracker crumb mixture, stirring well. Spoon mixture into a well-greased 1-quart casserole. Bake at 350° for 35 to 40 minutes; sprinkle casserole with cheese while hot. Yield: 2 servings.

Layered Corn Pie

3 slices bacon, partially cooked
¾ cup soft breadcrumbs, divided
1 cup peeled and sliced tomatoes
½ green pepper, minced
½ teaspoon salt
⅛ teaspoon pepper
½ teaspoon sugar
1½ cups fresh corn
1 tablespoon butter or margarine

Place 1½ slices of bacon in bottom of a 1-quart casserole. Place remaining 1½ slices around sides. Spread ¼ cup breadcrumbs over bacon; top with half of tomato slices and half of green pepper.

Combine salt, pepper, and sugar; sprinkle half of mixture over green pepper. Top with half of corn. Repeat layers. Top casserole with remaining ¼ cup breadcrumbs, and dot with butter. Bake at 375° about 35 minutes. Yield: 2 servings.

Broiled Eggplant

1 small eggplant
Olive or vegetable oil
Salt and pepper
Dried oregano leaves, crushed

Peel eggplant; slice crosswise into ¾-inch-thick slices. Brush both sides of slices with olive oil. Arrange on broiler pan. Sprinkle with salt, pepper, and oregano. Broil 3 to 5 inches from heat about 4 minutes or until lightly browned. Remove from oven; turn slices over and sprinkle with salt, pepper, and oregano. Broil about 3 minutes or until lightly browned. Yield: 2 servings.

When you are out of canned tomatoes for your recipe—do not panic! Try substituting 1 (6-ounce) can tomato paste plus 1 cup water.

Eggplant with Cheese

1 small eggplant
2 to 4 tablespoons butter or margarine, melted
Salt and pepper
½ cup (2 ounces) shredded Monterey Jack cheese

Peel eggplant; cut into slices ¾-inch-thick. Brush both sides of slices with butter. Arrange slices in a single layer in a greased baking dish; sprinkle with salt and pepper. Press cheese onto each slice. Bake at 375° for 10 minutes or until eggplant is tender and cheese is melted. Yield: 2 servings.

Creamy Grits

⅓ cup uncooked regular grits
1¼ cups milk
¼ teaspoon salt

Combine grits, milk, and salt in top of a double boiler. Cover and cook over low heat 20 to 25 minutes, stirring occasionally. Serve with butter or gravy. Yield: 2 servings.

Creamed Mushrooms

1 small onion, chopped
¼ pound fresh mushrooms, thinly sliced
2 teaspoons butter or margarine
Salt and pepper to taste
1½ teaspoons chopped fresh parsley
⅛ teaspoon paprika
1 teaspoon lemon juice
½ cup commercial sour cream
3 slices bacon
1 English muffin, halved and toasted

Sauté onion and mushrooms in butter until tender. Add salt, pepper, parsley, paprika, lemon juice, and sour cream. Place over low heat until warm (do not allow to boil).

Fry bacon, and place on muffin halves. Spoon sauce over bacon. Serve immediately. Yield: 2 servings.

Sauteed Mushrooms

1 tablespoon minced onion
2 tablespoons butter or margarine
½ pound fresh mushrooms, thickly sliced
½ teaspoon lemon juice
¼ teaspoon salt or seasoned salt
Dash of pepper

Sauté onion in butter until tender. Add mushrooms; sauté over medium heat, stirring occasionally, 10 minutes. Sprinkle with lemon juice, salt, and pepper; stir lightly. Yield: 2 servings.

Mushroom Sauce over Vermicelli

⅓ cup chopped onion
1 clove garlic, minced
¼ cup butter or margarine, divided
½ pound fresh mushrooms, sliced
1 cup frozen English peas, thawed
2½ teaspoons lemon juice
½ teaspoon salt
⅛ teaspoon pepper
⅛ teaspoon dried oregano leaves (optional)
1 (6-ounce) package vermicelli
Grated Parmesan cheese

Sauté onion and garlic in 2 tablespoons butter 3 minutes, stirring occasionally. Add mushrooms; cook 5 minutes, stirring occasionally. Stir in peas, lemon juice, and seasonings; cook over low heat 5 minutes.

Cook vermicelli according to package directions; drain. Add remaining 2 tablespoons butter, and stir well. Spoon mushroom mixture over vermicelli. Serve with Parmesan cheese. Yield: about 2 servings.

Stuffed Peppers for Two

2 medium-size green peppers
½ pound ground beef
¼ cup uncooked instant rice
1 (8-ounce) can tomato sauce with
  cheese, divided
1 tablespoon chopped onion
½ teaspoon salt
Dash of pepper
½ teaspoon Worcestershire sauce
1 egg, beaten

Cut off top of each green pepper; remove seeds. Cook 5 minutes in boiling salted water to cover. Drain; set aside.

Combine ground beef, rice, ¼ cup tomato sauce, and remaining ingredients. Stuff peppers with mixture, and place in a small baking pan.

Pour remaining tomato sauce over stuffed peppers. Cover and bake at 350° for 50 to 60 minutes or until meat is done, basting peppers twice with drippings. Yield: 2 servings.

Okra and Tomatoes

½ pound okra
All-purpose flour
2 slices bacon, coarsely chopped
Bacon drippings
1 cup peeled and chopped fresh
  tomatoes
Salt and pepper to taste

Wash okra well; drain. Cut off tip and stem ends; cut okra crosswise into ½-inch slices, and dredge in flour.

Cook bacon until crisp; remove from skillet, and set aside. Fry okra in bacon drippings, turning often until browned; add bacon drippings as needed.

Add tomatoes to okra; stir in bacon, salt, and pepper. Simmer until tomatoes are tender, stirring often. Yield: 2 servings.

Fried Okra with Cheese

½ pound okra
1 egg, beaten
All-purpose flour
1 teaspoon paprika
Vegetable oil
½ cup (2 ounces) shredded Cheddar
  cheese
Salt and pepper to taste

Wash okra well; drain. Cut off tip and stem ends; cut okra crosswise into ½-inch slices. Dip okra in egg, then in flour seasoned with paprika. Fry in hot oil until brown and crisp; drain slightly.

Add cheese, salt, and pepper to okra; stir gently to coat. Serve immediately. Yield: 2 servings.

Herb-Stuffed Potatoes

2 medium baking potatoes
Vegetable oil
3 tablespoons butter or margarine
1 teaspoon chopped onion
1 teaspoon chopped fresh parsley
3 tablespoons evaporated milk
⅛ teaspoon crushed basil leaves
⅛ teaspoon crushed tarragon leaves
½ teaspoon salt
⅛ teaspoon pepper
Butter or margarine

Scrub potatoes thoroughly, and rub skins with oil; bake at 400° for 1 hour or until done.

Allow potatoes to cool to touch. Slice skin away from top of each potato. Carefully scoop out pulp, leaving shells intact; mash pulp. Add 3 tablespoons butter, onion, parsley, milk, and seasonings to potato pulp, mixing well. Stuff shells with potato mixture, and dot with butter. Bake at 350° about 30 minutes. Yield: 2 servings.

Bacon-Stuffed Potatoes

2 large baking potatoes
Vegetable oil
4 slices bacon
¼ cup chopped green onion
2 tablespoons grated Parmesan cheese
½ cup commercial sour cream
½ teaspoon salt
¼ teaspoon pepper
¼ teaspoon paprika

Scrub potatoes thoroughly, and rub skins with oil; bake at 400° for 1 hour or until done.

Allow potatoes to cool to touch. Slice skin away from top of each potato. Carefully scoop out pulp, leaving shells intact; mash pulp.

Cook bacon until crisp; drain and crumble, reserving 1½ tablespoons drippings in skillet. Sauté onion in bacon drippings until tender. Combine potato pulp, bacon, onion, cheese, sour cream, salt, and pepper, mixing well. Stuff shells with potato mixture; sprinkle each with ⅛ teaspoon paprika. Bake at 350° for 15 to 20 minutes or until heated thoroughly. Yield: 2 servings.

Herb-Fried Potatoes

2 tablespoons butter or margarine
2 medium potatoes, peeled and cut into ⅛-inch strips
⅛ teaspoon ground oregano
1 tablespoon chopped parsley
¼ teaspoon instant minced onion
⅛ teaspoon salt
Pepper to taste

Melt butter in a 10-inch skillet; add potatoes. Cover and cook over medium heat 10 minutes. Turn potatoes carefully; cook, uncovered, about 10 minutes more, turning occasionally to brown all sides. Sprinkle with remaining ingredients during last 5 minutes of cooking. Yield: 2 servings.

New Potatoes in Butter

6 small new potatoes
¼ cup butter or margarine, melted
1 teaspoon dried dillweed
1 teaspoon sugar
1 tablespoon lemon juice
Salt to taste

Cook potatoes in boiling water until tender; drain. Cool slightly and peel. Combine remaining ingredients, and pour over potatoes. Yield: 2 servings.

Potato Pancakes

4 eggs
⅓ cup all-purpose flour
1½ teaspoons instant minced onion
½ teaspoon salt
¼ teaspoon baking powder
3 cups frozen Southern-style hash brown potatoes, thawed
½ cup (2 ounces) shredded Cheddar cheese
Parsley sprigs (optional)
Spiced apples (optional)
Commercial sour cream and/or applesauce (optional)

Beat together eggs, flour, onion, salt, and baking powder. Stir in potatoes and cheese. For each pancake, pour ½ cup batter onto hot, well-greased skillet or griddle. Cook until golden brown on one side; turn and brown other side. Garnish with parsley sprigs and spiced apples, if desired. Serve hot with sour cream or applesauce, if desired. Yield: about 6 pancakes.

Candied Sweet Potatoes

2 tablespoons butter or margarine
2 teaspoons bacon drippings
2 medium-size sweet potatoes, peeled
  and thinly sliced
3 tablespoons water
¾ cup sugar

Melt butter and bacon drippings in a large heavy skillet. Add sweet potatoes and water; sprinkle sugar over mixture. Cook, uncovered, over medium heat, stirring frequently, until potatoes are tender and a thick sauce forms (about 30 minutes). Yield: 2 servings.

Stuffed Baked Sweet Potatoes

2 medium-size sweet potatoes
3 tablespoons orange juice
1 tablespoon butter or margarine
½ teaspoon salt
½ (8-ounce) can crushed pineapple,
  drained
1 tablespoon chopped pecans

Scrub potatoes thoroughly; bake at 375° for 1 hour or until tender.

Allow potatoes to cool to touch. Slice skin away from top of each potato. Carefully scoop out pulp, leaving shells intact.

Combine potato pulp, orange juice, butter, and salt; beat at medium speed of electric mixer until fluffy. Stir in pineapple. Stuff shells with potato mixture, and sprinkle with pecans. Bake at 375° for 12 minutes. Yield: 2 servings.

Basic Rice for Two

½ cup uncooked regular rice
1 tablespoon butter or margarine
1 or 2 chicken- or beef-flavored
  bouillon cubes
1 cup hot water

Sauté rice in butter over low heat in a stovetop, ovenproof casserole until golden brown.

Dissolve bouillon cube in hot water; add to rice, and bring to a boil. Remove rice from heat; cover and bake at 350° for 20 to 25 minutes or until all liquid is absorbed. Yield: 2 servings.

Shrimp and Sausage Rice

1 Basic Rice recipe
¼ pound medium shrimp, cooked,
  peeled, and deveined
⅓ pound Polish sausage or smoked
  sausage, cut into ¼-inch slices
2 medium tomatoes, peeled and
  chopped
⅛ teaspoon pepper
¼ teaspoon paprika

Prepare rice according to Basic Rice recipe except stir in remaining ingredients before baking. Cover and bake at 350° for 20 to 25 minutes or until all liquid is absorbed. Yield: 2 servings.

Chicken Rice

1 Basic Rice recipe
2 to 3 tablespoons raisins
1 tablespoon toasted sliced almonds
¼ teaspoon curry powder
1 to 1½ cups chopped cooked chicken

Prepare rice according to Basic Rice recipe except for baking. Stir in remaining ingredients. Cover and bake at 350° for 20 to 25 minutes or until all of the liquid is absorbed. Yield: 2 servings.

Cooking vegetables with the least amount of water possible will preserve vitamins and maintain flavor. Save the cooking liquid, and add to soup stock or gravy for additional food value and flavor.

Vegetable Rice

1 Basic Rice recipe
1 small onion, chopped
½ green pepper, chopped
¼ cup chopped celery
½ cup sliced fresh mushrooms

Prepare rice according to Basic Rice recipe, sautéing vegetables in butter along with rice. Yield: 2 servings.

Note: Any combination of the vegetables may be used.

Mushroom-Walnut Rice

2 tablespoons butter or margarine
½ cup uncooked regular rice
1 (10¾-ounce) can chicken broth
¼ teaspoon salt
⅓ cup finely chopped walnuts
⅓ cup finely chopped mushrooms

Melt butter in a skillet over medium heat; add rice, and stir until well browned. Add broth and salt; cover and cook until rice is tender (about 30 minutes).

Stir walnuts and mushrooms into rice; cook 2 to 3 minutes longer, stirring occasionally. Yield: 2 servings.

Stir-Fried Rice

1 egg, slightly beaten
1¾ cups cooked rice, chilled
½ cup diced cooked pork, ham, chicken, or beef
2 tablespoons sliced green onion
¼ cup water chestnuts, drained and sliced
½ cup sliced fresh mushrooms
2 tablespoons butter or margarine
1 tablespoon soy sauce
¼ teaspoon sugar

Sauté egg, rice, meat, onion, water chestnuts, and mushrooms in butter. Stir in soy sauce and sugar. Serve hot. Yield: 2 servings.

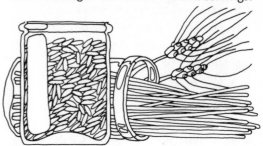

Green Rice

¼ cup chopped green onion
¼ cup chopped green pepper
2 tablespoons butter or margarine
½ cup uncooked regular rice
1⅓ cups beef or chicken broth
¼ cup chopped parsley
Salt and pepper to taste

Sauté green onion and green pepper in butter until tender; add rice, and stir until rice is well coated with butter (about 5 minutes). Add broth; cover and cook 20 to 25 minutes or until rice is tender. Stir in remaining ingredients; cook about 1 minute longer. Yield: 2 servings.

Wine-Baked Rice

2 tablespoons chopped onion
1 tablespoon chopped green pepper
1 stalk celery, diagonally sliced
1 tablespoon butter or margarine
½ cup uncooked regular rice
¾ cup water
¾ teaspoon chicken-flavored bouillon granules
¼ cup white wine
Salt and pepper to taste

Sauté onion, green pepper, and celery in butter until tender; stir in rice, and cook until lightly browned. Add remaining ingredients, stirring until bouillon granules are dissolved. Transfer to a lightly greased 1-quart casserole. Cover and bake at 350° about 25 minutes or until all liquid is absorbed. Yield: 2 servings.

Stir-Fry Spinach

1 pound fresh spinach
1 tablespoon vegetable oil
2 teaspoons soy sauce
½ small onion, thinly sliced
¼ pound fresh mushrooms, sliced

Wash and drain spinach; tear into bite-size pieces.

Combine oil and soy sauce in a skillet or wok. Add onion and mushrooms; cook, stirring occasionally, until tender. Add spinach; cook 2 to 3 minutes or until spinach is crisp-tender; stir occasionally. Yield: 2 servings.

Scalloped Spinach

¾ pound fresh spinach, washed and drained
1 tablespoon butter or margarine
1 tablespoon all-purpose flour
½ cup milk
¼ cup shredded Cheddar cheese
¼ teaspoon salt
Dash of pepper
1 tablespoon grated onion
¼ cup soft breadcrumbs
1 tablespoon butter or margarine, melted

Cook spinach in a small amount of salted water 8 to 10 minutes or until tender. Drain, and spoon into a lightly greased 1-quart casserole; set aside.

Melt 1 tablespoon butter in a heavy saucepan over low heat; blend in flour, and cook 1 minute, stirring constantly. Gradually stir in milk; cook over medium heat, stirring con-

stantly, about 6 to 8 minutes or until sauce is thickened and bubbly. Add cheese, salt, pepper, and onion, stirring until cheese melts.

Spoon sauce over spinach. Combine breadcrumbs and remaining butter; sprinkle over cheese sauce. Bake at 375° for 20 minutes or until bubbly. Yield: 2 servings.

Hot Spinach Salad

1¼ to 1½ cups unsalted cooked spinach, drained
½ teaspoon minced onion
3 tablespoons butter or margarine
¼ teaspoon prepared mustard
1 tablespoon vinegar
¼ teaspoon salt
Dash of pepper
1 hard-cooked egg, chopped

Place spinach in a 1-quart casserole; keep warm.

Sauté onion in butter until tender. Add remaining ingredients except egg. Heat thoroughly. Pour mixture over spinach; sprinkle with chopped egg. Serve immediately. Yield: 2 servings.

Glazed Acorn Squash

1 acorn squash
Salt
2 tablespoons butter or margarine
1 tablespoon brown sugar
¼ cup chopped pecans or walnuts

Rinse squash; cut in half lengthwise and remove seeds and membrane. Sprinkle each half lightly with salt, and fill each with 1 tablespoon butter, 1½ teaspoons brown sugar, and 2 tablespoons pecans. Place squash in a baking dish; add ½-inch water to dish. Cover and bake at 350° for 1 hour and 15 minutes or until squash is tender. Yield: 2 servings.

Pork-Stuffed Acorn Squash

1 large acorn squash
¼ pound ground pork
1 large apple, peeled, cored, and
  chopped
1 tablespoon brown sugar
¼ teaspoon ground nutmeg
¼ teaspoon ground cinnamon
½ teaspoon salt
Butter or margarine

Cut squash in half; remove seeds and membrane. Cover and cook in boiling water for 10 minutes. Scoop out pulp from shells, leaving a ½-inch margin.

Cook pork until brown; stir in apple and pulp. Cook over medium heat for 10 minutes, stirring often. Add sugar, nutmeg, cinnamon, and salt; mix well. Spoon into squash shells; dot with butter. Place shells in a shallow pan; bake at 350° for 30 minutes. Yield: 2 servings.

Squash and Cheese Casserole

4 medium-size yellow squash
2 slices bacon
½ small onion, chopped
1 egg, beaten
½ cup (2 ounces) shredded sharp
  Cheddar cheese
Salt and pepper to taste
1½ teaspoons Worcestershire sauce

Cook squash in a small amount of boiling salted water until tender; drain well, and mash. Cook bacon until crisp; drain well and crumble, reserving drippings. Sauté onion in reserved drippings.

Combine all ingredients, stirring well; spoon into a lightly greased 1-quart casserole. Bake at 350° for 20 to 30 minutes. Yield: 2 servings.

Marinated Yellow Squash

2 medium-size yellow squash, thinly
  sliced
¼ cup thinly sliced green onion
¼ cup chopped green pepper
¼ cup sliced celery
3 tablespoons vegetable oil
¼ cup cider vinegar
1 tablespoon wine vinegar
¼ cup plus 1 tablespoon sugar
½ teaspoon salt
¼ teaspoon pepper
1 small clove garlic, crushed

Combine squash, green onion, green pepper, and celery in a large mixing bowl; toss lightly. Combine remaining ingredients; stir well and spoon over vegetables. Chill about 12 hours, stirring occasionally. Drain and serve. Yield: 4 servings.

Note: This may be stored in container in refrigerator for two weeks.

Spaghetti Squash

1 small spaghetti squash
2 tablespoons butter or margarine,
  melted
1 tablespoon chopped parsley
Salt and pepper to taste
Grated Parmesan cheese

Wash squash and pierce in several places with a large fork. Place in a medium saucepan. Add water to cover the squash. Bring to a boil; cover and cook 25 minutes.

Drain squash; cut in half lengthwise and remove seeds. Remove spaghetti-like strands with a large spoon. Stir strands into melted butter in a large skillet over medium heat. Add parsley, salt, and pepper. Heat, tossing gently to coat strands with butter. Top with Parmesan cheese to serve. Yield: 2 servings.

Onion-Stuffed Zucchini

2 medium zucchini
½ cup finely chopped onion
2 tablespoons butter or margarine
½ teaspoon salt
2 tablespoons shredded mozzarella or Monterey Jack cheese

Place zucchini in saucepan; cover with water. Bring to a boil. Cook 4 to 6 minutes or until squash can be easily pierced with a fork. Drain and allow to cool slightly. Slice a thin layer off top of squash. Scoop out insides to form a ¼-inch-thick shell. Finely chop squash pulp; set aside.

Sauté onion in butter until translucent. Add chopped squash and salt. Stir to combine. Fill shells with onion mixture. Place squash in a small lightly buttered pan. Top each with cheese. Broil about 3 inches from heat until cheese is melted. Yield: 2 servings.

Zucchini with Sour Cream Sauce

3 medium zucchini, sliced
½ cup sour cream
1 egg yolk
1 teaspoon tarragon vinegar
¼ teaspoon paprika

Arrange sliced zucchini in steamer basket. Place in a Dutch oven containing ½-inch

water. Cover; bring to a boil and steam 4 to 6 minutes, or until crisp-tender. While zucchini is steaming, combine remaining ingredients in a small saucepan. Cook over low heat, stirring constantly with a wire whisk, until thick and smooth.

Place zucchini in a serving bowl; top with sauce. Yield: 2 servings.

Fresh Tomatoes and Stuffing

¼ cup diagonally sliced celery
¼ cup (1- × ½-inch) green pepper strips
1½ teaspoons instant minced onion
½ teaspoon dried basil leaves
¼ to ½ teaspoon salt
⅛ teaspoon pepper
3 tablespoons butter or margarine
½ cup herb-seasoned stuffing mix
2 tomatoes, each cut into 8 wedges
1 teaspoon sugar

Sauté celery, green pepper, onion, and seasonings in butter until vegetables are crisp-tender. Stir in stuffing mix. Add tomatoes and sugar; stir gently. Cover and cook over low heat 10 to 12 minutes. Yield: 2 servings.

Vegetable Stir-Fry

2½ tablespoons vegetable oil
10 to 12 large mushrooms, sliced
1 medium onion, sliced and separated into rings
1 medium zucchini, thinly sliced
1 tablespoon soy sauce
½ teaspoon salt
¼ teaspoon pepper
¼ teaspoon sugar

Heat oil in a large skillet or wok. Add remaining ingredients; stir-fry over high heat 3 to 5 minutes or until zucchini is crisp-tender. Yield: 2 servings.

Index

Fish *(continued)*
  Mackerel, Baked, 188
  Salmon and Cheese Casserole, 188
  Steamed Fish Fillets, 186
French Toast, Overnight, 19
Frittata, Spinach, 167
Frostings, Fillings, and Toppings
  Buttercream Frosting, 173
  Caramel Frosting, Easy, 173
  Chocolate Frosting, 175, 177
  Chocolate Whipped Cream Topping, 174
  Cocoa Frosting, 172
  Cream Cheese Frosting, 57, 171
  Creamy Nut Filling, 177
  Fudge Frosting, 174
  Lemon Frosting, Creamy, 110
  Lemon Glaze, 175
  Meringue, 181
  Prune-Orange Filling, 28
  Rum Cream, 140
Fruits
  Compote, Gingered Fruit, 226
  Creative Desserts, 170
  Custard with Fruit, Italian, 112
  Fruitcake, 19
  Mélange, Summer Fruit, 37
  Muffins, Fruit, 154
  Pork Chops with Rice, Fruit-Glazed, 84
  Salad, Avocado Fruit, 225
  Salad, Fruited Cottage Cheese, 226
  Spiced Fruit, 53
  Summer Fruits and Cream, 49
  Winter and Spring Fruits, 107
  Winter Fruits, Chilled, 97

Gazpacho, 83
Grapefruit
  Fruit-Filled Grapefruit, 178
  Sherried Broiled Grapefruit, 27
  Warmed Grapefruit, 53
Grape Salad, Green, 226
Grits
  Cheese Grits, Quick, 22
  Creamy Grits, 246
Guacamole, 43, 161

Ham
  Baked Ham Slice, 211
  Biscuits, Ham-Filled, 127
  Burgers, Beef and Ham, 199
  Casserole, Chicken and Ham, 217
  Eggs Florentine, 41
  Eggs Special, Ham and, 61
  Fried Country Ham Slices, 23
  Grilled Ham, 211

Noodles and Ham, Green, 212
Omelet, Ham and Cheese, 162
Omelet, Sour Cream-Ham, 20
Quiche, Ham and Cheese, 168
Roll-Ups, Ham and Cheese, 31
Salad, Ham and Avocado, 230
Sandwiches, Ham and Swiss Cheese, 146
Sandwiches, Ham and Turkey, 146
Sandwich Special, 32
Sauce, Creamy Ham, 122
Shortcake, Ham, 212
Spread, Ham-and-Egg, 145
Stir-Fry, Ham and Zucchini, 211
Stuffed Eggs, Deviled Ham-, 159

Kabobs
  Chicken Kabobs, 217
  Shish Kabobs, 109
  Steak and Mushroom Kabobs, 86
  Steak Strip Kabobs, Island, 205

Lamb
  Chops, Baked Lamb, 210
  Chops, Chinese Lamb, 210
  Chops, Grilled Lamb, 210
  Shish Kabobs, 109
Lemons
  Bars, Lemon Yogurt, 110
  Bars, Picnic Lemon, 35
  Bread, Lemon-Nut, 151
  Butter, Lemon, 240
  Custard in Meringue Cups, Lemon, 103
  Frosting, Creamy Lemon, 110
  Glaze, Lemon, 175
  Muffins, Lemon, 130
  Pears, Lemon Poached, 84
  Pie, Luscious Lemon Meringue, 181
  Pie, Whipped Lemon, 181
  Pudding, Lemon, 75
  Sauce, Lemon, 71
  Soup, Egg and Lemon, 108
  Veal, Lemon-Sauced, 111
Liver
  Baked Liver, Crunchy, 46
  Chicken Livers over Rice, 222
  Chicken Livers, Sherried, 222
  Chicken Livers, Tarragon, 222
  Chicken Livers, Wine-Sauced, 77
  Onions, Liver and, 209
  Stroganoff, Liver, 210

Macaroni
  Salad for Two, Macaroni, 228
  Soufflé, Macaroni and Cheese, 169